POSITIVITY BIAS

PRACTICAL WISDOM

for

POSITIVE LIVING

MENDEL KALMENSON

Inspired by the life and teachings of
The Lubavitcher Rebbe

POSITIVITY BIAS

7th Printing—July 2021

Chabad.ORG
718-735-2000
editor@chabad.org

Published by
Ezra Press
770 Eastern Parkway, Brooklyn, New York 11213
718-774-4000 / Fax 718-774-2718
editor@kehot.com

Order Department:
291 Kingston Avenue, Brooklyn, New York 11213
718-778-0226 / Fax 718-778-4148
www.kehot.com

EZRA PRESS

Ezra Press is an imprint of Kehot Publication Society.
The Ezra logo is a trademark of Kehot Publication Society.

7 9 11 13 15 16 14 12 10 8

ISBN: 978-0-8266-9008-1

Printed in The United States of America

ב"ה.

PREFACE

The Rebbe, of righteous memory, is widely known for his profound piety and immense love for God and His Torah; for his fearless leadership and breathtaking innovation; and especially for his daring post-Holocaust renaissance of the Jewish people, revolutionary social vision for the world, and Torah genius.

For many, the Rebbe's immense love for every single one of God's children towers above all. He would treat each one as if he or she were his own child, and revealed from deep inside them robust reservoirs of faith, courage and strength.

Through personal written correspondence, one-on-one conversations, and thousands of hours of public teaching, the Rebbe guided and empowered countless individuals to transform their every challenge into catalysts for good. Remarkably, he shared the tools and underlying principles to do so with all, so everyone can achieve a life of joy, meaning and purpose.

If these teachings were ever vital and life-saving, they are arguably most so today.

Indeed, an ever-growing stream of millions—from all walks of life and from all across the globe—regularly beat a path to Chabad.org in search of the Rebbe's profound insight and practical advice for their most existential dilemmas and concerns.

In *Positivity Bias: Practical Wisdom for Positive Living,* distinguished author Rabbi Mendel Kalmenson encapsulates some of the extraordinary positivity undergirding so much of the Rebbe's approach. This book was met with overwhelming interest, prompting repeated printings to keep up with demand. We are very pleased to present herewith a newly updated edition.

We pray that the goodness certain to result from this newest expression of the Torah's timeless blueprint herald the ultimate positivity—that of our world transformed, with the coming of the righteous Moshiach speedily in our days.

Chabad.org

10 Shevat, 5780
Celebrating 70 Years of the Rebbe's Leadership
Brooklyn, N.Y.

With everlasting
gratitude and appreciation
for your endless devotion to Chabad.org,
its team, and its mission to empower
all of G-d's children.

Dedicated to Chabad.org pillars

Moris and Lillian Tabacinic

You are shining examples of
הצנע לכת עם אלקיך
humbly doing the work of Hashem.

May Hashem grant you
endless *nachas* from your loved ones,
immense success in all of your endeavors,
with *gezunt* and *menuchah*,
now and forever!

• THE REBBE •

The Rebbe, Rabbi Menachem Mendel Schneerson (1902–1994), of righteous memory, is widely regarded as one of the most influential religious personalities of modern times.

Seventh in the dynastic lineage of Chabad-Lubavitch leaders, leadership was thrust upon the reluctant Rebbe 70 years ago, catalyzing a post-holocaust spiritual revival whose effects are felt ever more widely and deeply with the passage of time.

The Rebbe's ubiquitous mitzvah campaigns catapulted Jewish learning and practice to the very center of Jewish life, and his holistic Torah prescription for personal fulfillment and global harmony uplifts and empowers from the halls of power to the forgotten and downtrodden. People of all faiths, nationalities and backgrounds travel from across the globe to pray at his resting place for blessing and inspiration.

To Learn more about the Rebbe visit TheRebbe.org.

TABLE OF CONTENTS

INTRODUCTION

DURING A PRIVATE AUDIENCE with the Lubavitcher Rebbe, R. Menachem M. Schneerson, of righteous memory, a bureau chief for a national Jewish newspaper extolled his periodical: "Our publication is independent and completely objective!"

The Rebbe responded pointedly: "Independent, perhaps—but objective? There is no such thing. It is humanly impossible to be completely objective.

"Every person has a bias of some kind."[1]

I understand the Rebbe's words to mean that while one can live without an agenda, one cannot live without bias.

Through a mix of nature, nurture, and free will, we each possess a certain lens that frames and forms the way we see ourselves, others, and the world around us. It is simply not possible to erase all traces of our personality, past experiences, and deeply-held beliefs from our observations, expressions, or actions—no matter how hard we may try.

This frame that we adopt, whether consciously or unconsciously, deeply impacts the way we perceive reality.

This matrix of understanding becomes our operating system, so to speak—the default mechanism through which we construe and contextualize, react and reinforce, interpret and identify every event and interaction we experience.

Based on this fact of subjectivity, the following questions arise:

What are our biases? What are the default frames through which we see the world? How can they be adjusted to better serve ourselves and others?

If our biases inevitably color the way we interpret and experience the world, it follows that a primary focus of life should be to assess and reset our biases.

In the penetrating words of the Rebbe to an individual who was wont to complain about his life circumstances:

> In our world, everything is a mixture of good and bad. Human beings must choose which aspects they will emphasize, contemplate, and pursue...
>
> How instructive is that which our Sages tell us, that Adam was an ingrate. Even before he was banished from the Garden of Eden, [while living in a literal paradise] he complained about his circumstances. On the other hand, there were Jewish men and women who thanked and blessed the Creator and recited the morning blessings while living through the most horrifying times in the German concentration camps. Ultimately, everyone's circumstances will be somewhere between these two extremes....
>
> My point [in saying this is not to admonish you; it] is simply to underscore the reality [that]:
>
> The type of lives that we live, whether full of satisfaction and meaning or the opposite, depends, in large measure, on our willpower, which dictates whether we will focus on the positive or on the negative.[2]

Our perspectives are so powerful, they can lead us to find fault with Paradise or to express gratitude even while in a state of extreme suffering.

In a rare personal disclosure to one of his Chasidim and a trusted confidante, R. Berel Junik,[3] the Rebbe once alluded to his focus on seeing things positively as stemming from his harrowing past, saying, "I worked on myself to [always] look at things in a positive light; otherwise I could not have survived."

This deceptively simple statement encapsulates the basic premise of this book; namely, that living a life of positivity is a matter of *choice, not circumstance,* and derives from *perspective, not personality.*

It is not the events of our lives that shape us, but the meanings we assign to those events.

In other words: *If you change the way you look at things, the things you look at change.*

Ultimately, the greatest testing grounds for any theory is the Laboratory of Life.

And that is what makes this book on positivity different from many. For if, as the saying goes, history is philosophy teaching through examples, this book teaches the philosophy of positivity by way of a living example, demonstrating how the Rebbe interacted with real people reacting in real time to real-life situations.

It is important to note that the redemptive perspectives presented in this book are not those of a man who lived a life of peace and privilege. They are the insights of a man who lived through waves of pogroms, the killing fields of World War I, a typhus epidemic, a refugee crisis, the persecution and forced exile of his father, whom he never saw again, the Bolshevik Revolution, the rise of Communism, World War II, the brutal murder of his brother, grandmother, and numerous other relatives at the hands of the Nazis, and a life of childlessness.

They are the teachings of a man who personally absorbed and carried the crushing pain of hundreds of thousands of individuals who sought him out for healing, comfort, love, acceptance, help, and sometimes, simply a reason to live.

And finally, they are the working principles of a man who made an active choice to consciously curate a philosophy and habits of thought, speech, and action—firmly rooted in 3,000 years of Jewish wisdom, understanding and knowledge that all coalesce into what we refer to in this book as the Rebbe's "Positivity Bias."

Once pointed out, the Rebbe's Positivity Bias is impossible to miss. As the hundreds of stories, letters, anecdotes, and vignettes in the following pages bring to life, the Rebbe's Positivity Bias illuminated every corner of his thoughts, every nuance of his speech, and infused his every action, reaction, and interaction with the power of Positive Living.

Ultimately, however, this book was not written to tell the story of one man's courageous effort to design a life of positivity despite the dark and difficult times in which he lived, nor does it seek to detail how he inspired a global task-force of dedicated "lamplighters" to share his message of positivity and providence with every person they encountered along their path.

Instead, this book aims to provide you, dear reader, with the principles and practices, wisdom and tools, insights and inspiration that will empower you to personalize, internalize, and actualize your very own Positivity Bias.

Each chapter, each story, and each teaching contained within these pages is but another key to access your higher vision, and to open your eyes to a better and brighter world.

Mendel Kalmenson
28 Sivan 5779
London

CHAPTER 1

The World is G-d's Garden

1951. 770 EASTERN PARKWAY, BROOKLYN, NEW YORK.

ON THE TENTH DAY of the Hebrew month of Shevat, a small group of Chasidim huddled together in the middle of winter, anxiously waiting to hear the first words from their new Rebbe.

This humble gathering represented the meager remnant of the once glorious Chasidic dynasty known as Chabad-Lubavitch, which in the past had numbered in the hundreds of thousands, with centers and outposts active across much of Eastern Europe.

Many of those present had lost much of their families to Stalinist purges, or during the war, while others had ventured across the Atlantic earlier and had begun to assimilate into the surrounding American culture to varying degrees. And yet, here they all were, waiting and wondering—what would become of them and their way of life in this new land? What would be their marching orders into the future?

It had been exactly one year since the sixth Lubavitcher Rebbe, R. Yosef Yitzchak Schneersohn, had passed away, creating a leadership vacuum in this tight-knit community of pious scholars and mystics, simple Jews, and survivors. During the interim period, the future of the movement had been uncertain, as the new Rebbe had consistently rejected all invitations to assume the position.

Numerous debates and deliberations ensued. Who would lead them? Where would they turn for comfort, strength, and guidance in life and Torah?

With these questions up in the air, coupled with the traumas of life under Soviet Regime and aftershocks of the war, it is easy to imagine this small group of largely Yiddish-speaking immigrants feeling profoundly distraught and disoriented.

Within this relative chaos, the Rebbe revealed a hidden order. Picking up precisely where his father-in-law, the sixth Rebbe, had left off, the new Rebbe began his inaugural address with the well-known words from Song of Songs, *Bati L'gani* (*I have come into My garden*).[4]

These were the very same opening words quoted by R. Yosef Yitzchak in his final discourse, amounting to a last will and testament of sorts for his followers, published exactly one year earlier to the day. This subtle act of spiritual connection—threading the proverbial needle from one Rebbe to the next—was so important to the Rebbe, that for the next four decades, the Rebbe would continue to review and reveal deeper and higher aspects of R. Yosef Yitzchak's final teaching every year at the annual Chasidic gathering marking the anniversary of his father-in-law and predecessor's passing.

Ultimately, both Rebbes interpreted the verse of *Bati L'gani* in a profoundly creative and inspiring way: Despite all of the eruptive uncertainty and destructive chaos punctuating the recent past and still defining the times in many ways, the world is not a cruel and meaningless mass hurdling blindly through space. The world is G-d's garden, His finest creation and chosen abode.

Realizing and living this truth largely depends on how one views and understands the world around and within them.

When you look out at the world and into your soul, do you see a wasteland or a wonderland, a desert or an oasis?

According to Chasidut (Chasidic philosophy), we each have the power to define and influence our experience based on our perception. Knowing this with every fiber of his being, the Rebbe rigorously developed and consistently expressed what I would call a profound and programmatic Positivity Bias to life, to the Torah, and to people, leading him to seek and find the pure and positive essence within everyone and everything.

Always seeing the Temple beneath the ruins, actively seeking the positive aspect or opportunity in any given situation, believing deeply in G-d's ultimate goodness and immanent presence, living with purpose, responsibility and meaning—these qualities provide the psycho-spiritual foundation of the Rebbe's radical theory and redemptive practice of life.

Cultivating this consciousness was his way of tending

G-d's Garden, while helping each of us become better, holier and happier gardeners ourselves.

Quite simply, this Positivity Bias, which is the key to unlocking G-d's Secret Garden, became a cornerstone of the Rebbe's teachings over the next four decades, expressing itself in myriad ways, especially as he continued to elaborate on *Bati L'gani* year after year.

What a Wonderful World

In a well-known address delivered twenty-two years later, on 10 Shevat, 5732 (1972), the Rebbe again expounded on *Bati L'gani*, addressing the potential cognitive dissonance one may experience when comparing the contention of this teaching, that the world is G-d's garden, to the world they actually live in. The Rebbe explained:

> When we look about with physical eyes, we only perceive the physical aspects in all that we see and we naturally wonder: What is happening with the world? The situation is steadily deteriorating—from one generation to the next, and even from one year to the next. Goodness does not prevail, conditions are not improving, holy and spiritual values do not dominate....
>
> Such thoughts easily lead to the conclusion that this world is but a jungle dominated by selfish beasts, and that it certainly does not even remotely resemble a garden that yields delectable fruit....
>
> "Such thoughts also lead to dejection and despair. How can we hope to affect and change the world

> for the better if the situation is consistently degenerating?

The shape of our thoughts directly impacts the color of our emotions, the tone of our speech, and even the efficacy of our actions. Certain thoughts are more likely to lead us down dark and destructive pathways, while other thoughts have the power to inspire and strengthen us in pursuit of our highest purpose.

Therefore:

> We must know that the world...is a garden! Not just a [utilitarian] field that yields grain [which is necessary in order to subsist], but a luxuriant garden that yields precious fruits [that provide color, aroma, flavor, beauty, and pleasure].
>
> Moreover, this world is not just anyone's garden; it is G-d's garden. As the verse states, I have come to My garden. [Its goodness is therefore measured according to His infinite terms....]
>
> With this perspective, we [are able to] view the world differently; we begin to notice things that we may have missed upon first glance. When we realize that it is our responsibility to constantly search [for G-d and for the good], we endeavor to look around us and perceive that which is beneath the shell, the fruit that is under the peel.[5]

Furthermore, despite all evidence to the contrary:

> We are confident that we will successfully uncover the garden that is latent in creation, because the

> Torah tells us that it is indeed there, waiting to be discovered....
>
> Knowing that a precious treasure awaits discovery, we remain focused on our task and do not allow ourselves to be sidetracked by other endeavors....
>
> We must know that we inhabit a wonderful world. And through contemplating the above, we may assuredly traverse through life...secure in the knowledge that we will find the fruits of G-d's garden.

Easy for You to Say

Regardless of how well-intentioned they are, such statements often leave one feeling as if the person saying them must never have experienced true suffering.

However, let's recall that the Rebbe lived through waves of pogroms, a typhus epidemic, a refugee crisis, the killing fields of World War I, the Bolshevik revolution, the rise of Communism, the forced exile of his father, who ended up passing away while in exile, World War II, and childlessness. Additionally, as a Rebbe, and even before—as we will see—his life was dedicated to absorbing and carrying the pain of hundreds of thousands of individuals who came to him for healing, advice, blessing, support, love, acceptance, help, and even a reason to live.

Similarly, R. Yosef Yitzchak, who first introduced the idea that the world as we know it is yet "G-d's garden," also lived a life of unimaginable pain and suffering, both personal and historical.

After all, R. Yosef Yitzchak was imprisoned, tortured,

exiled, and sentenced to death by the Soviets, survived the carpet-bombing of Warsaw at the beginning of World War II, suffered from multiple sclerosis, lost a daughter in the Treblinka death camp, witnessed the members of his movement drastically dwindle due to Communism and the Holocaust, and saw the widespread assimilation of American Jews upon his arrival.

In the Rebbe's own words:[6]

> All of the above are the views of a *man who has seen affliction* (Lamentations 3:1), who underwent unspeakable suffering, both before and after arriving on the welcoming shores of America....

And yet, as the Rebbe pointed out in 1972, he was still able to see G-d's garden beneath all of man's destruction and desecration.

The Rebbes had lived through the violent paroxysms of a world gone mad and witnessed up close the "most civilized of nations" as it was transformed almost overnight into the cruelest of killing machines.

Suffering alongside millions of their brethren, they looked on broken-heartedly as European Jewry was destroyed, all while the "developed" and "enlightened" world stood silently by and wondered what to do about "the Jewish question."

These men had every right to be cynical about the world and the human condition and lose faith in the progress of history and humanity.

And yet, despite all they'd been through, both Rebbes steadfastly maintained this fundamental teaching throughout the period of their leadership: "The world is inherently good, intentionally crafted, and not only that, but beautiful too. Reality itself is a veritable work of sacred art!"

Both, in their own way, committed every fiber of their beings to healing the broken spirit of a battered people, and helping rebuild and renew their faith in G-d, His world and creations, one day at a time, and one good deed at a time.

Time and again, no matter what they faced in life, they stated loud and clear: This world is a garden! Its upkeep has been left in our care.

No matter how littered the past is with our collective monstrosities and personal mistakes, we are each, in essence, eminently capable of revealing the holy sparks of light that lie scattered beneath the surface of a shattered world.

Toward this end, we must each make sure to attune our perception to never lose sight of life's pristine beauty, nor forget Whose hand fashioned its design!

This is our redemptive work as faithful gardeners, for which the Rebbe never stopped preparing us: To always see good in the world, to always see G-d in the world, and to tend to His garden.

This fundamental spiritual mission statement, full of holy *chutzpah* and hope, came to the forefront of Jewish consciousness when it was most needed, rising like a phoenix from the smoldering ashes of hatred, fear, and genocide to inspire an army of like-minded illuminators.

This was the Rebbe's way—to banish darkness through light.

CHAPTER 2

Dwell on the Positive

HAVE YOU EVER WONDERED why newspapers are so full of bad news? Or why people often spend so much more time fretting about what's wrong in their lives instead of appreciating what's going right? Why do painful experiences take up so much real estate in our memory? And why are they so much easier to recall than pleasurable ones? Why do we often feel that it is our negative experiences that define us rather than our positive ones?

Scientists have coined the term "negativity bias" to describe this phenomenon of how human consciousness relates to the world. Essentially, our negativity bias ensures that experiences of a more negative nature have a greater effect on our psychological state and consequent behavior than neutral or positive ones, even when they are of equal intensity.

According to neuroscientists, our brains have developed specialized circuits that register negative experiences immediately in emotional memory so that we can learn from them.

On the other hand, most positive experiences flow through the brain like water through a sieve; we experience them, enjoy them, and quickly forget them.

Accordingly, we use much more brain space to scan and process negative experiences than positive ones, because negative stimuli, if not registered and responded to appropriately, can be fatal.

Out of necessity, we have become masters of fixating on the negative aspects of our lives and environments.

This is only natural.

This negativity bias is what allows us to remain vigilant in our efforts to register and respond to any potential dangers and imminent threats to our well-being—ideally, before it is too late.

The problem is that this negativity bias has a side effect.

Since we are always on high alert for potential dangers, the positive aspects of our lives tend to get less attention. When we receive a compliment, for instance, we feel nice for a moment, but then the brain shifts back to a more defensive mode and we forget those warm, positive feelings.

Similarly, if we have nine positive experiences or interactions during the day and one negative experience, it is most likely that at the end of the day we will remember the negative experience most vividly.

We may therefore walk around in a low-level state of

hypervigilance and anxiety. As a result, we tend to blow our negative experiences out of proportion and fail to contextualize them within the positive aspects of our life that we have forgotten in moments of stress.

Establishing a positive mindset is therefore quite difficult, as it goes against the grain of our established nature. And yet, maintaining a positive perspective in the midst of hardship is essential to elevating one's quality of life.

The Rebbe was well aware of the natural tendency of human consciousness to dwell on the negative. Nevertheless, he consistently insisted that we could change our experience of life for the better by making conscious and concerted efforts to focus and dwell on the positive.

Indeed, as mentioned, the Rebbe once referred to his focus on seeing things positively, saying, "I worked on myself to look at things in a positive light, otherwise I could not have survived."[7]

When one considers the immense challenges and devastating events the Rebbe experienced in his lifetime, this statement is truly remarkable.

It is worth pointing out that the Rebbe's approach to dwelling on the positive, or what we refer to throughout this book as his Positivity Bias, was never meant to be a naive white-washing or covering up of actual reality. In fact, what was so unique about the Rebbe's worldview and motivational theology was that it did not ignore or deny the harsh realities of life; rather, it acknowledged and addressed them head-on.

One example among many is the following response the Rebbe penned to someone who wrote despairingly of their life.

No Satisfaction

The Rebbe writes:[8]

> I received your letter in which you describe your economic circumstances and certain other conditions which are the causes of [your] dissatisfaction and lack of spiritual gratification.
>
> If you have a copy of your letter, and will re-read it again in a more objective frame of mind, I think you will come to the conclusion that human life on this earth unfortunately is not free from various factors which bring about unhappiness; and that this is universal, though the causes vary.... To go through life in complete happiness is not destined for man. One of the basic things, however, is to have a clear vision on the fundamental issues, and to cultivate [appropriate expectations and] attitudes.

The ultimate goal is not to completely avoid or remove all challenges or conflicts in one's life. That, according to the Rebbe, is impossible. And, as we will see, it would not even guarantee our happiness, because so much depends on our perspective in relation to our actual circumstances. It is, however, within our power to "cultivate attitudes" in order to process and integrate all of our experiences, including the negative, in a way that liberates rather than limits our potential for success and happiness. Seeing life from a wider angle than just our own immediate experience is a crucial first step in shifting our negative response patterns.

Doctor's Orders

Interestingly, the Rebbe makes a similar point regarding Maimonides.

In a letter written by the Rebbe to someone regarding the necessity of maintaining an optimistic outlook, he wrote:[9]

> It is clearly observable that to a great and discernible degree, the effect of one's life events depends largely on how one reacts to them. And who is a better example of this than Maimonides, whose outward life was filled with misfortune, turbulence, suffering, and tragedy—may the Merciful One save us—to a greater degree than the average person. Nevertheless he maintained a very positive—and in today's vernacular, optimistic—view on life, as articulated in his work, *The Guide for the Perplexed.*

The Rebbe here refers to the following passage from *The Guide for the Perplexed* (3:12):

> People often think that the evils in the world are more numerous than the good things; many sayings and songs of the Nations dwell on this idea. They say that a good thing is found only exceptionally, while evil things are numerous and lasting. Not only common people make this mistake, but even many who believe that they are wise.
>
> This error results from judging the whole universe by what occurs to a single person. Only an ignorant person believes that the whole universe exists for him alone, as if nothing else required any consideration. If, therefore, anything happens to him con-

> trary to his expectation, he at once concludes that the whole universe is evil. If, however, he would take into consideration the whole universe, form an idea of it, and comprehend what a small portion he is of it, he will find the truth.

When one is able to zoom out from a narrow self-orientation, it becomes possible to appreciate that, all-in-all, Creation is overwhelmingly good and "in order." Stars in their orbits, seasons turning, mountain heights, ocean depths, birdsong in the morning.

Of course, our lives are also full of worries, dangers, and dramas, but we must not get stuck in our own circumference and fall prey to negative projections and self-fulfilling prophecies.

Contemplating one's place within the vast wonders of Creation is a time-honored practice of dwelling on the positive.

Don't Forget What You Have

One significant side-effect of the negativity bias is that we tend to fixate on what is lacking in our lives rather than on what we have.

In another pointed letter,[10] written to an individual who was struggling financially and complained that he had "never experienced goodness in his life," the Rebbe wrote:

> In response to your letter…in which you write about your current situation and that throughout your life you have not experienced any good….
>
> It seems that you do not sense the contradiction in

> your letter. For a man whom G-d has blessed with a wife and children to say that he has never seen any good is ungrateful to an alarming degree.... Hundreds, even thousands, of people pray every day to be blessed with children and would give everything they own to have a single child but have not as of yet merited this....
>
> But you, the recipient of this blessing, which it seems came to you without you having to especially pray for it, don't recognize the wealth and happiness in the blessings you have, and you write twice in your letter that you have never experienced any good!

It is worth noting that the Rebbe himself never had children and deeply understood this particular pain on a personal level. He was therefore in a unique position, not just spiritually but existentially, to point out the magnificent blessing that this person had received, and that they were, judging from the Rebbe's response, taking for granted.

Too often we simply don't keep the good things in our life at the forefront of our mind; we are too busy scanning for threats and dangers. They therefore tend to quietly and quickly recede into the hungry shadows of our long-suffering complaints. These complaints, if left unchecked, naturally override our awareness and skew our evaluation of life.

Count Your Blessings

In another letter to someone who complained about their life, the Rebbe alludes to the blessings recited every morning. These particular blessings take note of and thank G-d for some of the very basic amenities of human existence: The gift of a new day, the ability to see, the clothes we wear, the earth beneath our feet, and the strength to carry on.

Actively beginning each day by acknowledging the blessings we often take for granted allows us to gain the proper perspective on our life so that we are not overwhelmed by gnawing negativity and anxiety. To the contrary, we are filled with gratitude for all the tiny miracles in our life!

> I read [your letter] with great shock. If you pay attention to the simple meaning of the eighteen morning blessings, in which you bless G-d at the beginning of every day, you will see that you have been blessed with all of them. In addition, you have been blessed with good health, good parents, good education, a good community, a good profession, livelihood, and more.
>
> If so, what is the justification for your complaints?![11]

No matter what else is going on in your life, if you are alive you have something to be grateful for; you just need to take the time to recognize and appreciate it.

One way to focus and dwell on the positive is to literally count your blessings every day, no matter how small they may seem. Toward this end, our Sages instituted that we recite (at least) 100 blessings each day.[12]

This practice of near-constant expressions of gratitude throughout the day has the power to sensitize us to G-d's gifts and presence all around us, if we would but take the time to stop and notice. Over time this conscious attention to the blessings in our lives, both large and small, can help shift our default setting from an ungrateful negativity bias to a Positivity Bias focused on appreciation.

Choose Gratitude

R. Dovid Schochet—the president of the Council of Orthodox Rabbis of Toronto—had his first audience with the Rebbe in 1952, when he enrolled in the central Lubavitcher *yeshivah* in Brooklyn. What he remembers most from that initial meeting was the Rebbe's guidance on actively appreciating life.

"Don't take life for granted," the Rebbe said. "In the morning, when you wake up, thank G-d for everything that has been given to you." Many people go to sleep at night and, when they wake up in the morning, they expect their shoes to be by their bed where they left them the night before. As they are getting dressed, they complain that the weather is too cold or too hot. They are essentially criticizing G-d, because who creates the weather? Instead, they should be grateful that they are still alive, that their possessions are still with them, that a new day is beginning where they have an opportunity to do many good deeds.

According to Rabbi Schochet, this was a lesson he never forgot.[13]

It is important to remember, as explored previously, that the Rebbe spent time as a refugee fleeing across Europe and the Atlantic Ocean during World War II. He knew firsthand what it meant to lose almost everything. For him to be able to give such advice after experiencing such horrors speaks volumes to his belief in and commitment to this practice of actively invoking and dwelling on the positive.

Indeed, the Rebbe saw the cultivation of an attitude of gratitude as a pillar of Jewish consciousness and spiritual practice.

The Rebbe's Favorite Prayer

As the following story conveys,[14] the Rebbe cherished Judaism's daily practice of not taking things for granted above all else.

When R. Nochum Stillerman was a teenager growing up in the Crown Heights section of Brooklyn, he used to deliver groceries to community members, including the Rebbe's mother, Rebbetzin Chana Schneerson, of blessed memory.

She was always very kind to him and would often invite him into her home for cookies and milk.

On one such occasion, he mustered the courage to ask, "Rebbetzin, what is the Rebbe's favorite prayer?"

She answered, "Of course, all the prayers are important, but yes, there must be one that is closest to the Rebbe's heart. I don't know which one that is, but the next time he is here, I will ask him on your behalf."

The following week, when young Nochum saw the Rebbetzin, she said, "I am so happy to have an answer to your question. It's a very short prayer. It's the first prayer we say in the morning, *Modeh ani lefanecha*—'I offer thanks to You, living and eternal King, for You have restored my soul within me with mercy; Your faithfulness is great.'"

"That's it?" he asked.

"Yes," she said. "That's his favorite."

Nochum was surprised by this answer. *Modeh Ani* is such

a short prayer and doesn't even contain G-d's name! Indeed, it is the one prayer we recite while still in bed, before getting dressed and formally starting our day. Surely, one of the more elaborate and sophisticated prayers that are recited later in the day must be more important!

But this prayer, above all others, was the Rebbe's favorite,[15] alerting us to the cardinal importance he accorded to actively focusing one's attention on the gift of life, and making this appreciation the cornerstone of one's consciousness.[16]

Vessels for Blessing

One final point worth making is that from the Rebbe's perspective, dwelling on the positive is not just about generating a feeling of psychological well-being; it is also an actual investment in our future.

According to Chasidut, the words and feelings of gratitude that we express to G-d for the blessings we already have in our lives actually become the vessels and vehicles for new blessings and abundance to flow into our lives.

In a certain sense, the expression of gratitude in the present begets what to be grateful for in the future.

In response to a strongly-worded letter written by someone who bitterly complained that they lacked any positive aspects in their life due to their myriad struggles, the Rebbe wrote:[17]

> I'm not implying that one is supposed to struggle for a living or not enjoy perfect health [G-d forbid]. My point is that perhaps the reason for your weak health and your difficulties in earning a living is

> your failure to appreciate G-d's blessings to you in a far more basic matter than perfect health and abundant sustenance—the blessing of sons and daughters who follow the ways of G-d [for instance]. When one does not recognize the explicit good bestowed [on them] from Above, particularly when one's lack of recognition is so extreme that it results in statements such as you express in your letter, is it any wonder that [more] blessings are not forthcoming from Above in other matters?
>
> My hope is that these few lines will suffice to open your eyes to see your situation in its true light. And when you begin to serve G-d with a true and inner joy, surely G-d will increase His blessings also in regard to health and sustenance...

In another letter,[18] the Rebbe makes a similar point and highlights the importance of expressing appreciation to G-d for the blessings one has in one's life already before asking for more:

> Obviously you must pray that G-d fulfill all your needs from His full hand...but it must be preceded by thankfulness for His abundant kindness to you.

If we want more good in our lives and in the world, we must actively acknowledge and deeply integrate the positive aspects of life that we are already experiencing and be grateful to G-d, who provides that good.

To do this we must counter the natural tendency to focus on the negative aspects of life surrounding us. Not that we should blind ourselves to the many threats and dangers in our midst, but we must learn to actively dwell on the positive that we do possess so that we are not overwhelmed by constant anxiety and feelings of lack, which block the flow of blessings that G-d wants to funnel into our lives.

Heartfelt appreciation opens the gates for G-d's abundance!

CHAPTER 3

What are Humans Made Of?

VIENNA, 1960. VIKTOR FRANKL, the world-famous author and psychologist, was ready to uproot his whole life—his research, his clinical practice, his family—and move to Australia.

Having survived the unimaginable horrors of the Holocaust, emerging from the ashes of Auschwitz with an unorthodox and daring theory of human psychology, he could no longer endure the constant derision of his life's work by his colleagues in the field. Frankl's view of human nature differed in certain key areas from the party-line views that dominated the discipline of psychology after the war, making him and his work a consistent target of public scholarly ridicule.

It was this very diminution of his deepest held beliefs

regarding the inner makeup of the human being that was the last straw. He could survive the attacks of the Nazis on his body, but he could no longer bear the attacks of his peers on his soul.

It was at that moment when Marguerite Kozenn-Chajes (1909-2000), a well-known opera singer and descendant of Vizhnitz Chasidim, knocked on his door in Vienna.[19] When Dr. Frankl came to the door he found a sharply dressed woman whom he had never met before standing on his doorstep.

She announced herself as the bearer of a personal message addressed to him by a Chasidic Rebbe, R. Menachem Mendel Schneerson, from Brooklyn, New York. Upon hearing this startling explanation for her visit, and recognizing the name of the Rebbe, Dr. Frankl promptly invited Mrs. Chajes inside to speak privately.

"The Rebbe asked me to tell you," she began, "that you must not give up. You must be strong. Do not be disturbed by those who ridicule you. You will succeed and your work will achieve a major breakthrough."

Upon hearing this reassuring voice from afar, Dr. Frankl broke into tears. Dispirited, he had just recently been filling out his immigration papers to Australia. He had given up—but the Rebbe's words of encouragement brought Dr. Frankl back to life.

After regaining his composure, Dr. Frankl responded vigorously with a renewed commitment to continue his life's work. And, indeed, he did. Following this fateful meeting, Dr. Frankl redoubled his efforts in spreading his unique insights and therapeutic approaches to healing the human psyche. Not long afterward, his magnum opus, Man's Search for Meaning, was translated into English, sparking immediate popular interest in his work and worldview that has continued to this very day. That work alone has been translated into 28 languages and sold over ten million copies, giving birth to an entire genre of self-help literature as well as the field of logotherapy, Frankl's unique philosophy and practice of psychological health and healing.

History tells us that Viktor Frankl went on to become one of the most influential thinkers of the 20th century; he lived through the hell of the Holocaust and nevertheless found the strength to put forth an inspiring view of the human psyche that diverged in fundamental ways from the accepted norms of his time. But why was the Rebbe so concerned with Dr. Frankl and, particularly, with the fate of his work? There were plenty of psychologists at the time, what was it about Dr. Frankl's view of the human psyche that so piqued the Rebbe's interest and attracted his personal attention and support?

To answer that question, we must dig deeper into the beginnings of psychoanalysis itself. In the 1920s, Viktor Frankl was a prized student of Sigmund Freud. Indeed, from the very inception of the field of psychoanalysis, Frankl was an early adopter and gifted adept of Freud's radical theories and practices. However, after a time, their ideas about the shape and substance of human nature began to diverge.

In Freudian thought, the human self is defined by—and entangled in—a perpetual struggle to balance competing drives and desires, conscious and unconscious. Frankl, by contrast, emphasized the soul's potential to transcend the limitations of the self through a search for deeper meaning and acts of loving kindness.

This fundamental rift between their perspectives only grew wider and more pronounced over the years.

Sigmund Freud, having passed away in 1939, was never forced to face the ultimate inhumanity of the Holocaust; one can only imagine how that might have complicated or clarified his initial insights into the psychic nature of the human being.

Viktor Frankl, on the other hand, survived Auschwitz. He heard its terrible sounds and saw its dark visions; he tasted its putrid waters and smelled its rotting corpses, but he also witnessed miraculous deeds of utter selflessness and caring.

"If Freud were in the concentration camps," Frankl wrote,[20] "he would have changed his position. Beyond the basic natural drives and instincts of people, he would have encountered the human capacity for self-transcendence. We who lived in concentration camps can remember the men who walked through the huts comforting others, giving away their last piece of bread. They may have been few in number, but they offer sufficient proof that everything can be taken from a man but one thing: The last of the human freedoms—to choose one's attitude in any given set of circumstances; to choose one's own way."

It was thus within the crucible of that horrific concentration camp that Frankl came to refine and crystallize his earlier intuitions concerning the underlying realities of human psychology. Once the war was over, Dr. Frankl could not avoid the inevitable collision with the founding principles and devoted followers of his former teacher.

The essential question is whether an underlying, integral spiritual essence—a soul—exists beneath it all. Are we defined by the limited circumstantial ingredients that make up our particular personality, or is there something deeper and infinite within our makeup that we can access and activate to transcend our own limitations?

Freud and Frankl, each in his own way, sought to uncover what lies hidden within our psychic depths beneath the masks we show the world. They both wanted to know what truly defines and drives human behavior—who are we really? And, more importantly, who can we be?

In response to these questions, both Freud and Frankl posited the existence of a stratified structure of human consciousness. Meaning, that each human contains multiple levels of awareness, including, of course, the unconscious regions of the psyche that exert primal influences upon our behavior and express themselves in mysterious ways through dreams and language.

Dr. Frankl believed that underneath the varying self-serving or socio-adaptive drives there is something deeper—an inner essence, a soul that transcends and includes the complex elements of the psyche and mind.

This level of our being is primarily driven by a "striving to find meaning in one's life." Hence the title of his best-selling book—Man's Search for Meaning.

This fundamental difference of opinion between Freud and Frankl concerning what lies at the root of the human psyche is beautifully encapsulated in a conversation between the Rebbe and a well-known professor who complained to the Rebbe about the twisted nature of people:

"From my encounters in life, I have noticed that people might seem nice and charming at the outset. They may express concern for you, show interest in your life, and even openly admit that they love you! But if one digs just a little deeper than the outer surface—some require more digging than others—at their core, everyone is exactly the same—selfish, arrogant, and egotistical. Why is this the nature of mankind?"

The Rebbe responded with a parable:

"When one walks on the street, things often look so elegant and appealing—tall flowery trees, fancy houses, paved roads, and expensive cars. But if one takes a shovel and begins digging beneath the surface, he discovers dirt and mud, nothing like the beautiful but 'deceptive' world above ground."

At this point the professor was nodding his head in agreement.

"But—if he weren't to give up," the Rebbe concluded, "and would continue digging deeper, he would eventually encounter precious minerals and diamonds."

The Rebbe acknowledged the fact that beneath the surface of people's outward personalities, there often lies a much less flattering psychic reality. However, the Rebbe further stressed that beneath all the "dirt and mud" there is something deeper, something beautiful and holy: There is a soul.

This is perhaps why the Rebbe took such a strong interest in Dr. Frankl and his work. Frankl's view of the human psyche corresponded quite closely with that of Chasidic understanding: We have a soul beneath the surface of the self. This soul forms the very core of our being and connects us to other souls and to a Higher power. Activation of this core point within is what allows us to transcend our baser nature and become a force for good in the world.

Throughout the years following his initial motivating message to Dr. Frankl, the Rebbe wrote admiringly about Frankl's approach:[21] "It is obvious [that] some doctors have helped and healed their patients in straight ways, especially since one professor (Frankl) found the courage in his soul to declare and announce that, contrary to the opinion of the famous founder of psychoanalysis (Freud), faith in G-d, and a religious inclination in general, which gives meaning to life, etc., is one of the most effective ways of healing."

Additionally, the Rebbe continued to support and endorse his work,[22] even suggesting to other scholars and psychologists[23] that Frankl's work would be a good place to find and forge further connections between the views of psychology and the teachings of Chasidism.

What's more, despite the fact that Dr. Frankl rarely engaged the Jewish community in any public way, he became a consistent supporter of Chabad's work in Vienna for the rest of his life.

It is clear from all of the above stories that ultimately, despite Freud's uncontested influence in the field of psychology, the Rebbe felt a kinship toward Dr. Frankl's ideas and approach to healing and motivating the human being to become more human. The Rebbe agreed with Dr. Frankl that each person has the potential to be so much more than just their body and their ego. By activating their inner point of ultimate meaning, a person can escape the quicksand of self-centered obsessions and truly become holy.

CHAPTER 4

Who is a Good Jew?

IN THE PREVIOUS CHAPTER, we explored the different views of Viktor Frankl and Sigmund Freud concerning human nature in general. What are people made of? What really lies beneath the surface of the masks we wear and present to the world? Are we splintered selves motivated by competing desires, or are we aspiring souls seeking deeper meaning and connection with others?

The answers to these questions that we subscribe to are not just theoretical or academic, they define in our minds what it is to be human, which in turn validates or challenges what we take to be acceptable or achievable goals and behaviors. In so many ways, our lives are our personal answer to that most existential of questions: Who and what am I?

In this chapter, we will continue this line of inquiry as

we analyze a further extension of the Rebbe's Positivity Bias as it applies to the Jewish soul in particular.

Hypocrite Redefined

A man once told the Rebbe that he felt like a hypocrite when he went to shul on Yom Kippur because he didn't go the rest of the year. The Rebbe responded by saying that the natural place for a Jew to be is in shul. "You're not a hypocrite when you go to shul on Yom Kippur," he said. "You're a hypocrite when you don't go to shul the rest of the year."[24]

So many Jews struggle with their Jewish identity. Based on how they were raised or what kind of life they lead, they tend to think of themselves as "bad Jews" or "good Jews," religious or secular, and so on. This self-definition then influences their decisions to participate in the life and rituals of the community or not. According to the Rebbe, however, being Jewish means that fulfilling the *mitzvot* is the most natural and truly authentic thing for one to do. Anything else is just another expression of exile from one's indigenous soul.

The Rebbe further emphasizes this point in a letter written to someone who had sought his counsel:

> There can be no question of hypocrisy when a Jew learns Torah and conducts his life in accordance with the Torah and *mitzvot,* even if some of his other actions, even feelings, do not always harmonize with his Torah study and observance; because the incongruity lies not in acting according to the Torah and *mitzvot,* rather it lies in acting contrary to the Torah and *mitzvot.*[25]

The Rebbe saw the Jewish soul as being healthiest and most fulfilled when in alignment with Torah. This is indeed a Jew's most natural state of vitality, and anything else is a stress and shock to their system. Accordingly, he worked tirelessly as a kind of spiritual chiropractor, realigning an entire generation and reconnecting each of us to our true source of power and purpose.

Family Tree of Life

In a letter written to a youngster who informed the Rebbe about his upcoming bar mitzvah, the Rebbe added the following postscript:[26]

> Regarding that which you write that you "stem from a secular family": certainly the "secular-ness" is an ancillary condition and an external "garment" that covers your essence and core. For every member of your family is a son of Abraham, Isaac, and Jacob, and a daughter of Sarah, Rebecca, Rachel, and Leah; and, following them were tens of generations of followers of Torah and its precepts.
>
> G-d gave Man choice with regards to his actions; however, he cannot whatsoever change the essence and core of his truest nature.

Our families and our lives may appear staunchly secular on the surface. But this betrays our bedrock disposition as "believers and children of believers." According to the Rebbe, faith is the cornerstone of our individual and collective consciousness. Everything else is just cosmetic additions onto a facade, so to speak.

In a related letter,[27] the Rebbe clarifies this point further:

> I must take exception to what you call at the conclusion of your letter, "my lost Judaism." The expression "lost" does not really fit here, for no person can lose something that is his or her true essence and inner nature. What is possible is that this true essence of a person is sometimes in a state of "suspended animation," or covered over with various layers of foreign substances, even those that are at variance with this essence. But this essence can never be "lost"; it can only be dormant, as it were, instead of being active and expressed on the surface as it should be.

In this letter, the Rebbe draws a distinction between a person's actions or outward appearances and their essence or innermost aspect. According to Chasidut, as well as psychology, a human is a geological being, with strata upon strata of psychic and spiritual sediment settled beneath the surface. In the Rebbe's view, beneath all of our competing urges, influences, appetites, and drives there is something unified, whole, and infinite—an eternal soul created in G-d's image. This—rather than the various forces within clamoring for our attention—is what defines us; this is who we truly always are, if only we could quiet the storms of self to hear the still voice of the soul.

Of Roots and Fruits

The Rebbe was once asked by Professor Velvl Greene whether the Freudian notion of conscious and subconscious has a parallel in Judaism.

In response,[28] the Rebbe referred to Maimonides' explanation of a particular halachic question,[29] in which the rabbinic court is allowed to influence a person's behavior to act in accordance with the prescribed law. On the surface, this may appear as "tampering" with a witness or defendant to elicit the desired answer or outcome. However, the Rebbe creatively employs Freud's division of the human psyche to reveal the deeper psycho-spiritual dimensions of Rambam's halachic ruling.

> ...To use contemporary terminology [as requested in your original question]: The conscious state of a Jew can be affected by external pressures that induce states of mind and even behavior that is contrary to his subconscious, which is the Jew's essential nature. When the external pressures are removed, it does not constitute a change or transformation of his essential nature, but, on the contrary, is merely the reassertion of his innate and true character....

The Rebbe viewed the Jewish soul as intrinsically whole and holy at root, and it is therefore only on the surface that the fruits of our actions may become rancid. Our essence, however, is always pure and predisposed to divinity.

A disciple from a neighboring Chasidic community once visited the Rebbe for a blessing. After discussing his personal issue, the Chasid asked a question: "The Talmud states[30] that 'even the "sinners of Israel" have as many good deeds as a pomegranate has seeds.' But isn't that statement contradictory? If someone is truly a 'sinner of Israel' how can the

Talmud say that he is full of good deeds?" The Rebbe closed his eyes and nodded, quietly beginning to cry.

"I have a question on the very same passage," replied the Rebbe. "If the Jew we speak of is truly 'full of good deeds,' *how can he be called 'a sinner of Israel'*?"[31]

Obviously, these different viewpoints have nothing to do with the percentage of good deeds versus sins performed by those whom the Talmud calls the "sinners of Israel." For everyone knows that even those who sin have some merits as well, and by the same token even righteous people have shortcomings.

The real question raised by this story is therefore one of essence: Are these Jews essentially sinners who have performed a few good deeds, or are they wholly righteous at their root, regardless of the fact that they have made some mistakes? In other words, what defines the essence of a Jew—the inclination to do good or the opposite? Which force is intrinsic to the Jewish soul and which is imported?

The Rebbe argued time and again, often in the face of opposition, that it is the goodness and G-dliness of the Jewish soul that defines who and what a Jew is, regardless of their level of religious observance. As the Talmud teaches:[32] "Even when the Jewish People have sinned, they are still called Israel." Any momentary deviation from this pure essence is just that—a deviation from the eternally established norm. As the *Tanya* further explains: "Even while the sin is being committed, the Divine soul always believes in the One G-d and remains faithful to Him."[33]

Here then is a classic example of two individuals looking at an identical text but seeing something vastly different.

What becomes clear from this story is not just the spiritual state of the Jews under discussion in the Talmud, but also the mind state of the people having the discussion itself. For each is choosing what to focus their attention on—the negative or the positive aspects at play.

As illustrated by this story, we are all inescapably biased in some way. The question is: What is your bias? When you judge others, or even yourself, are you actively looking to emphasize positivity or its opposite? It's up to you to decide.

For, at the end of the day, we see what we are looking for.

Spirit of Folly

Yet the above discussion raises an important and unavoidable question: If I am so good, where does sin come from?

In response, the Talmud answers profoundly,[34] "A person does not commit a transgression unless a spirit of folly enters him." Far from being needlessly metaphorical, the Talmud here weighs in precisely on our question regarding the makeup of a human being.

Unlike others—whether religious or secular—who believe that mankind, due to some original stain or disposition, are selfish sinners by nature, the Talmud suggests that we are in essence righteous beings who are nevertheless vulnerable to the wiles of an external "spirit of folly." If undetected, this spirit can lead us astray from our inner soul-essence, which is purely good. However, the Torah teaches[35] that G-d created man in His image. Just as G-d is inherently good, so too is the being He created. Thus, in Jewish thought, it is evil, not goodness, which is alien to man; a foreign product smuggled in from the outside, a forbidden fruit grafted onto our holy root. Goodness, righteousness, holiness—this is who we are by Divine design, and what we naturally want to express in life.

It is essential for our own mental health and self-image to distinguish between our actions, which may waver from good to bad, and our essence, which is always good. We may sometimes be hijacked or led astray, but that does not change who we are on the deepest level. However, it does raise the issue: How do we regain control and realign our actions with our essence?

Return to the Land of Your Soul

The famed medieval Spanish Kabbalist and Biblical commentator, R. Moshe ben Nachman, known as Nachmanides or Ramban (1194–1270) had a disciple named Avner. Following a crisis of faith, Avner rejected his Jewish faith, left the community behind, and became a government official.

One Yom Kippur, Avner sent guards to summon his former teacher to appear before him. Spitefully, he then proceeded to slaughter, roast, and eat a pig in front of Ramban, on the holiest fast day of the year.

The Ramban asked him, "What brought you to this point? What caused you to reject the holy ways of your ancestors?!"

"You did, Rabbi!" Avner retorted venomously. "Your teachings were exaggerated and had no basis in reality. You once taught us that in the brief Torah portion of *Haazinu*, a mere 52 verses, the Torah encodes the entire history of the Jewish People until the coming of Moshiach.

"This is just ridiculous!" scoffed Avner. "How could 3,000 years of history (and literally millions of names) be condensed into just 614 words?"

"But it's true," replied Ramban, holding his ground.

"Then show me my name and my fate," Avner challenged incredulously.

The Ramban fell into a state of meditation and prayed silently to G-d to reveal this secret.

"Your name, Avner, can be found in the third letter of each word in the verse, (אמרתי) אפאיהם אשביתה מאנוש זכרם."[36]

The verse reads: *I [G-d] said in my heart that I would scatter them, causing their memory to cease from mankind,* referring to those who had rejected Torah and a Jewish way of life.

Avner's face turned pale as heavy tears began to fall.

"Is there any hope for me?" he sobbed. "What can I possibly do to rectify my unthinkable sins?"

"The verse itself has provided the rectification," said Ramban. "It says that G-d will scatter them until their memory is erased. You, too, must scatter those distracting, alien thoughts and impulses that have held you captive for too long, until they are forgotten. Relocate to a new environment, free from your former associations and addictions, and in this way you can return to your essence anew and be remembered for good among your people."

At a *farbrengen* in 1982,[37] the Rebbe shared that as a child he was taught this story by his teacher. The traditional point stressed by his teacher was the uniqueness of Parshas Haazinu and the infinite nature of the Torah. How, indeed, could the Torah contain such esoteric codes and secrets? "However," the Rebbe added, "there is another layer of depth to the story that has been overlooked. If you notice, the words quoted by the Ramban begin not with an *alef*, for Avner, but with a *reish* (*Amarti*). The letter *reish* is often used as a formal prefix for 'Reb,' an honorific term. Therefore, his name as quoted in this verse is Reb Avner, revealing how he is actually seen in G-d's eyes through the lens of the Torah—as a spiritual being deserving of respect and reverence."

This self-revelation, like a lightning flash, instantly brought R. Avner back into alignment with his higher nature. In fact, the moment he was exposed to the error of his ways, a spirit of *teshuvah* was immediately awakened within him. After having left his faith, even going so far as to mock and taunt its devout leaders on its holiest day, the vision of his soul that was reflected back from within the Torah instantly aroused a yearning within him to return to his roots.

Jewish thought is essentially positive in its assessment of the soul; there is no need to be "born again" or to "turn over a new leaf" in the process of the spiritual journey. Even if a person sins and seeks absolution, there is never any need to become something completely different.

In fact, the Hebrew word *teshuvah,* which is commonly translated as repentance, actually means to return.[38] This existential orientation further reinforces Judaism's core principle: The soul is eternally, essentially, and unalterably pure, no matter what; this is our root. We may sometimes branch out in various ways, but we are always attached to that root. To rectify our actions and reconnect to our soul, we merely need to reclaim and return to who we truly are and always will be—a spiritual being eternally connected to our Divine Source and Essence.

You Are What You Seek

"I came here to look for some *Yiddishkeit*," said a philanthropist who had traveled overseas to visit the Rebbe. "You didn't have to come all the way here for that," said the Rebbe. "You only had to look deep inside your own heart."

In the Rebbe's view, Jewishness or Jewish faith is not something to be sought or superimposed; rather, it emerges and expresses itself from deep within. In fact, the Talmud teaches[39] that each baby is taught the entire Torah while in the womb, which is then forgotten at the moment of birth. Torah is thus already integrated into the deepest levels of our beings; it merely seeks further expression in the world through sanctified thoughts, speech, and action.

R. Tzvi Hersh Weinreb moved with his family to Maryland to pursue a career in psychology. At one point he was going through a difficult time and decided to call the Rebbe for guidance. The Rebbe's secretary answered the phone and asked the caller to identify himself. Not wanting to disclose his name due to the sensitive nature of his questions, Rabbi Weinreb replied only, "A Jew from Maryland." He went on to outline the questions for which he wanted the Rebbe's guidance—uncertainties regarding his life, his career, and his faith. Suddenly, Rabbi Weinreb heard the Rebbe's voice in the background: "Tell him there's a Jew in Maryland with whom he can speak. His name is Weinreb." The secretary repeated the Rebbe's words. "Yes," he exclaimed to the secretary, "but... my name is Weinreb!" Rabbi Weinreb then heard the Rebbe saying gently: "If that's the case, he should know that sometimes a person needs to speak to himself."[40]

This radical faith in each Jew led the Rebbe to see holiness and sanctity in every person, even when they themselves might not.

In a candid interview with Israeli author Shlomo Shamir, the Rebbe shared some of his thoughts on faith and the Land of Israel:[41]

"Every single Jew living in Israel today is a great believer," he said. "Sometimes without even knowing it. The Land of Israel is a 'barrel overflowing with faith,' just waiting for the spark to ignite it into a great flame.

"Take, for example, a Jewish man who lives in *Eretz Yisrael* and is a member of the Communist Party. He's apparently a communist, right? I believe that he is a great believer. There he is, living with his wife and children in a country surrounded by enemies who wish to annihilate him and his children. What's keeping this Jew in *Eretz Yisrael*? Faith in Marxism? No, I don't think so. He lives in *Eretz Yisrael*, and every once in a while rises up to defend it, because—perhaps unbeknownst to him—he believes in G-d and in the fact that *Eretz Yisrael* was given to the People of Israel. We only have to awaken inside of him the awareness of his own faith…."

"How do we do it?" asked Shamir. "How do we find a path to these great and precious believers? Need we launch a campaign of religious *hasbarah* (publicity and promotion)? Must we first acquire good and wise leaders?"

"No," said the Rebbe. "There's no need for religious *hasbarah*, and great leaders are only needed to create something when there is nothing. The faith exists already. It's inside each Jew, just waiting to be liberated."[42]

It's Yours!

In an inspired attempt to summarize the essence of Judaism for students and seekers of all ages, the Rebbe selected twelve Torah passages from the entire corpus of Jewish literature and presented them as a crystallized curriculum of Jewish faith.

The very first passage states: *The Torah that Moses commanded us is the inheritance of the congregation of Jacob.*[43]

The Torah, given to us by Moses, does not belong just to rabbis or scholars, it belongs to every single Jew. Every Jew has his or her portion in the Torah. In fact, the soul of every Jew is like a letter in the Torah, which is only complete when all letters are present and accounted for.

The Torah is our inheritance; our birthright. And like an inheritance, the inheritor is entitled to it whether or not they know all its intricacies and details. It is all theirs, all at once, even before they know what it is. They do not have to earn it, but they do have to claim it.

As the Rebbe once said in reference to this *inheritance of the congregation of Jacob*: "What's the value of a priceless inheritance if you don't claim it and cash it in?"

Are You Jewish?

The view that the Torah and *mitzvot* are the automatic inheritance of every Jew regardless of prior learning or level of observance led the Rebbe to initiate a host of outreach programs whose sole purpose was to provide Jews with as many access points and opportunities to perform *mitzvot* as possible. Whether it was wrapping *tefillin,* lighting Shabbat candles or hearing the *shofar,* the Rebbe set about distributing the inheritance of the Jewish People, even going against the expressed opinions of many other religious authorities of his time who felt that *mitzvot* should only be performed by the "properly prepared."

Like the companies that comb through public legal and financial records searching for unclaimed inheritances to distribute to their rightful recipients, the Rebbe's emissaries, on his orders, position themselves on street corners around the world asking passersby, "Are you Jewish?" What they're really saying is: "I may have something meant for you, something precious, something priceless. Don't you want to claim your birthright?"

CHAPTER 5

Bringing the Close Closer

JEWISH LIFE IN EASTERN Europe during the 1700s was particularly precarious, amid persistent outbursts of extreme violence directed at whole communities. The Jewish People were still reeling from the shock and destruction left in the wake of the Chmielnicki Massacres, which left over 100,000 Jews dead across the Ukrainian landscape. Additionally, the failed messianic fervor of Shabbetai Tzvi, who eventually converted to Islam, dealt a crushing blow to Jewish spirit and morale from Europe to North Africa all the way to the Middle East.

Internally, the Jewish world was also at odds with itself and coming apart at the seams. The social gap between the educated elite and the unlettered masses was a seemingly unbridgeable chasm, leaving the majority of Jews to feel spiritually unworthy and incompetent, relegating the pursuit of G-d and Torah to the privileged few. Additionally, the Enlightenment was beginning to impact the lives of young intellectuals throughout Europe, causing many to leave religion and community behind in search of vaguely promised universal truths and individual freedoms. As a result, both the bodies and souls of the Jewish People were nearing total exhaustion and bordering on breakdown.

The great healer, teacher, and lover of the Jewish People known as the Baal Shem Tov, founder of the Chasidic movement, publicly appeared on this fraught historical stage in the middle of the 18th century. Functioning as a spiritual first-responder, the Baal Shem Tov sought to gently uplift the beaten and battered Jews of his time, reviving them from their near-pulverized state. In the face of suffering, he spread joy; in the face of power, he spread peace; and in the humble lives of simple Jews, he saw the highest light and the deepest sparks of Divinity. Through a variety of innovative approaches, including songs, storytelling, simple faith, and ecstatic spiritual practices, the Baal Shem Tov aimed at nothing less than a full-scale renewal of the Jewish spirit. To accomplish this he turned Kabbalah (the esoteric teachings and spiritual secrets of Torah) inside-out, sharing with the masses what used to be exclusive to a religious elite, thereby sparking a popular revolution of piety and passion that reverberates to this day.

Let's fast forward almost 200 years to 1951, less than a decade after the horrors of the Holocaust, and a few short years after masses of Middle Eastern Jews had been expelled from their home countries. This was the moment when the Rebbe assumed leadership. Similar to the times of the Baal Shem Tov, spiritual calamity, confusion, trauma, and displacement were sweeping the Jewish world. The horrors of genocide and forced expulsion were leaving people with profound theological and theodical questions left unanswered. Once again, Jewish spirit and morale were in ruins.

In addition to such geo-political upheaval, internal denominationalism, assimilation, and secularization had further unraveled the fabric of the people. For the most part, religious Jews kept to themselves, as did secular and progressive Jews. Left to its own devices, this socio-spiritual chasm would have continued to grow, possibly stretching the seams of the Jewish People to the point of no return.

Within this divided time, the Rebbe addressed himself first to his immediate followers, but also to the Jewish world as a whole, seeking to restore purpose, passion, cohesion, and confidence to a broken and fragmented people. Toward this end, the Rebbe came up with a daring and risky strategy, which is best summarized by R. Jonathan Sacks, former chief rabbi of England: "To search out every Jew in love, the way they were once hunted down in hate." This led him to devise various programs to engage and energize the wider Jewish world outside his own circle of followers and the religious community at large. This open-armed approach, sought to existentially expand the tent of holiness to make room for every Jew, no matter their background, level of knowledge, or observance.

From this perspective, it becomes clear that Judaism is not so much a religion as it is a family. You are not a member of a family on account of your behavior. You are a member of a family in an irrevocable way. Even the "wicked son" mentioned in the Haggadah is still part of the family. Of course, it is always unfortunate when family members are estranged—but it doesn't make them any less family. We all have a seat at the table.

According to Chasidut, every Jewish soul is essentially pure and incorruptible at its core, and nothing can ever sever the eternal bond with the Divine. It is from that inner point of essence that the Rebbe sought to connect and build up each individual whom he encountered.

A Single Point

In 1951, Gershon Kranzler came to interview the newly appointed Rebbe on behalf of the *Orthodox Jewish Life* to hear what his plans were for the future. Throughout the course of their conversation, in which the Rebbe laid out many of the core principles he would put into practice throughout the next four decades, he directly addressed this topic of reaching out to non-religious Jews based on an inherent soul-connection:

> It has always been the belief of Chabad that there is not a single Jew, as far as he may seem or thought himself to have drifted from the center of *Yiddishkeit,* who does not have some good point, some particular mitzvah that by nature or by inclination he may promote. This spark of good in each soul can and must be utilized for the good.[44]

Pilot Light

"What do you do?" the Rebbe asked a young man who came to meet with him.

"I'm a student at university," he responded. "I'm studying for a Master's degree in education."

"I, too, attended university many years ago," the Rebbe replied.

Somewhat surprised, the young man asked, "And what did you study? Theology?"

"No. I studied electrical engineering," the Rebbe responded with a smile. "But I prefer to turn on the lights in people's souls."

Seeing the young man's confusion and curiosity, the Rebbe explained that every human being has a soul, a divine spark that burns inside them. Sometimes a person moves away from their inner light—it might even seem that the light of their soul has been snuffed out. But the soul is like a pilot light—it never goes out completely. All it needs is for someone to turn up the flame, to ignite it into a blaze of illumination. This is my goal—to illuminate Jewish life through the soul by brightening and fanning its flame, until it burns bright again....[45]

Here we see the Rebbe stating his goal explicitly—to directly address the Jewish soul on its own terms and help rekindle its fire against all odds. In fact, it was this very belief and grounding in the soul of the Jewish People that inspired the Rebbe to reach out and welcome all who crossed his path, whether in person or through one of his many emissaries across the globe.

Plugging In

Drawing a parallel between the times and mission of the Baal Shem Tov and his own, the Rebbe once told a group of visiting Hillel students:[46]

> We can understand what the Baal Shem Tov did through the relationship of an electric powerhouse with a lamp that is connected to it by a wire.... It was the Baal Shem Tov's mission to explain and proclaim that every Jew, without exception, is connected with "the powerhouse," and every one of them has a switch in his innermost [depths] that will be found if searched for.
>
> "So [too], every one of us must try to find the switch in the soul of every Jew. One can never know what will make the connection—perhaps one word. But by this, you open up the well or inner fountain of their soul.

The Rebbe boldly insisted that all Jews alive after the Holocaust had the privilege and responsibility to strengthen each other's soul-expression and connection to G-d and the Jewish People. We all have something special to offer the world. You don't have to be a rabbi or a Rebbe to do this holy work. Each of us possesses a unique G-d-given soul that can refract the infinite light like no other. In the quest to uncover and unleash the power of the soul, one can choose to fixate on the darkness that surrounds it or focus on the inherent light within.

Geology 101

In a separate conversation with a group of students, when asked, "What does a Rebbe do?" the Rebbe replied:[47]

> The Jewish People are like the earth, which contains nature's treasures hidden underneath. One needs to know, however, where to dig. Dr. Freud dug in the human soul and found swampy waters and mire. Dr. Adler found rocks. Contemporary psychiatry searches for ills and traumas that must be uprooted. But when a Rebbe digs, he finds gold, silver, and diamonds.

Our methods and maps of reality determine what we seek and find within ourselves and others.

The prevailing values of the day included defining religiosity based on the level of a person's acquired knowledge and practice; their learning and observance were thus seen to create their connection to G-d. However, Chasidut in general, and the Rebbe in particular, stressed that it is the soul that is primary. Torah study and mitzvah observance are the spiritual tools and language that help express our internal connection to the Divine and each other. But we each inherently possess this internal connection, and it is always present deep down! There is simply no such thing as a "bad Jew," contrary to what some may claim. There are just different dimensions of goodness when seen in the right light.

In this spirit, the Rebbe lovingly addressed all Jews on either extreme. To secular Jews he essentially said: *You're not as secular as you think. You have an ancient tradition and an indomitable point of infinite holiness within you that yearns to serve, sing, and soar.*

This was exactly the kind of accepting, affirming, and empowering message that those estranged from Jewish life and faith needed to hear. G-d and Torah were already inside them; they just needed to "turn on the light," so to speak!

Two Lectures

In January, 1962, a woman wrote to the Rebbe. She had been raised in a "non-believing," home. Now she had attended two lectures on Torah-true Judaism that touched her deeply and presented her with a dilemma. "In what should I believe?" she asked the Rebbe. "In the path along which I have been raised and educated over many years or in that which I heard from a stranger in the course of two evenings?"

What follows is a freely-translated excerpt of the Rebbe's reply:[48]

> ...Certainly you have heard of the expression "return to roots." I'm sure that you are also aware that an education does not work in a vacuum, since in each and every individual there are [spiritual dynamics] that are rooted in the soul prior to the onset of the educational process—things that stem from the innermost heart of the soul. Furthermore, no education or conditioning can change these things; they can only suppress them for a longer or shorter period of time. This has been repeatedly demonstrated in the field of education, as well as in medical science, biology, and other fields.
>
> This is the reason why we often see that a single lecture or a short discussion—an "education" of an

> extremely brief duration—might affect a most basic change in a person. All this person needed was a catalyst that would initiate the removal of whatever has been covering up that which already exists in the inner reaches of his soul.
>
> The above is the answer to your question, "What should I believe?" The very fact that you were so deeply impressed by what you heard in the course of two evenings attests to the truth of what our Sages told us thousands of years ago: "All Jews are believers, the children of believers";[49] it is only that their faith might, at times, be obscured by a layer of foreign elements.
>
> My hope is that these few lines will suffice to shed light on the matter.

The Rebbe sought to instill in all receptive hearts this redemptive belief in the Divine point within every Jew. This helped inspire and initiate the miraculous return of so many to Jewish faith and life in the second half of the 20th century. In many ways this belief was predicated on the viewpoint that a Jew's faith, spiritual state, and ultimate value in G-d's eyes are not something that one must earn as a reward; rather, they must be claimed as an inheritance. The Rebbe's overwhelming message was: *You already belong. You are already holy. You are already loved. Now you too must love, and by loving, help others feel that they also belong.*

No Background

George Rohr is a businessman who actively supports many

Lubavitch activities. He once shared with the Rebbe that he had organized a Rosh Hashanah service for over 200 Jews "without any [Jewish] background."

The Rebbe gave him a piercing look and said, "You will explain to all of these people that they have a real background of Abraham, Isaac, and Jacob, and Sarah Rebecca, Rachel, and Leah.[50]

This very point—that even Jews with little to no traditional learning, experience, or observance had a place, not just at the table, but at the head of the table—was a cornerstone of the Rebbe's curriculum for communal rejuvenation and spiritual renaissance.

Once again we see the Rebbe focusing on the inherent light of the soul rather than on religious behavior or accomplishments as defining a Jew's essence. Every Jew is an illustrious child of our holy Patriarchs and Matriarchs, with equal access to the spiritual inheritance they bequeathed us. This was the Rebbe's empowering message to those who felt far from any meaningful Jewish life or identity.

At the same time, the Rebbe was telling the multitudes of religious Jews that they aren't as separate as they think. All of Israel is bound together—with each other, with G-d, and with the Torah.

In the Rebbe's own words, spoken on the eve of his inauguration: "*My 'mission statement' is to communicate the essential truth that love of G-d and Torah without love of your fellow Jew is not lasting or true. You cannot fully have one without the other.*"[51]

Echoing the Baal Shem Tov, time and again we find examples of the Rebbe reminding the more punctilious among our people of the enduring soul within each and every Jew, regardless of their external life experiences and choices up to that point. In fact, the ideas that we are all G-d's children and that no one other than G-d can judge the state of another's soul had always been a fundamental principle of Chasidic teaching over the centuries, as we can see from the following stories.

Soul-Maven

R. Monya Moneszon was a Chabad Chasid and successful diamond merchant. During a private audience with R. Shalom DovBer, the fifth Lubavitcher Rebbe, the Rebbe praised several individuals who appeared on the surface to be simple and unremarkable. This surprised R. Monya. When he voiced his surprise, R. Shalom DovBer replied, "They possess special qualities." "I don't see it," said R. Monya, and with that the conversation moved on to other topics.

At a later point in the conversation, R. Shalom DovBer suddenly asked R. Monya whether he had a pouch of diamonds with him. R. Monya took out a pouch and displayed the diamonds, pointing out the incredible quality of one specific stone. The Rebbe remarked, "I don't see anything special about it." R. Monya replied, "[For that] one must be a maven."

R. Shalom DovBer responded pointedly, "When it comes to seeing the special qualities of a Jew's soul, one must also be a maven."[52]

Anyone can make a snap judgment based on surface, external markers, such as outwardly expressed learning and religious observance. But a Jew is like a diamond, which can be buried and covered in dirt and sediment on the outside while at the same time shining brilliantly on the inside.

The way you view others determines in large part *what* you see in them.

Are you focused on the outer coal or on the inner flame that is just waiting to be kindled into a holy fire?

Every Jew a Diamond

One hot Sunday afternoon in the summer of 1991, an elderly woman was patiently waiting her turn in the long line of people from all walks of life who had come to receive the Rebbe's blessing and a dollar bill to give to *tzedakah*.

When her turn finally arrived, she could not contain herself and blurted out, "Rebbe! I've been standing here for only an hour and I'm already exhausted. You have been standing here for hours and hours, how do you not get tired?"

The Rebbe smiled gently and said, "When you are counting diamonds, you don't get tired."[53]

No matter the external appearance, the Rebbe saw what is buried deep within.

In this way, the Rebbe applied the Talmudic saying, "Know before Whom you stand," which is generally applied to one's awareness of G-d's presence, to a more interpersonal realm.

By foregrounding the spiritual essence of the one with whom you are interacting, an immediate awe and appreciation for the utter uniqueness of their being is brought into focus. All further interactions then flow from this infinite and loving point.

Based on this spiritual understanding of the nature of the

Jewish soul, the Rebbe would continue to offer corrective insight, even to those already "on-board" and engaged in the wider project of Jewish "outreach." This is because there is a perpetually lurking danger in the holy work of outreach to see oneself as better than or above those whom you are "reaching out to."

Bringing the Close Closer

Rabbi Yisrael Meir Lau, the former Chief Rabbi of Israel, once mentioned to the Rebbe that he was actively involved in "Kiruv Rechokim," bringing back lost Jews who have strayed afar.

The Rebbe corrected him, saying, "We cannot label anyone as being 'far.' Who are we to determine who is far and who is near? They are all close to G-d!"[54]

On another occasion, a representative of a Brooklyn Synagogue visited the Rebbe to seek his blessing.

During the course of their conversation the man praised Lubavitch's mission of "*kiruv rechokim*—bringing close those who are far from Judaism." The Rebbe replied, "People commonly use the expression of '*kiruv rechokim*' despite the fact that they say every morning before prayers that they are accepting upon themselves to fulfill the mitzvah to love your fellow as yourself. This means that no one can truly be far. However, even one who is already close can be drawn even closer." The Rebbe then proceeded to give them a blessing in their work to bring those who are close even closer.[55]

Based on the spiritually affirmative model and method of his spiritual ancestor, the Baal Shem Tov, coupled with his undying love and concern for the Jewish soul in a world turned upside-down, the Rebbe turned Judaism inside-out, putting the soul front and center.

From this place, all are holy, each in their own mysterious way. And it is ultimately only when each lamp is lit, when each voice is heard, and when each soul is seen for what it truly is that we will deeply know and understand that *All Your people are righteous*.[56] Only then will we merit to be called a "light unto the nations."

The Baal Shem Tov and the Rebbe—each in their own day and way—brought that day one hour closer through their unceasing love of G-d, the Torah, the Jewish People, and the whole world in all of its myriad expressions of ultimate unity.

CHAPTER 6

Limud Zechut: Seek Merits, Not Mistakes

TOWARD THE END OF the life of R. Yosef Yitzchak, the sixth Lubavitcher Rebbe, he gathered together some of his oldest and most trusted Chasidim and said to them: "We're looking for someone who will seek out the merits of the Jewish People and advocate on their behalf."[57]

It was only after the Rebbe accepted the mantle of Chabad leadership that they fully understood the full scope and significance of that simple statement.

From his first public address, it became clear that the Rebbe sought to make *ahavat Yisrael*—the unconditional love and acceptance of one's fellow—the cornerstone of his unceasing effort to heal and revitalize the Jewish People in the aftermath of the horrors of the Holocaust.

R. Yosef Yitzchak saw the need for, and the Rebbe set into motion, a radical new approach to uplift and activate the Jewish People, emphasizing joy over judgment, compassion over condemnation, and empowerment over exclusion.

Toward this end, the Rebbe set out to accomplish nothing less than a full-scale revolution of Jewish values by utilizing the foundations of the Chasidic movement, which sought to illuminate and activate the inner soul of the Jewish people.

A deep belief in the indomitable presence of a redemptive spark within each individual led the Rebbe to constantly strive to acknowledge and amplify whatever point of goodness a person might possess.

This is referred to as *limud zechut*, finding merit in others. In addition to "judging others favorably," as the Mishnah demands,[58] *limud zechut* literally means, the "study of another's merit," which implies a conscious, concerted, and creative effort to discover the often-hidden merits in others and bring them to the fore.

As we will see from the examples below, a hallmark of the Rebbe's Positivity Bias was his stubborn insistence on always seeing and highlighting the good in others. In this way, he took his place in the illustrious line of great Jewish leaders who sought to uplift and unify the people.

Remember the Ten Percent

A certain vice president of a prominent college was known for generously volunteering his time on behalf of Jewish education, which was one of the Rebbe's deepest concerns.

Specifically, he used his experience with the local

bureaucracy to assist Jewish institutions by preparing the necessary applications for state and federal funding. Over the years he received much satisfaction from seeing numerous schools and institutions awarded necessary funding on account of his efforts.

However, at some point he began noticing a marked drop in his success rate. After looking into matters, he discovered that his applications had not even reached the federal offices. In fact, they were regularly being flagged and disqualified by a Jewish state clerk who deliberately sought petty flaws in every application.

One Sunday afternoon, while receiving a dollar from the Rebbe for charity, he briefly described the situation. In fact, he became so agitated in the course of his retelling that he blurted out: "In the past, when a person stood in the way of benefitting the Jewish People, our leaders would intervene 'on High' to make sure they could interfere no longer. This is what I am asking regarding that clerk..."

The Rebbe listened patiently and then responded: "Even if one considers another person to be ninety percent lacking in goodness and merit, one must nevertheless remember that he still maintains ten percent of positive virtue."[59]

Here the Rebbe defends a seemingly indefensible individual by claiming that no matter how bad he seems, there is surely a portion of him that is righteous, and it is that innermost reality, his true essence, that we should focus on, connect with, and strive to reveal and activate.

One particular area in which the Rebbe consistently refused to judge other Jews harshly because he would focus on their essence was in relation to their personal level of ritual observance. This willingness to publicly defend those Jews who, for whatever reason, had strayed from the fold of Jewish law set the Rebbe apart from much of the prevailing religious leadership and establishment.

Thankfully, despite the enormous opposition he faced over the years, today there is hardly a segment within the Orthodox Jewish community that has not adopted, to some extent or another, the embracing and non-judgmental attitude he embodied and advocated, transforming inclusivity into the norm.

The next few stories testify to these special qualities embodied and espoused by the Rebbe.

It All Counts

The Rebbe once received a letter from an individual who, in the course of his travels, had encountered something that upset him. Specifically, he was perturbed by a man in a far-flung community who would come to *shul* to make the *minyan*, but then proceed to read his newspaper during the prayers.

The Rebbe replied:[60]

> ...I see in [this situation] the extreme Jewish attachment that one finds in every Jew. For here is a person who has wandered off to a remote part of the world and has become so far removed, not only geographically, but also mentally and intellectually, as to have no concept of what prayer is or what a house of G-d is; yet one finds in him that Jewish spark, or as the Alter Rebbe, the founder of Chabad,

> expressed it in his *Tanya*: "The Divine soul, which is truly a part of G-d."
>
> This Divine soul, which is the inheritance of every Jew, seeks expression as best it can, and in the case of this particular Jew, it seeks expression in at least enabling other Jews to pray congregationally, and he therefore goes out of his way to help them and at the same time to be counted with them.

The Rebbe's insight into the essential goodness of the innermost self reveals that the person is not an arrogant heretic, mocking G-d and Jewish tradition; he is a holy Jew in exile, responding to G-d's call in whatever way he knows how.

Yom Kippur: Fifteen Minutes of Faith

In another incident told by R. Yehoshua Moshe Stockhammer,[61] during a private audience with the Rebbe, when he raised the topic of the Rebbe's unique approach toward outreach, the Rebbe said earnestly:

"If a Jew wakes up in the morning on Yom Kippur, and *Heaven forbid,* shaves, eats a full meal, gets in his car and drives to synagogue for services (all of which are severe violations of the holiest day on the Jewish calendar), and sits there for all of an hour or two, those hours spent in synagogue carry great value in and of themselves. In the first instance, during that time, he has abstained from further violations of the sacred day, and furthermore, during that time he has absorbed and internalized the sanctity of the day, and even if this does not have an immediate effect on him, it may well impact his descendants and future generations to come...!"

Here we see the Rebbe, while emphasizing the seriousness of the transgression, exemplifying his approach to those who were uninitiated, choosing to highlight and celebrate their spiritual progress, however little, rather than focusing on and condemning them for whatever they were not doing, or doing "wrong."

Laughing All the Way to the World to Come

Shimon Dzigan was a famous Israeli comedian, known particularly for his humorous, though somewhat satirical, characterizations of traditional Judaism. In the eyes of much of the religious establishment he was less than an ally.

Surprisingly, not long after his passing, the Rebbe mentioned a story from the Talmud during a public gathering:[62]

"The Talmud (*Taanit* 22a) relates that there were 'two jesters' who 'were joyous and would bring joy to others,' and therefore 'they are meritorious of the World to Come.' The Talmud doesn't tell us that they merited the World to Come because of their scholarship and the like; rather, it was simply because 'they were joyous and brought joy to others.'"

In this seemingly random aside, we see the Rebbe going out of his way to evaluate someone's life and legacy in a positive light. Furthermore, in this case it was a public figure who was known to sometimes satirize the religious world whom the Rebbe finds such merit in, making it all the more astounding.

Notably, in this story, as in many others, the Rebbe made

a point of rooting his *limud zechut* in classic Jewish sources, perhaps to demonstrate that he was not truly revolutionizing Judaism, but rather returning it to its original ethos.

The above story was not an isolated incident. In fact, the Rebbe took many opportunities to exhibit *limud zechut* in various polarizing public debates and pronouncements that often pitted him against other leaders of the Chasidic and Orthodox world.

We may learn from this that the Rebbe valued this trait of *limud zechut* even more than his own public image, as he was willing, time after time, to stand up for Jews under attack at the expense of his own reputation.

Heroes or Heretics

It was 1976. A full flight from Tel Aviv to Paris was hijacked by the PLO, landing at Entebbe Airport in Uganda. Over the next seven days there were reports of hostages, demands, negotiations, and plans that culminated in a daring 90-minute raid carried out by the IDF on July 4, which successfully freed 102 of the 106 Jewish hostages and killed all of the terrorists.

Following this week-long international rollercoaster there ensued a public uproar heard throughout the halls of the UN as well as throughout various Chasidic and Ultra-Orthodox Jewish courts and communities, as everyone wrestled with the political implications and spiritual significance of the events.

More emotionally charged than the legal debates between various ambassadors and diplomats, however, were the theological critiques of certain rabbis.

As most of the IDF soldiers were secular, these rabbis simply couldn't see how anything G-dly or miraculous could manifest through the medium of non-religious Jews.

Into this fray the Rebbe offered his own perspective, which was radically positive, and redemptive.

In a public talk given on August 16, 1976, the Rebbe applauded the courage and selflessness of the IDF, "who flew thousands of miles, putting their lives in danger for the sole purpose of possibly saving the lives of around one hundred Jews."

Furthermore, he declared the Israeli soldiers to be an instrument for the deliverance of the Jewish People, even stating that a miracle had occurred through them. As a result, according to the Rebbe, they were undoubtedly righteous and "their portion in the World to Come is guaranteed."

For this loving expression of *limud zechut*, the Rebbe was vilified. "How could he publicly praise those who deviate regularly from Jewish law?!" Although he would respond to such attacks firmly, the Rebbe refused, on principle, to call out his detractors by name.

Instead, he would seek to understand and explain their position: For example, a rabbi who treated non-observant Jews with contempt may have perhaps been born and raised in an unloving home.

In that case, it would be necessary to re-educate this rabbi who was angry or quick to condemn—not to write him off as a bad leader.

No matter the issue or the nature of the debate, the Rebbe seemed virtually incapable of not finding a point of goodness or source of merit within anyone or anything.

How Low Can You Go

In perhaps one of the most radical applications of *limud zechut,* the following story relates how the Rebbe sought to redeem the memory of even those considered by many as the lowliest of our people—kapos, Jews who served as guards in concentration camps.

In 1964, the Rebbe was visited by well-known author Harvey Swados for an interview.[63] As a writer particularly interested in how ideas translate into actions and how leaders interface with the masses, Mr. Swados was predominantly interested in the Rebbe's views on some of the thornier ethical questions that emerge from the Holocaust, including the reports of self-serving compliance and cooperation with the Germans by certain Jewish communal leaders.

In Mr. Swados' own words:

"I began by asking his opinion of the causes of the Holocaust that resulted in the extinction of six million European Jews—and of the controversy about the behavior of the German masses and the Jewish leadership, which has tormented the Western World, particularly since the appearance of Hannah Arendt's book on the Eichmann trial.

"His reply made no reference to abstractions, whether theological or philosophical, nor did he remark—as had another Chasidic Rebbe—on the sins the victims must have committed to be punished so terribly by G-d.[64]

"He pointed instead to political realities, [and] to the incredible difficulties in maintaining one's faith under a totalitarian regime. 'The miracle,' he said, 'was that there was any resistance, organization, or leadership at all.' This was not exactly what I had expected."

In the Rebbe's view, the very leaders who betrayed their own people were credited with simply doing the best they could in an unthinkable situation.

It wasn't surprising that there was treason in the ranks—that was, in fact, understandable given the horrific circumstances.

What was surprising was that anyone at all could rise above such short-sighted temptation, and it was these heroic cases that should be acknowledged and amplified.

The Rebbe continued to push the point, turning the tables and posing nuanced questions to the author about his own socially-conscious work.

"He seemed particularly interested in *On the Line,* a book in which I had attempted, by means of a series of fictional portraits of auto assembly workers, to demonstrate the impact of their work on their lives.

"'What conclusions did you come to?' the Rebbe asked. 'Did you suggest,' he persisted, 'that the unhappy [and exploited] workers, chained to their machines, should revolt?'

"'Of course not,' I replied. 'It would have been unrealistic.'"

The Rebbe was silent.

Suddenly, Harvey realized that he had been led to the very understanding that he was seeking.

In conclusion, the Rebbe then said:

"You could not conscientiously recommend revolution for your unhappy workers in a free country or see it as a practical perspective for their leaders. Then how could one demand it from those who were being crushed and destroyed by the Nazis?"

Case closed. Compassion carries the day.

Amazingly, in this story the tables have been turned.

The same Rebbe who made it his life's mission to reveal each person's highest potential manages, through profound empathy and generosity of spirit, to lighten the crushing load of judgment and indictment weighing on individuals who were subjected to the most inhumane circumstances one could imagine.

In this way, the Rebbe was a master of not only recognizing the good that exists within a given person, but also having compassion for the challenges they may have experienced.

In other words, no one was ever without some merit or cause for understanding, even those we normally characterize as the lowest of the low.

This Is All He Has

One final example[65] of the Rebbe's efforts to see others in the best possible light came in his response to an underhanded political maneuver.

The Rebbe had founded an organization to counter attempts by Christian missionaries and fringe religious cults to recruit Jews. He did so anonymously in order to attract support from Orthodox communities outside Chabad-Lubavitch. The Rebbe's role became known, however, and one of the organization's leaders removed his name and started his own effort along the same lines, which leached support and donations from the original group.

The original organization's manager, a non-Lubavitcher Chasid, was appalled by the rival leader's politically motivated action and confronted him with written evidence in hand, but the rabbi in question flatly denied being involved with forming the newer organization.

Frustrated and disillusioned, the original manager consulted the Rebbe and told him the story. How could this rabbi put politics before principles, he asked the Rebbe in anguish.

The Rebbe responded by citing a Talmudic[66] discussion that disqualifies a king or a high priest from serving as a judge when it comes to establishing a leap year. The king has a vested interest in whether a year has twelve or thirteen months, because he pays his soldiers' wages by the year, which means that the treasury gains when a year has thirteen months.

Similarly, the high priest has a vested interest in this, because he has to immerse in the *mikveh* five times on Yom Kippur and might be partial to a calendar that places that day in warmer weather.

Such is human nature, the Rebbe said, that we are all prone to subconscious calculation of self-interest, whether we know it or not—even a Jewish king and a high priest!

The Rebbe then reminded the manager that the rabbi he was judging for his conduct had been the leader of a large community and *yeshivah* in Europe that had been completely wiped out during the Holocaust. Now he was trying to establish a *yeshivah* in New York for which he was dependent on certain donors who were ideologically opposed to Lubavitch. "This is all he has," the Rebbe said. "Can you blame him for wanting to ensure the success of his important work and life-legacy at all costs?"

Faced with the account of a rabbinic leader who was engaging in petty politics against him when he should have been modeling integrity, the Rebbe not only put a positive spin on the rabbi's tactics—he was trying to protect the remnant of his community—but acknowledged the rabbi's status by citing a Talmudic discussion relating to figures in the most honored positions: a Jewish king and the high priest.

Even in a case that directly impacted him and his work for others in a negative way, the Rebbe refused to make an enemy of any Jew. Even if publicly attacked and slandered, the Rebbe personally responded out of love and hope for unification.

CHAPTER 7

Of Virtuous Villains and Sinful Saints

ELISHA BEN AVUYAH WAS a great Talmudic Sage who went on to become a famous heretic in Jewish history. Following his rejection and repeated public desecration of Jewish law and community norms, he was held in such contempt by the community that he was stripped of his name and referred to only as Acher, which means other. Elisha ben Avuyah has thus come to represent a particular facet of the archetypal "other" in rabbinic thought and mythos: A person who not only grows up within the community and chooses to leave and live beyond its borders, but one who continuously flouts and flaunts his apostasy publicly.

However, as always, there is more to the story. The Talmud[67] relates that one Shabbat, R. Meir was walking behind Elisha ben Avuyah to learn a Torah lesson from him, while Elisha was riding upon a horse—a public desecration of Shabbat. At a certain point, Elisha stopped and pointed out for R. Meir's benefit that, according to his count of their steps, they had reached the Shabbat boundary, and should thus go no further; a most meticulous display of rabbinic acumen and halachic sensitivity.

We see expressed in this brief Talmudic vignette the numerous shades of existential complexity that exist simultaneously within each human identity, making it all the more difficult to one-dimensionalize and judge the character or worth of any "other" from our finite perspective. So, how are we supposed to read this story?

In 1982, at a *farbrengen* on Shabbat *Parashat Emor*,[68] the Rebbe referred to Elisha ben Avuyah and his student R. Meir. Citing the inclusion of a teaching of Elisha ben Avuyah in *Pirkei Avot* (Ethics of our Fathers), the Rebbe juxtaposes Elisha ben Avuyah's teaching with a quote from R. Meir, which appears in close proximity to Elisha's, reading them both through the lens of their complex personal biographies.

Reflecting on his own inner journey and struggle, Elisha ben Avuyah taught:[69] "He who studies Torah as a child, to what can he be compared? To ink written on fresh paper; and he who studies Torah as an old man, to what can he be compared? To ink written on paper that has been erased." In the context of his story, the Rebbe suggests that despite the outward appearance of Elisha ben Avuyah's total disavowal of the ways of Torah, his prodigious Torah study is still present on some level, and that no matter how far he may go, he carries an imprint of holiness deep within him that can never be fully erased.

Similarly, reflecting on his own experience (as one who continued to learn from such a heretic), R. Meir teaches:[70] "Look not at the vessel, but at what it contains." This explains how R. Meir was allowed to learn Torah teachings from "Acher"—because R. Meir did not regard the "vessel," rather what it contained, and accepted a teaching which Acher had learned as a child, which remained for eternity because it was as "ink written on fresh paper."

In the Rebbe's teachings, we see him following in the footsteps of R. Meir, an exalted Sage of Israel who never gave up on the incorruptible soul of an "other," no matter how far they may have strayed from the community.

Judging by Your Intentions

According to Chasidut, the stories in the Torah are existentially instructive. Far from being just historical records of remarkable individuals from a bygone era, each incident, and even each individual, expresses a psycho-spiritual template or dynamic that is constantly present and spiritually relevant throughout all time. Similarly, every person, like the Torah, is a nested being; our deepest inner soul is concealed beneath literal and metaphorical flesh, bones, and garments—thoughts, words, and actions. It is therefore up to us to probe and penetrate the external fronts that obfuscate the transcendent spiritual nature within, whether in relation to Torah or people.

Based on this understanding, and on a belief in the eternal

purity of the soul, the Rebbe was committed to actively seeking and finding the inner point of holiness within each person. However, he did not stop there. In fact, so given to this interpersonal aspect of his Positivity Bias, the Rebbe applied that generosity of spirit to personalities and characters throughout the entire corpus of Jewish literature.

If, as the saying goes, people tend to judge others by their actions and themselves by their intentions, the Rebbe did the opposite, revisiting and redeeming character after character in Scripture and tradition by focusing on their noble intentions rather than their misguided actions.

In this spirit, the Rebbe would revisit stories of individuals who were traditionally seen as scandalous or villainous, recasting them in a new, redemptive light by looking beneath the surface and considering their inner intentions. According to the Rebbe, their intentions were rooted in holiness, even if still in need of rectification. Traditionally, the inclusion of such shocking stories and disreputable characters in the Torah itself was understood as providing us examples for how *not* to behave. But through the redemptive eyes of the Rebbe, misguided actions reveal noble intentions worthy of our acknowledgment and even emulation.

In this way, the Rebbe practiced a form of intergenerational "love of one's fellow man," dedicating himself to the redemption and elevation of not only those souls who lived in his generation, but of all souls to have ever lived. Throughout the rest of this chapter we will explore just a small sampling of the many Biblical characters and historical figures whose stories were transformed as a result of the Rebbe's rigorous process of revaluation and redemption.

Testing, Testing...

Let's start at the beginning. The story of humanity's first failure, as recounted in the Torah, is arguably the most far-reaching tragedy of all time. Adam's inability to obey G-d's command to refrain from eating the forbidden fruit, and his subsequent banishment from the Garden of Eden, are generally understood to be the root source of human negativity and corruption.

The Rebbe taught[71] that this story has been read superficially and its deeper, positive message missed. Adam was the first human, created by the Hand of G-d Himself. He was the ultimate human prototype, literally "created in G-d's image." He was placed in the Garden along with the snake, who represents the force in Creation that constantly pulls us away from all that is good and holy, toward what is destructive and meaningless. But what is the deeper purpose of the snake and its test?

Before Creation, all that existed was G-d's Infinite Oneness. There was no other, no possible relationship, only One. A desire stirred within G-d to share and relate with something other than Himself. In order to make space for a finite Creation to exist, G-d constricted His Infinite Presence, thus creating a fertile void within which one might emerge. This act of cosmic contraction is referred to by Kabbalah as *tzimtzum*.

The world and all that is in it was formed within the vacuum created by this act of Divine retention. However, as a result of *tzimtzum*, G-d's presence was no longer overtly apparent. The Hebrew word *olam* (world), is etymologically related to the word *he'elem* (concealment), indicating that

G-d's presence is concealed within the world—to be revealed by man. Like a cosmic game of hide and seek, the Infinite One was now hidden within the finite multitudes of Creation. This was how the world worked, until the sixth day, when Adam was created. With the birth of humanity, a new stage of creation became possible—the conscious relationship between Creator and creation that G-d initially desired. This, then, was the test of Creation. Would a finite human being, endowed with free will on account of G-d's apparent absence, consciously choose to live in an honest relationship with the Infinite One, in loving alignment with His will?

Adam's test was whether he could fulfill a single Divine command without the revealed presence of G-d looking over his shoulder. This was the archetypal test of the human condition. The Garden of Eden was the proving ground. Adam's every move would impact and set the course for human history from here on out. The stakes couldn't have been higher.

> It was precisely because of the enormity of Adam's mission [the very first command from Creator to creation] that the snake [symbolizing the inclination in humans to negativity] exerted such enormous energies and focused all of its strength on disturbing Adam's mission, which was simply to abstain from the Tree of Knowledge.... This was indeed a most worrisome moment for the snake, whose entire purpose and reason for existing was to stop man from serving his Maker. To validate his purpose, one can imagine the tremendous effort the snake invested in causing Adam to sin.[72]

The Talmud[73] teaches that Adam was created on the sixth day of Creation, which was divided into twelve hours. Every hour of the day, humanity went through another stage of development, until Shabbat, the seventh day. In the ninth hour of the sixth day, Adam was commanded not to eat from the Tree of Knowledge, but he ate from it only one hour later! On the surface this would seem to demonstrate a weakness within the nature or constitution of Adam, and thus within humanity. *He couldn't go more than a single hour without disobeying G-d's will.*

However, if we consider the cosmic stakes on the line, it becomes clear that Adam actually exhibited nearly superhuman restraint by holding off as long as he did.

According to the Rebbe's treatment of this story, the question is no longer, *How could Adam succumb to sin so soon?* Instead, it becomes, *How was Adam able to withstand the evil inclination's advances for as long as he did?*

Rather than highlighting humanity's weakness, Adam's story comes to symbolize and inspire our resilience and tenacity in striving to live a spiritual life in a physical world, where G-d is present but hidden behind the veil of dualistic knowledge. Additionally, Adam's example, when seen through the Rebbe's Positivity Bias, teaches us that the more resistance we encounter when it comes to doing the right thing, the more essential that action may be to our purpose in life.

Spark Seeker

Few characters from the Torah are presented as negatively in the Talmud as Jacob's brother Esau. He is characterized as a brute, a murderer, or a glutton incapable of curbing his appetites. He represents ancient Rome, medieval Christianity, coarse physicality, and a host of other oppressive forces intent on subjugating the spiritual life and sovereignty of the Jewish People. As such, Esau is seen as the polar opposite of his brother Jacob, who represents a pure and simple spirituality in contrast to his brother's unencumbered carnality.

Yet, the Torah tells us that "Isaac loved Esau,"[74] preferring him to Jacob. How are we to understand this? What did Isaac see in Esau that we might easily overlook? Additionally, how are we to understand the fact that Jacob had to don the garments of Esau in order to procure his father's deathbed blessing?

In a Chasidic discourse delivered in 1963,[75] the Rebbe directly addressed this question and applied his signature Positivity Bias to redeem the soul and story of Esau. According to the Rebbe, Esau and Jacob represented possible approaches to spiritual life and service in the world, and in the final analysis, one without the other is incomplete.

Jacob, referred to as a "man of the tents of Torah study," represents a secluded spiritual existence focused on the World to Come. Esau, referred to as a "hunter of the field," represents someone who is not afraid to descend and engage with the material world on its own terms in order to elevate and expose its spiritual essence and origins.

Isaac, though supportive of Jacob's unsullied existence and one-dimensional focus on the ethereal, saw the ultimate point of the Jewish path as requiring an approach much closer to Esau's. For ultimately, the work of the Jew is to sanctify Creation, not to separate ourselves from it.

However, Esau's path also brought him into dangerous proximity with the temptations of this world. And without a firm enough connection to the spiritual realm, he fell prey to his lower nature and appetites, which ultimately brought him down. This is the shadow aspect of Esau, emphasized by centuries of rabbinic commentary. In the Rebbe's view, however, expounding on a theme emphasized by the Alter Rebbe and his successors, there is an additional dimension. Esau possessed an invaluable spark of holy energy that needed to be redeemed. From this perspective, Jacob had to integrate the essence of Esau in order to complete his character. Since we are children of Jacob, we too need to learn to integrate this spark of our estranged brothers and selves.

The Rebbe encouraged all of us to redeem the positive aspects of Esau—the willingness to engage the darkness in order to transform it into light, and the ability to seek out the spiritual spark contained within the earthly realm. We must each have one foot in the tent of Jacob, strengthening ourselves in Torah and prayer, with the other foot in the field of Esau, in active pursuit of the fallen sparks within Creation.

Bringing Heaven Down to Earth

This theme of balancing our spiritual and earthly drives and commitments is reflected in numerous other stories in Torah. Notably, the main characters in these stories are often, like Esau, taken at face value, thus blinding us to their deeper, positive aspects that are worthy of our consideration and even emulation. The Rebbe referred to the classic Chasidic interpretation of two stories in particular, to highlight this theme.

While the Jewish People were traveling through the desert, Moses sent out twelve spies to scout out the Holy Land ahead of their arrival. When they returned to the camp, ten of the spies delivered a devastating report about the prospects of inhabiting the Land, roiling the masses. The people wailed and despaired, causing G-d to respond with a deadly plague directed at those who had slandered the Promised Land, inducing rebellion and unrest within the Israelite camp. This event, known as the sin of the spies, is what elicited the Divine decree that the Jewish People would not enter the Land of Israel until the whole generation passed away, thirty-nine years later.

The most widespread interpretation of the spies is that they acted out of fear and doubt, thus signaling a lapse in faith. In their own words: *We are unable to go up against the people, for they are stronger than we* [and He, referring to G-d].

However, Chasidut offered a different perspective.[76] This was not a typical mutiny or sabotage, nor were these men struck by a gross lapse of faith in G-d's word and Providence. The spies, who were actually princes of Israel, were motivated by their responsibility to their charges. They felt that the change of environment from the idyllic spiritual reality in the desert to the mundane physical reality of civilization, with all that it entails, would severely diminish and distract the spiritual focus of their people. In the wilderness, G-d's Presence and Providence was openly revealed; manna was provided daily, water flowed from rocks, protection from the elements was provided by Divine clouds of glory, and Torah echoed through hearts and canyons. The spies worried that the daily tasks of establishing a settled life and society would interrupt this collective state of revelation and communion with G-d. It was the spies' fear of *success* (at *conquering* the land), rather than a fear of *failure* (resulting from an absence of faith in G-d's ability to lead them to victory) that motivated them to return with negative reports.

The Land is one that [spiritually] swallows its inhabitants was their argument.

The spies wanted to remain within the womb of the wilderness; they expressed a positive desire to live in the uncompromised embrace of truth and transcendence. This is, according to the Rebbe, the positive point within the intentions of the spies that must be redeemed. However, the Torah also teaches us that we must not abuse our spiritual life by using it to escape the world. We are meant to spend time in the tent of Torah, as well as within the desert of the soul, but we are also meant to bring those experiences and truths into the beautiful, often complicated mess of everyday life. The Torah does not divide physical and spiritual, body and soul; it unites!

On one occasion among many,[77] the Rebbe spoke as above, about the virtue of the spies, reflecting on the statement of our Sages that "due to the severity of their sin, they have no portion in the World to Come." The Rebbe explained that the spies do not have merely a *portion* in the World to Come; they have more! After the talk, Chasidim began to sing a Chasidic melody with the words: "*V'chol karnei resha'im,*" meaning that G-d will remove all wicked people in the Messianic times. The Rebbe stopped them from singing and asked: "We just spoke about the virtue of the spies, and now you have chosen to sing about sinners? Please exchange that song for '*Yifrach beyamav tzaddik*'"—a different song based on words relating to the righteous: *May the righteous one flourish in his days....*

Spiritual Overdose

Nadav and Avihu were two sons of Aaron the High Priest. As recounted in the Torah, they *offered a strange fire before G-d, which He had not commanded.* This elicited G-d's swift retribution, as it says, *A fire went out from G-d and consumed them, and they died before G-d.*

While the cause of death is clear from the text, the reason for their deaths is not. The Divine logic behind this tragedy has plagued commentators throughout the ages. Here are some of the reasons they offer, which, when combined, paint an overwhelmingly negative portrait of these two ill-fated young men:

a) They entered the Tabernacle's Holy of Holies without permission.[78]
b) They weren't wearing all of the necessary garments while performing the priestly service.[79]
c) They never married.[80]
d) They had no children.[81]
e) They were arrogant and many women remained unmarried while waiting for them. They said: "Our father's brother is a king, our mother's brother is a prince [Nachshon, the head of the tribe of Judah], our father is a High Priest, and we are both deputy High Priests; what woman is worthy of us?"

f) They offered up an "alien fire,"[82] i.e., an unbidden incense offering.[83]

g) They rendered a decision on a matter about which they should have consulted their teacher Moses.[84]

h) Each of them acted on his own initiative, not taking counsel from one another.[85]

i) They performed the Temple service while intoxicated.[86]

j) They entered the Sanctuary without washing their hands and feet.[87]

k) They already deserved to die at Mount Sinai, when they callously feasted their eyes on the Divine.[88]

In all cases, these brothers are essentially portrayed as self-centered, egotistical, spiritual thrill seekers, who deserved what they got. The Rebbe, however, highlighted[89] and developed a teaching of the *Or Hachayim*[90] and elaborated on in Chasidic sources. Aaron's eldest sons passed away from a "Kiss of G-d," a most positive description, used only for the highest souls. Each of the punishable actions enumerated in the Midrash was rooted in a single, positive source—intense passion and yearning for G-d. In the words of the Rebbe: "They approached the supernal light out of their great love of the Holy, and thereby died. Thus they died by 'Divine kiss,' such as experienced by the perfectly righteous.... This is the meaning of the verse, *They came close to G-d and died.*" From this perspective, it becomes clear that Nadav and Avihu died of a spiritual overdose—too much of a good thing.

Jewish tradition teaches that we are here for a reason, which is to elevate and sanctify the material world, not only to transcend it.

While not condoning their approach of unfettered and

irresponsible spiritual indulgence, we can and must emulate Nadav and Avihu's willingness to give up everything, even life itself, in pursuit of spiritual truth. With our feet firmly planted on the earth, our souls are free to reach for the heights to bring the infinite light of the Divine down into our daily life and tasks.

Moshiach Now!

Another one of the archetypal villains of the Torah was a man named Korach, who led a rebellion against Moses and Aaron in the desert; he is also understood by classical Chasidic teaching, elaborated on by the Rebbe, as being motivated by righteous principles. Rather than a power-hungry and disrespectful insurrectionary who sought to seize control of the masses to satisfy his ego and delusions of grandeur, which is how he is often seen, there are two aspects of Korach's personality in particular that are worth elevating and emulating.

On one hand, Korach was motivated by a spiritual urge. Korach was a Levite, and while he could participate in the Divine service, he could not perform the service of the High Priest. He intensely desired such an intimate experience of G-d, and he was therefore willing to take up Moses' challenge the following morning to offer incense before G-d, despite knowing that it could be fatal.[91]

On the other hand, Korach was socially motivated. He saw the world in its Messianic state of utopian universalism, a world in which we are all spiritually equal, when G-d *will be revealed as the water covers the sea*.[92] This led him to foment an ideological revolution in the camp meant to destabilize the prevailing power structure and hierarchy of leadership, questioning Moses directly: *Aren't we all holy?*[93]

From one perspective, Korach was absolutely right; this is where the world is ultimately headed. However, as is true for many visionaries, he was ahead of his time and suffered the consequences of trying to implement the Messianic transformation of history and humanity before the world was ready.[94]

Nevertheless, the Rebbe points out that we must not lose sight of the holy vision and spiritual yearning of Korach!

Dynamic Duo

Two colorful characters in Korach's rebellion in particular have also been singled out as being particularly corrupt. Dathan and Abiram are regarded as the prototypical pair of inveterate trouble-makers. According to the Talmud,[95] they were wholly wicked "from beginning to end." They are identified[96] as the two quarreling Jews in Egypt, and it was they who caused Moses' flight to the desert by denouncing him to Pharaoh for killing the Egyptian taskmaster and revealing that he was not the son of Pharaoh's daughter.[97] They incited the people to return to Egypt,[98] both at the Red Sea and when the spies returned from Canaan.[99] They transgressed the commandment concerning the manna by keeping it overnight,[100] and they accused Moses of bringing the Jewish People out of Egypt to die in the desert. Finally, Dathan and Abiram became ringleaders of the rebellion under the influence of Korach and died as a result.

The Rebbe explains this,[101] based on classic commentary,

so that a different picture emerges. It's not that these two did not instigate any trouble; there was more to them than that. In fact, they had a point of goodness within. While this goodness was generally muted, it nevertheless shone brightly on certain occasions, revealing that beneath the layers of rebellion there existed a core of righteousness worth examining.

Based on a Biblical commentary,[102] Dathan and Abiram were actually deeply involved Jewish leaders concerned about the welfare of their people. Although they had all of the personal failings mentioned above, they were also part of the group of Jewish officers who risked their lives to confront and challenge Pharaoh for ceasing to provide the Jewish slaves with straw for their bricks. *They cried out to Pharaoh, saying, "Why do you do this to your servants?"*[103]

Furthermore, they were among those officers willing to take a beating for the Jews when they did not fill their quotas: *And the officers of the Children of Israel whom Pharaoh's task-masters had appointed over them were beaten.*[104]

Moreover, they challenged Moses and Aaron directly for making things worse for the people, as conditions rapidly deteriorated for them as soon as Moses started instigating against Pharaoh. *May the Lord look upon you and judge, for you have brought us into foul odor in the eyes of Pharaoh and in the eyes of his servants, to place a sword into their hand[s] to kill us.*[105]

Indeed, Moses validated their claim by bringing their challenge to G-d on behalf of the Jewish People!

Read through the Rebbe's deeper insight, despite their many shortcomings, Dathan and Abiram also emerge as vigilant guardians of the people, faithfully protecting them from all potential threats, whether from within or without.

You Can Take the Jew out of the Temple, But...

A particularly fascinating example of this aspect of the Rebbe's Positivity Bias was expressed during a *farbrengen* in which he spoke about a woman named Miriam bat Bilgah. The Talmud[106] relates that Miriam bat Bilgah abandoned Judaism, married a Greek officer, and accompanied the Greeks as they stormed the Holy Temple (in the era leading up to the story of Chanukah). In that very moment of one of our deepest and darkest national tragedies, as the Greeks were defiling the Holy Temple, she went and pounded on the Holy Altar with her sandal, taunting G-d and mocking the Jewish People: "Wolf, Wolf! You consume the people's wealth, but you don't answer them in their time of need!" For this vile act of contempt and utter disrespect, the Sages punished her entire family.

Be that as it may, during a public gathering in honor of the anniversary of his mother's passing,[107] the Rebbe spoke at length about Miriam bat Bilgah and the meaning of her story. Miriam's outburst was not out of contempt; it was out of compassion for the suffering of her people. In a voice audibly strained by emotion,[108] the Rebbe broke into tears as he explained. Despite the fact that she had intermarried and renounced the ways of her people—joining and even encouraging their enemy all the way to the desecration of the Temple—upon reaching that innermost sanctum, her innermost truth was activated, and she was overcome with the feeling of an unbreakable bond between herself and her people. This moved her to protest to G-d on their behalf, even as her husband ransacked and defiled the Holy of Holies.

Herein lies a profound message: It may appear that a Jew is cut off from everything Jewish, but the Torah says, "No! What you see is only superficial." The fact remains that they are and will always remain a Jew. As R. Schneur Zalman of Liadi teaches:[109] "A Jew neither desires nor is capable of being separated from G-dliness, G-d forbid." Even after Miriam bat Bilgah apostatized and joined the enemy, what was it that ultimately bothered her? "Why is the Altar not protecting the people?" After all was said and done, she cried out in pain for her fellow Jews. So why does the Talmud tell us this story? Not, G-d forbid, to disparage a Jewess, but to the contrary: To teach us about the beautiful and unbreakable bond that exists among the Jewish People.

Infidelity or Inspiration

In addition to Adam's sin in the Garden, the sin of the Golden Calf is one of the most notorious and far-reaching stories in the Torah. A mere forty days after experiencing the revelation at Mount Sinai and hearing from G-d, Himself, "I am the L-rd, your G-d, do not worship another," the people fashioned an idol and served it. It is hard to find anything redemptive in this seemingly irredeemable episode.

Nevertheless, the Rebbe quotes classic commentaries[110] that enable us to see the light within such tremendous darkness. Through a close analysis of the text of the Golden Calf incident itself, it becomes clear that the greatest blemish on our national record and history does not actually begin as a story of religious betrayal and infidelity.

The Jewish People were not (initially) seeking out a new god to worship; rather, they were seeking a new spiritual leader who would guide them in their service of G-d.

This becomes clear from the verse that introduces the Golden Calf incident, which states: *The people saw that Moses delayed in descending the mountain,* and therefore *gathered around Aaron and said to him, "Rise up, make for us an Elokim who will go before us."*[111] It is important to point out that *Elokim* is a multivalent Hebrew word that can either refer to deities or to powerful human leaders. The Jewish People then proceeded to push for their request by exclaiming: *For* this man, Moses, *the man who brought us up from the land of Egypt, we do not know what became of him*!

The people desired—and felt they required—someone or something to replace Moses, who, according to their mistaken calculations, had gone missing. In other words, the Jewish People were not looking for a deity that would replace G-d; rather, they were looking for someone (or something) who would replace Moses.

Essentially, the Jews were lost and looking for sustainable inspiration and a channel of revelation. When they thought that their source of leadership and spiritual guidance was gone, they sought a replacement. Without wasting a moment or sparing any cost, they set about creating a new collective focus for spiritual practice. Instead of taking time off from their intense spiritual experience while waiting for Moses to return, they didn't allow a moment to pass before seeking out a new means of inspiration!

Needless to say, the Rebbe is not condoning the creation of the Golden Calf itself, which was a forbidden act and quickly devolved into idol worship. Rather, he is acknowledging a Divine spark within their initial intention, which was to ensure that they always had a point of spiritual focus.

This brings us to our final area of inquiry, indirectly introduced in the episode of the Golden Calf: The role of a true spiritual leader in relation to the people.

Expanding the Tent

The leading scholars of Mezhibuzh once visited the Baal Shem Tov in his *sukkah*. After closely inspecting the structural design of his *sukkah*, the scholars unanimously declared it invalid.

In response, the Baal Shem Tov began bringing various proofs to demonstrate that his *sukkah* did fulfill the mitzvah as prescribed by the Torah. The two sides debated back and forth—the Baal Shem Tov maintaining the validity of his *sukkah*, the scholars maintaining their opposition.

Finally, the Baal Shem Tov opened his hand. Inside lay a small piece of parchment. The scholars took the parchment and found it to be a note from heaven. "The *sukkah* of R. Yisrael [Baal Shem Tov] is kosher," they read. The note was signed by the archangel Metatron, keeper of the "inner spheres."

On Sukkot, 5727 (1966), the Rebbe recounted this extraordinary tale and asked the obvious question: While the story demonstrates the Baal Shem Tov's unique spiritual clout—his ability to pull heavenly strings to prove a point—we are left wondering why this saintly Jewish leader would construct his *sukkah* in such a questionable manner to begin with. Why invite the suspicion and judgment of the other rabbis by dwelling in a seemingly impermissible *sukkah*?

The Rebbe explained that what motivated the Baal Shem Tov was the desire to find merit for the masses. Knowing that there was a large amount of unlearned Jews who did not know how to properly construct a *sukkah*, the Baal Shem Tov built his *sukkah* in the most lenient manner possible in order to validate every *sukkah* with issues similar to his own, and to thus declare the practice of less-educated Jews to be within the pale of Jewish observance.

The moral of this story is clearly less about the kosher status of one man's *sukkah* than it is about the role of a Jewish leader. The Baal Shem Tov was trying to impress upon the scholars of Mezhibuzh that a true Jewish leader must be willing to make not just material, but also spiritual and social sacrifices for his people.

People Before Principles

We will close this chapter by looking at the archetypal leader in Jewish history, Moses. At the conclusion of the Torah we find a concise eulogy for the only man whom all Jews refer to as "*Rabbeinu*," our Teacher, to this day.

And there was no other prophet who arose in Israel like Moses, whom the Lord knew face to face, as manifested by all the signs and wonders, which the Lord had sent him to perform in the land of Egypt, to Pharaoh and all his servants, and to all his land, and all the strong hand, and all the great awe, which Moses performed before the eyes of all Israel.[112]

In his commentary to this verse, Rashi asks: "What great thing did Moses do before the eyes of all Israel?" His answer may be surprising. The great act of Moses that the Torah refers to *in its very last words*, according to Rashi, is the shattering of the Tablets when he came down from Mount Sinai and saw the Jewish People dancing around the Golden Calf. The idea that Moses' greatness lies in his "breaking of the law," needs to be unpacked to be properly understood.

Toward the end of Moses' forty days on top of the mountain receiving the Ten Commandments directly from G-d, the Jewish People became anxious that Moses had abandoned them and constructed a Golden Calf, as discussed above. Upon seeing this desecration, Moses threw down the tablets, shattering them in front of the people. G-d then tells Moses to step aside so He can destroy the people and start afresh. Moses responds on their behalf: *If you would, bear their sin; if not, then erase me from your book.*[113]

When Moses came down from the mountain and saw the Jewish People dancing around the Golden Calf, he knew that it was an offense punishable by death—according to the very Tablets he was holding. In that moment, Moses did the only thing he could think of to save his people—he broke the Tablets, nullifying the contract that made them liable. When faced with a choice between the survival of the Jewish People or the survival of the Torah, Moses chose the people.

For a Jewish leader who loves Torah almost more than life itself, this is the ultimate expression of unconditional love. That is why the Torah, which is called *Torat Moshe*, "Moses'

Torah," ends on this very note, lest we forget the ultimate point behind all of its principles—that the way to love G-d is by loving His people.

It is thus the eternal love and commitment to the Jewish People that Moses exhibited in this very instance—even challenging G-d—that forever engraved him in our hearts as the ultimate leader.

The Talmud[114] goes even further when it informs us that G-d, Himself, was "in accord with the mind of Moses" in this instance, even going so far as to offer him congratulations, "*Yeyasher kochacha sheshibarta* (Strength to you for breaking the tablets)!"

R. Schneur Zalman of Liadi makes a similar point. He was asked, "Which takes precedence, the love of G-d or the love of Israel?" He replied, "Love of Israel takes precedence—for you are loving whom your Beloved loves."[115]

In a world where real people are perpetually put in the service of abstract principles, whether religiously or politically, Moses made a revolutionary statement: It is not a matter of having to make a choice between loving people or loving G-d, because it is G-d's essential will that the best way to love Him is to love His children. This is the greatness of Moses—his commitment to the people he was entrusted to care for and guide through the wilderness of life, no matter what they may have done. And this too is the greatness of Torah—that it is not afraid to supplant its own supremacy for the sake of the Jewish People, because the Jewish People is its essential purpose. In this eternal moment, as illuminated by our Sages, the Torah is teaching us that a Jewish soul, no matter how brilliant or broken, is not a means to an end—it is in fact an end unto itself. This is the Torah's last word, its crown jewel.

This, too, is the super-rational principle underlying the Rebbe's relationship to all of G-d's children, those whom he encountered personally as well as those recorded in our history. The Rebbe never stopped looking for the good points within each one of us and never stopped advocating on our behalf, despite whatever failings or frailties we may have had. This is the essence of Jewish leadership. This is what makes a Rebbe.

CHAPTER 8

A Good Eye

R YOCHANAN BEN ZAKKAI, A great Talmudic Sage and leader, once sent his students out into the world to ascertain the best advice for living a righteous and fulfilling life. When his student R. Eliezer ben Horkenus returned from his travels, he reported: "I have searched, and I have found that the best advice is to develop an *ayin tov*, a good eye."[116]

When your eye, your lens on life, is good, what you see will be good, no matter what.

Of course, the opposite is also true. Therefore, it is of paramount importance to work on developing the capacity to see G-d and the good in all. This is the essence of a good eye.

When you view the world in such a way, you will tend to find positive interpretations of events and experiences, as well as judge others in the most favorable light. Every human being possesses this capacity for redemptive vision, but achieving and maintaining it requires effort.

Between You and Eye

One area in particular that benefits from an *ayin tov* is personal relationships, whether at work or within the family or community. Interpersonal relationships are complicated and messy, as we each have very different views, definitions, associations, narratives, word choices, insecurities, and projections, creating near-constant opportunities for misunderstanding and judgment.

When we speak with others, we are often unconsciously importing the energy of our previous encounters, and we sometimes carry over the residue of angst and resentments from the past. In any conversation or encounter there is the possibility for misappropriation of meaning and intent, giving rise to unnecessary skepticism, and ultimately suspicion of others. A person can easily fall into a default mode in which they immediately assume the worst about people.

Imagine how positive and kind our daily encounters could be if we would adopt a good eye and condition ourselves to view others more generously. Imagine a world in which the baseline of human interaction is the benefit of the doubt. Such a world would draw forth and activate the inherent kindness of our nature in a never-ending loop of mutual reinforcement.

It is important to remember that there is always more than one way to view a person. A study explored this phenomenon using a famous optical illusion, "My Wife and Mother-in-Law" (*pictured left*), which portrays a young woman or an old woman, depending on how it is viewed. The researchers found that the social standing and expectations of the subjects predicted which image they saw first, the young figure or the old. In other words, the way they saw directly impacted who they saw.

This shows that who we are colors our expectations of others, which in turn contributes to their character sketch in our eyes. Often this image of the other has more to do with us than with them. As the Baal Shem Tov, the founder of the Chasidic movement, taught: You see what is inside of you. Therefore, the more you condition yourself to look for the good in others, the more good in others you will see.

The good news is that you can rewire your neurological pathways and shift your patterns of perception to consciously focus on the positive in others.

With practice, you can reconfigure the fundamental way in which you approach and interpret your interactions with others, leading to the development of an interpersonal Positivity Bias. This will allow you to be more fully present to receive others with greater understanding, empathy, and trust.

In this chapter we will explore various demonstrations of the Rebbe's good eye, and the transformative effects of this particular application of his Positivity Bias on the people he encountered.

A Precious Kiddush

The Jewish People have struggled mightily throughout history to maintain its identity, tradition, and physical existence in the face of occupation and exile. However, among all the many tragic events in this history, the saga of Soviet Russia could be seen as one of the most forceful and successful attempts at stomping out the Jewish spirit. In other, earlier episodes of oppression, persecution by our enemies actually served to elicit our spiritual resistance, which called forth an even stronger adherence to tradition. In Soviet Russia, however, it seemed to be a continuous fall with no rebound. Therefore, it was natural for many who were looking in from the outside to view Soviet Jewry as a lost cause—an entire generation of Jews who were all but completely disconnected from their Judaism and identity, and therefore not worth the effort to reach out to and reconnect with.

The Rebbe saw things differently, vehemently rejecting such a dismal and cynical analysis. With his characteristic good eye, the Rebbe pointed out time and again that there were indeed many resisters—Jews who tenaciously clung to their tradition, creating underground Torah academies and prayer services, and holding Jewish weddings and circumcisions, all in secret and at the risk of their lives. Even as the general Jewish population appeared to have given up their Jewishness, the Rebbe saw hidden rays of self-sacrifice penetrating the Iron Curtain. Instead of focusing on the widespread desecration and destruction, the Rebbe chose to highlight Soviet Jewry's heroism and holiness.

In one conversation[117] with another Chasidic Rebbe who bemoaned the state of Soviet Jewry, the Rebbe went so far as to compare 20th century Soviet Jews to the Jewish People enslaved in Egypt, who never changed their Hebrew names or Jewish appearance despite unimaginable prejudice and oppression.

To further his point, the Rebbe cited the story of Chananya, Mishael, and Azarya, three Jewish youths captured by the cruel, idolatrous Babylonian king, Nebuchadnezzar in 441 BCE. During their long internment, they were brought into the palace and educated in foreign ways. However, through it all, they never let go of their Jewish practices and heroic loyalty to G-d. The Rebbe then quoted the Talmud, which says that if Chananya, Mishael, and Azarya had been tortured they may not have withstood the test. "But," he added earnestly, "the Russian Jews have been held captive and tortured for over sixty years and have still maintained their spiritual integrity and soul!"

The Rebbe continued with great emotion to describe the numerous letters and photographs he had received depicting secret Jewish weddings and underground *yeshivot,* smuggled to him from behind the Iron Curtain. He mentioned one letter in particular from a man who had managed against all odds to acquire a job that allowed him to avoid prohibited activities on Shabbat, although to observers he did seem to be doing his work. However, he was concerned whether his halachic status permitted him to recite Kiddush over wine or whether he should rather recite it over bread, although it is not the ideal way of reciting Kiddush.

The Rebbe's voice trembled as he recalled the sincerity of this anonymous Jewish hero: "He is willing to risk his life to keep Shabbat, and he is further risking his life just to send me a letter! And in it, all he is concerned with is whether he may recite Kiddush in the most stringent way possible."

Where others chose to focus on the devastation that Communism wrought upon the Jewish spirit, the Rebbe, with his *ayin tov*, highlighted the tremendous response of self-sacrifice that the Soviet regime elicited from Soviet Jewry.[118]

It's not that the devastation wasn't occurring, it's just that at the exact same moment there were also isolated, but inspiring, points of the highest goodness. Following the dictum that "A little bit of light dispels much darkness,"[119] the Rebbe made a point of acknowledging and amplifying those divine sparks amidst the wreckage in order to strengthen people's resolve and response to the plight of Jews in the Soviet Union.

The Future of American Jewry

Viewing other people and the world through the lens of a good eye endows us with a certain degree of optimism. From this perspective, every glass is half-full, not half-empty. A person is not defined by their lacks and weaknesses but by their strengths and potentials. Even a generation or historical period is judged according to its merits rather than its deficiencies.

Once, when giving a speech, Pulitzer Prize-winning novelist Herman Wouk referred to the Rebbe as "the most optimistic Jew of our time."

To support this assertion, he recounted how, during a visit with the Rebbe in the 1950s, he had commented on the sad state of American Jewry, bemoaning the lack of traditional observance and high rates of assimilation.

The Rebbe, in characteristic fashion, replied: "While many Jewish leaders are pessimistic about the present and future of American Jewry due to their struggles with observance, I'm upbeat and hopeful. Given the challenging situation of Jewish education in America, it's amazing that they still observe what they do observe. It is a very good community.

"While you cannot *tell* them to do anything," concluded the Rebbe, "you can *teach* them to do everything!"[120]

Instead of focusing on the lacks, or perceived vices, of the American Jewish community, the Rebbe chose to focus on its advantages and virtues, seeing promise and potential where others saw only deviation and despair. In the positively biased eyes of the Rebbe, even such a classically American trait as radical independence, which in many ways can seem to run counter to upholding past traditions, is seen in a redemptive light.

The above serves as a perfect example of what the world looks like when seen through a good eye. But what happens when one encounters something or someone who is intentionally hurtful?

The Fortitude to Differ

While we may find it feasible to see the good in someone neutral, how do we recast and redeem someone who has made their negative pretension or intolerance clear? In the following stories, the Rebbe looks past outer appearances or expressions of negativity in order to connect with the spiritual integrity and potential hiding within.

For almost two decades, Levi Yitzchak Freidin and his cameras were frequent visitors to the Chabad headquarters and synagogue at 770 Eastern Parkway in Brooklyn, preserving many solemn, spiritual, and elated moments there. In 1976, he held an exhibit called "770" at Tel Aviv's journalists' center, Beit Sokolov, and then at Bar Ilan University. These exhibits gave a wide range of unaffiliated Jews their first look at the Rebbe and the spirit, reverence, and joy of Jewish spiritual life.

The exhibit was very well received. However, one journalist commented sharply in the guest book: "With all due respect to the superb photography, the subject you have chosen is extremely clerical and takes us back to the primitive darkness of the Middle Ages."

Freidin later related: "During my next visit to the States, I presented the Rebbe with the guest book. Leafing through it quickly, he noticed that negative remark. 'Please compliment the journalist on his strength of character,' the Rebbe said. 'It takes fortitude to differ from all of the other responses.'"

The Rebbe then concluded with a further positive spin: "But tell him also that not everything in the Middle Ages was dark."[121]

Problem or Prodigy

By 1960, Yale Butler, the son of one of the leading Orthodox families in Pittsburgh, had developed a personal relationship with R. Yossi Shpielman, a local Lubavitcher rabbi. Young

Yale was an individualist, and a creative one, at that. In seventh grade, he became editor of the school newspaper. He wanted his first edition to attract attention throughout Pittsburgh's community, so he thought of a spoof.

One of the more active figures in Pittsburgh's Jewish community was a Lubavitcher who often wore an army hat and jacket. This and his untrimmed beard reminded many of Fidel Castro. In fact, the association was so common that he was nicknamed "Castro" throughout the community. The real Fidel Castro's totalitarian, anti-American policies were not widely known at the time.

Yale decided to expand on and caricature the visual association between the rabbi and the revolutionary dictator. He wrote a fictional account about an invasion of Cuba in which Castro's troops were in danger of being wiped out. In desperation, Castro called for his brethren in 770. They contacted the Rebbe and the order was given: Chasidim were to march on the Brooklyn Navy Yard, commandeer several submarines, and sail to Castro's rescue.

Yale's story did attract attention, but not the kind he desired. Many read his article, but few approved. Even as a jest, it was simply out of place. Leaders of the traditional Orthodox establishment reprimanded the twelve-year-old for his lack of sensitivity and encouraged him to apologize to the Lubavitcher community. The first issue of the paper was thus its final one.

Rabbi Shpielman, however, did not reprimand him. "You have to meet the Rebbe," he told Yale. Yale was not unwilling, and Rabbi Shpielman arranged for a private audience.

One Sunday evening, Yale and Rabbi Shpielman entered

the Rebbe's room. The Rebbe motioned for Yale to sit down. As he did, he noticed Rabbi Shpielman leaving. At this point, he began to feel nervous—a seventh-grader sitting alone with the Rebbe.

The Rebbe spoke to Yale warmly, telling him that he knew of his family and their work on behalf of the Jewish community in Pittsburgh. Yale was moved. The Rebbe continued, complimenting Yale for his talent as a writer.

Up until this point, Yale had been mesmerized by the Rebbe's eyes, but then he noticed, to his terror, a copy of his article on the Rebbe's desk. The Rebbe, however, made no mention of the article. He spoke of a person's obligation to see his talents as a trust, meant to be used for the benefit of others. In particular, the Rebbe emphasized, a writer should use his abilities to promote Jewish unity and love of one another.

Yale began to relax, and his feelings of fear turned into feelings of empowerment. Instead of reproaching him for his disrespectful story, the Rebbe had recognized his potential, encouraged him to develop it, and gave him a positive and productive focus for the future.

By 1982, Yale had become a rabbi and also the publisher of a newspaper, *B'nai Brith Messenger*. In the paper, he used the talks of the Rebbe for the weekly Torah portion column. One night, as he sat reviewing the list of people who had purchased lifetime subscriptions, he came across the name M.M. Schneerson. He had been sending the Rebbe a paper each week without charge. The Rebbe, however, had felt the need to subscribe on his own accord and pay for it with a personal check.

Years later, the Rebbe remarked in a conversation that Yale—now Rabbi Butler—had shown unique skill as a writer "since childhood."[122]

In this story, as in countless others, the Rebbe's Positivity Bias allowed him to see through the veneer of youthful chaos and rebellion into the boundless potential for spiritual accomplishment waiting to be identified and activated.

The world, others, and even our own selves look differently depending on the way they are perceived.

We have the ability to choose the way we approach and interpret the world. This act of perception can impact what we perceive, bringing out the good within ourselves and within others—or its opposite.

As the saying goes, "If you change the way you look at things, the things you look at change."

Just like light in the famous wave-particle duality of quantum mechanics, all life can be seen as a jumble of independent, isolated particles, or as a unified wave form, with every part connected to every other part, depending on how we view it.

What color are your glasses?

CHAPTER 9

Lashon Tov

JUDAISM DOES NOT BELIEVE in freedom of speech. There are certain ways of speaking about other people that are forbidden or discouraged. This heightened sensitivity to language is based on a profound respect for its power.

Ultimately, words matter.

Kabbalah teaches that speech itself has an effect beyond the simple event in which one person says something to another. The very fact that the words were pronounced has a certain significance and makes an energetic imprint.

A negative example of this phenomenon is the case of *lashon hara,* which translates literally as evil tongue but includes any kind of detrimental speech, including gossip, even if it is true and well-intentioned.

The Torah forbids speaking[123] or even listening to *lashon hara*. Moreover, the Sages tell us[124] that in addition to negatively affecting the speaker and listener, gossip has a negative impact on the person about whom it is spoken beyond the obvious defamation of character, even if they did not hear it.

We can understand why the speaker and the listener of *lashon hara* are punished; they have committed a serious transgression.

But why should the person *spoken about* be negatively affected?

The Kabbalists explain that by speaking about a person's negative qualities one invokes their expression. Although the person might not even be aware that they are being spoken about, the fact that their character flaws are being discussed concretizes their content on a certain level.

In his book of *Hayom Yom*, the Rebbe illustrates the deleterious effect of such negative speech with a story about the Baal Shem Tov, the founder of Chasidism:[125]

"Once, two men had a quarrel while in the Baal Shem Tov's synagogue, and one man shouted that he would tear the other fellow to pieces like a fish.

"In response, the Baal Shem Tov told his pupils to hold hands and stand near him with their eyes closed. Then he placed his holy hands on the shoulders of the two disciples next to him. Suddenly the disciples began shouting in great terror: They had seen that fellow actually dismembering his disputant.

"This incident demonstrates that every potential has an effect—either in physical form or on a spiritual plane that can be perceived only with higher and more refined senses."

Based on such a subtle understanding of the power of speech to negatively impact others, we can only imagine the positive effects our words can have if spoken with consciousness and compassion.

In this spirit, our Sages tell us to "judge everyone for good," including empathetically trying to understand the source of other people's shortcomings and "walk a mile in their shoes."

Beyond this, we can actively find ways to praise each person. The spiritual effect of such *lashon tov*, positive speech, is to enable a person's good qualities—which may be hidden deep within them—to come to the surface.[126]

If *lashon hara* is ultimately meant to tear someone down, *lashon tov* is meant to build them up.

There are countless recorded examples of the Rebbe practicing *lashon tov*. Indeed, consciously focusing on and explicitly verbalizing the good that he found in each individual was a feature of the Rebbe's every encounter.

Beyond just a pleasant exchange of niceties, the Rebbe saw such positive words as strengthening or activating the hidden resources of each person with whom he spoke and interacted.

His positive words would constantly encourage people and were meant to have a spiritually empowering effect on them.

In the words of R. Mordechai Eliyahu, former chief rabbi of Israel:[127] "During our four audiences, the Rebbe always sought out the merit of others. No matter the subject we were discussing, the Rebbe steered the conversation so that he could praise others."

In this chapter, we will see numerous examples of how the

Rebbe expressed this meta-linguistic aspect of his Positivity Bias through the consistent speaking of *lashon tov*.

Compliments

One particular way the Rebbe would positively impact others in conversation or correspondence was to always look for an opportunity to compliment them. Receiving a compliment from anyone is uplifting, but all the more so from a world spiritual leader.

Today, You Were the Teacher

After becoming engaged to a Lubavitch girl in Brooklyn, Jack Hardoff and his fiancé were invited to a private meeting with the Rebbe. The Rebbe shared that, like Jack, he too had studied electrical engineering, completing his degree at the Sorbonne in Paris, and that upon arriving from Europe during the war, he had worked at the Brooklyn Navy Yard as an engineer.

The Rebbe then proceeded to ask Jack to fill him in on all the new developments in electrical engineering. What was supposed to be a fifteen minute meeting lasted for two hours. When the meeting was finished, the Rebbe blessed the young couple with many years of marital bliss. Then he said something unexpected:

"You know, Yaakov ben Eliezer (Jack's Hebrew name), [normally] when people come here to see me, I am the 'rabbi' and they are the 'pupils,' but today you were the teacher and I was the pupil."

In Jack's own words:[128] "I'll never forget this compliment he gave me. It is something I will remember all my life."

Better than the Original

Raphael Nouril was born in Iran and trained as a classical artist. Eventually he moved with his family to London, where he lived next to a Lubavitcher family who invited the new neighbors over for a meal. Upon entering their house, Raphael was immediately drawn to a picture of the Rebbe they had hanging on the wall. Inexplicably moved, he decided then and there that he wanted to paint a portrait of the Rebbe.

Whenever Raphael painted someone's portrait, he always got to know them in some way before beginning his work. This particular portrait, however, posed a unique problem for Raphael.

"I felt distant on a number of levels. In addition to being thousands of miles away from the Rebbe, as a secular person I didn't feel like I could relate to him on a personal level. In my quest to get closer to him, I began to pray, to put on *tefillin,* and even to keep Shabbat and the holidays."

Upon completion of the portrait, Raphael traveled to New York with his neighbor to show the Rebbe his handiwork. After commenting on the position of his hands in the painting, Raphael asked the Rebbe what he thought about the face.

"Very good!" he said three times, and then added with a smile: "Better than the original!"[129]

Praise It Forward

In a letter to Mrs. Rachel Altein, Camp Mother of Camp Gan Israel in Swan Lake, NY, the Rebbe wrote:[130]

> During my recent inspection visit at the Camp, I was gratified to see how happy the children looked, and the evidence of the good care and attention that they are receiving. No doubt you have a substantial part in this, as Camp Mother. Although I know that your work at the Camp is motivated by the highest ideals, so that an expression of thanks may be superfluous, particularly as I know your education and background, as well as those of your husband. Nevertheless, I want to tell you about my feeling on visiting the Camp, as I hope that the knowledge of your success will redouble your efforts on behalf of the children and the Camp.

Empowerments

Another way in which the Rebbe would positively impact people through speech was to empower them in the virtues they were already expressing, or even in pointing out to them some unrevealed potential.

A General in the Rebbe's Army

David Chase, a successful American businessman, had a very close relationship with the Rebbe and continually sought to support his projects. Once, at the annual meeting of the

Machne Israel Development Fund, he told the Rebbe how honored he was to be "one of the soldiers in his army."

The Rebbe raised him with this quick reply: "You are not merely a soldier; you are my general!"

A short while later, Mr. Chase encountered the Rebbe during Sunday Dollars. After greeting the Rebbe, he promptly received another promotion: "[I regard you] as a four-star general."

In these two short exchanges,[131] the Rebbe expressed his confidence in Mr. Chase's leadership abilities, thereby encouraging him to step out of his soldier's shoes and put on his general's uniform. He had dutifully followed orders long enough; it was now time for him to become a leader.

Beautiful on the Inside

Susan Schuster grew up secular in New York. She went through school, became a nurse, and married a successful plastic surgeon. Shortly thereafter, they moved to Florida and began to have children. One of her sons befriended a Lubavitcher family at his Hebrew school, which spurred her own family to become more religious together. Eventually they made a trip to Brooklyn to meet the Rebbe, which was, according to Susan, "beyond words."

After that first meeting with the Rebbe, they returned many times and continued to become more religiously involved. In a subsequent encounter, the Rebbe said to Susan, "Your husband is a plastic surgeon; he makes people beautiful on the outside. It should be your mission to make people beautiful on the inside."

Susan took these words to heart and began inviting people to their home for Shabbat meals in an effort to help them find spiritual meaning in their lives. In her own words: "I took great pains in preparing these meals and in making the table very beautiful, so that it would reflect the inner beauty of Judaism." As a result of the Rebbe's continuous encouragement and empowerment, the Schusters even started and ran a successful *minyan* for many years in their neighborhood, providing others with opportunities to come together and connect to a higher purpose.[132]

What's in a Name?

One very personal way that the Rebbe would empower others was to link his encouragements and blessings for success to their given name.

This practice is based on the Talmudic statement that R. Meir would find references to a person's character in his name, and on the Kabbalistic idea which asserts that any person or thing is on some spiritual level defined by and further revealed through the word(s) by which they are called, which means that their inner essence can be creatively explicated through the prism of their name.

To Influence the Whole World

During one of the many Sunday Dollars, R. Yitzchak Kaduri an influential Sephardi Kabbalist and teacher, asked the Rebbe for a blessing for the success of his new project, a Kabbalistic *yeshivah* in Israel. The Rebbe responded with abundant blessings for the project's success and potential impact "to influence the entire globe, which is appropriate for your name, Kaduri (meaning global). [Through your *yeshivah*] you will be able to influence not only in the Holy Land, but the entire world."[133]

From a Place of Love

Shortly after the Crown Heights riots in 1991, US Senator Alfonse D'Amato came to visit the Rebbe with the then US Attorney for the Eastern District of New York to assure him that they were very aware of the issues in the neighborhood and that they were taking the protection of the Jewish People very seriously.

The Rebbe offered many words of wisdom and blessing, which he consistently phrased as being intended for "all the people of New York and the United States," and then added a personal comment directed at Senator D'Amato.

"You know that the word "Amato" has a connection with the word love [in Italian]," said the Rebbe.

He then continued: "May G-d A-mightly bless you to do all these things with inner love, and then certainly [the entire] population of New York will [respond] to you [and your colleagues] with their feeling of real love."[134]

In the words of our Sages:[135] "Words that come from the heart, enter the heart."

Unifying the Multitude

R. Gedalya Schreiber served as the director-general of the

Religious Affairs Ministry in Israel—among other posts. In 1980, he came to New York for a wedding. During the trip, he took the opportunity to meet with the Rebbe.

One particular topic that came up was the issue of Jewish unity. "There are so many separate camps—*Ashkenaz, Sefard,* the Right and the Left—but the key to our future is unity," the Rebbe said.

He wanted to know what Rabbi Schreiber and others in the government were doing to bring the various factions together. After hearing about the many activities of the Religious Affairs Ministry to further that goal, the Rebbe urged Rabbi Schreiber to keep doing more, and not to be satisfied with what they had achieved thus far.

When it was time to leave, the Rebbe said, "Your name is R. Gedalya Schreiber. King David says in Psalms (55:15), *Into the house of G-d we walked with a multitude*. The Hebrew word for multitude—*ReGeSH*—is the acronym of your name, **R. G**edalya **Sch**reiber."

According to Rabbi Schreiber: "When I walked out of the room, I was a different person. This meeting with the Rebbe gave me strength of purpose, and the Rebbe's spirit and perception guided me throughout my life."[136]

Seeing Others for Who They Are

One final example of the Rebbe's use of *lashon tov* to positively impact all those he met was his way of making each and every person feel special and unique—from remembering the small details of a particular interaction to providing specific guidance based on a person's individual interests or circumstances. In the following cases we can see various ways in which the Rebbe treated each person as a one-of-a-kind soul rather than a character type or generality.

Sounding the Shofar

In March 1992, on the very last Sunday the Rebbe distributed dollars, Judge Jerome Hornblass of the New York State Supreme Court came to see the Rebbe,[137] with whom he had multiple previous interactions over the years.

Upon his approach, the Rebbe looked up and said, "Oh, *tekias shofar*," a reference to the blowing of the *shofar* on Rosh Hashanah.

This greeting didn't make any sense to Judge Hornblass until he later met R. Zev Katz, the *gabbai* of the synagogue at 770 Eastern Parkway.

Rabbi Katz said to him, "Maybe you remember me. My mother was a patient at Memorial Sloan Kettering Hospital this past Rosh Hashanah, and you came to blow the *shofar* in her room."

Suddenly, it hit him: "Did you, by any chance, tell the Rebbe about this?"

"Yes, I told him," said Rabbi Katz.

"When did you tell him?" asked the judge.

"Right after Rosh Hashanah," he replied.

Out of all the people he met and the stories he had heard in that time, the Rebbe remembered Judge Hornblass and his act of loving-kindness, and he was not going to let it go unacknowledged.

Precious Things

The wife of a distinguished New York rabbi came to the Rebbe one Sunday to receive a dollar for charity. The Rebbe greeted her warmly, saying, "It's so nice to see you. You have not been here for a while, but that's the way it is with really precious things. You see them only from time to time."[138]

G-d Loves You More

In yet another example of the Rebbe uplifting others by acknowledging their special spark or soul attribute, once during Sunday Dollars he asked a rabbi to explain to a convert the rabbi had brought with him to receive a blessing that he [the convert] is "more beloved by G-d than you or me."[139]

Perhaps the Rebbe was alluding to the fact that the Torah commands us to "love our fellow" only once but instructs us to "love the convert" no less than 32 times.

Ever sensitive to the feelings of others, in this story the Rebbe makes a point of elevating the spirit of an individual who might have seen and felt himself to be an outsider on some level. By highlighting the reality that in G-d's eyes the convert was perhaps even more of an insider than others as a result of the sacrifices he had made for his faith, the Rebbe was letting him know that he was truly deserving of the highest honor and recognition.

We can see from all of the above stories, which are just a drop in the ocean, the Rebbe's commitment to *lashon tov*. In every interaction he constantly sought out a way to compliment, inspire, or acknowledge each person's special talent, strength, or potential. This was a direct expression of the Rebbe's belief that speaking positively to or about others manifests and strengthens their inherent points of goodness.

CHAPTER 10

Positive Language

THE REBBE'S POSITIVITY BIAS extended deeply into his habits of speech. In Yiddish, Hebrew, English, and all the other languages he spoke, the Rebbe constantly strove to phrase every teaching, idea, question, reflection, or suggestion in the most uplifting way possible. He would often note a teaching from the Talmud showing how the Torah speaks in a roundabout way to avoid describing even the negative characteristics of non-kosher animals.[140] It is clear from the stories that follow that the Rebbe believed that words matter, and that they should encourage and exalt in all circumstances.

One story that illustrates the Rebbe's practice of positive language is told about the *Lag BaOmer* parade in Crown Heights:[141]

R. Jacob J. Hecht, the official emcee of the parade, was having a difficult time one year. Leading up to the parade, he had worried that people wouldn't turn out, and that even if they did, they and their children wouldn't be entertained. During the parade, Rabbi Hecht viewed the floats and crowds with a jaded eye, seeing only the flaws and problems. He was anxious and apprehensive when the Rebbe came outside to address the crowd.

All of a sudden Rabbi Hecht noticed things changing for the good. The Rebbe delivered a talk to the children, saluted the soldiers who joined the parade, and admired the well-prepared floats. Perhaps it was the Rebbe's smile, perhaps it was his aura of good will or simply his presence, but Rabbi Hecht felt a sudden feeling of elation and good spirits in that moment.

At the end of the parade, Rabbi Hecht thanked the police, the organizers, and all the parade staff. He turned to the Rebbe and asked if he had enjoyed the event.

"Very much," the Rebbe responded.

Then Rabbi Hecht thanked the Rebbe for the great favor he had done for him personally—for having *aroisgeshlept, shlepped* or dragged him out of his troubles.

The Rebbe raised his hand in surprise and replied, "*Arois-geshlept? Oifgehoiben*! (Schlepped you out? Uplifted!)" To the Rebbe, the idea of dragging him out implied that Rabbi Hecht had been in a bad place and had perhaps left it unwillingly. Whereas to be *oifgehoiben, uplifted,* suggested that Rabbi Hecht's state simply went from the everyday to much better.

The Big Idea

This seemingly random rephrasing of Rabbi Hecht's words in the midst of a conversation was far from an isolated incident. There are many stories of the Rebbe adjusting someone's language—whether spoken or written—ever so slightly to reflect a more positive predisposition. When taken as a whole, it becomes clear that each of these incidents represents an expression of the Rebbe's general theory and practice of putting thoughts into words: Our language defines us and the world we inhabit; our words can limit or liberate us. Therefore, we need to choose them carefully and consciously.

The idea that words are the medium through which thoughts become things is rooted in centuries of Kabbalistic teachings and based on a metaphysical understanding of the beginning of the Torah in which G-d speaks the world into being. Detailing the many ways in which the Divine cosmogonic power of speech trickles down to human expression is beyond the scope of this present volume. Suffice it to say that a heightened sensitivity to the power of language is a foundational principle that runs through every facet of rabbinic teaching and text—including the Torah, prayers, the binding nature of oaths, and the spiritual and interpersonal repercussions of gossip.

This in-depth understanding of the relationship between our words and our experience is not limited to Kabbalists. According to neuroscientist Andrew Newberg and Professor Mark Robert Waldman, words can actually change your brain. In their book, *Words Can Change Your Brain*, they write, "A single word has the power to influence the expression of genes that regulate physical and emotional stress."

For instance, MRI scans demonstrate that a single negative word can increase the activity in the amygdala, the fear center of the brain. In fact, just seeing a list of negative words for a few seconds will make a highly anxious or depressed person feel even worse, and the more you ruminate on them, the more you can damage key brain structures that regulate memory, feelings, and emotions, further impacting your sleep, appetite, and overall sense of wellbeing. Moreover, if you vocalize your negativity, even more stress chemicals will be released, not only in your brain, but in the listener's brain as well. Both people will experience increased anxiety and irritability,[142] undermining potential for mutual cooperation and trust.[143]

Conversely, research indicates that the longer you concentrate on positive words, the more you begin to affect other areas of the brain. For instance, functions in the parietal lobe start to change, which changes your perception of yourself and the people you interact with. Studies have shown that positive words such as "peace" and "love" can actually alter the expression of genes, strengthening areas in our frontal lobes and promoting the brain's cognitive functioning.

Over time, the structure of the thalamus, which is the part of the brain that acts as a center for perception, changes in response to your words, thoughts, and feelings, affecting the way in which you perceive yourself, others, and the world. Using the right words can literally transform your reality.

The Rebbe understood this metalinguistic dynamic in a very profound yet practical way. What follows are a number of stories and examples demonstrating this particular aspect of the Rebbe's Positivity Bias in a wide array of contexts, including casual conversations, public speeches, and written correspondence.

Common Words and Colloquial Phrases

The Rebbe consistently sought to avoid locutions that expressed attitudes of contempt, derision, or negative judgment. Even more strikingly, he would actively rephrase common words and colloquial phrases that many of us speak or write without a second thought.

For instance, he disliked the word deadline, with its connection to death, preferring due date, with its connotation of birth.[144] He wouldn't call a spiritual getaway a retreat, because "retreat" connotes regression and surrender; in the Rebbe's playbook, there was only one direction: onward and upward. He didn't "undertake" projects, possibly because he saw a connotation to half-heartedness in the prefix under or because he associated the word undertaker with death.[145]

Even terms used universally by Jews were subject to the Rebbe's preference for positive rephrasing. For example, there were times when he objected to the label for the Torah portion of *Metzora,* because the word refers to a skin affliction that was associated with negative speech, *lashon hara*. He thought it better to call the section *Parashat Taharah,* purity, after the process it describes, which helps restore ritual purity once the affliction had abated.

Despite the fact that the Rebbe essentially jumpstarted the *baal teshuvah* movement, as discussed in a previous chapter,[146] he preferred that this term not be used in reference to specific individuals, which means master of repentance.[147] He felt it was disparaging to label someone in a way that insinuated they had done something that required atonement.[148]

In an extreme example, the Rebbe didn't even like to characterize geographical places as far away. When a Chabad rabbi introduced the Rebbe to a donor from East Asia, the Rebbe said to the donor, "You come from a place in the East called the opposite of near."[149] He also objected to calling Australia a faraway land, preferring to call it "the opposite of close."[150]

Each of these examples reveals how seriously the Rebbe took this practice of positive language, applying it even to trivial dimensions of common parlance.

Self-Definition

Obviously, the Rebbe saw great importance in the psychological impact of words. He felt that the way a label or concept was framed linguistically was not only relevant intellectually but had great value in shaping a person's identity and outlook.

He objected strongly, for example, to the Israeli phrase for hospital, *beit cholim*, which means house of the sick. Why was the hospital not called *beit refuah*—house of healing—he asked? In a letter to Professor Mordechai Shani, director of the Sheba Medical Center in Israel, he wrote,[151] "Even though...this would seem to represent only a semantic change, the term *beit refuah* brings encouragement to the sick; it represents more accurately the goal of the institution...which is to bring about a complete healing. Therefore, why call it by a word that does not suit its intentions?" By changing the way we refer to hospitals, the Rebbe felt that we would strengthen and sanctify health rather than prioritizing illness.[152]

When a man from Curaçao described himself as "a small Jew" in a letter to the Rebbe, the Rebbe wrote back[153] that "there is no such thing as a small Jew," reminding him that the soul of every Jew is "part of G-d." Therefore, "a Jew must never underestimate his or her tremendous potential."

Another man came to the Rebbe and said, "Rebbe, something must be wrong with me." He began to bemoan his spiritual state of being. The Rebbe said, "Just as it's forbidden to speak disparagingly about someone else, even if one speaks the absolute truth, it's also forbidden to speak negatively about oneself."[154] The Rebbe wasn't accusing the man of a transgression; he was reminding him that the words we say manifest what we're speaking about. If it doesn't propel you forward, don't dwell on it.

The Rebbe suggested to Mrs. Chana Sharfstein, who had written a research paper about the Chasidic community of Crown Heights, that she change her wording from "the hard life of a Chasid" to "the hardships of life."[155] The Rebbe's reservation was not so much that she thought the lives of Chasidim were more difficult than those of people in the secular community; rather, it was because the phrase equated life itself with hardship, perhaps precluding joy. Better, the Rebbe thought, to acknowledge that while life does contain hardships, they should not define life as hard in and of itself.

On a more historical and national level, the Rebbe was reluctant to refer to the genocide of European Jews during World War II as the Holocaust, sometimes even referring to it as the so-called Holocaust. The word holocaust comes from the Greek for "completely burned," and the Rebbe may have objected to feeding the idea that the destruction of six million Jews had any connection to the idea of ritual animal sacrifice in which an animal is completely burned and reduced to ashes. He was opposed to the idea of even tenuously linking animal sacrifice, a holy act, with the murder of six million Jews. The Rebbe vehemently rejected the idea, held by some in the Jewish community, that there was any spiritual meaning or purpose in the genocide or that it was a retribution from G-d, and he wanted his language to reflect this view.[156]

The Problem with 'Inanimate' Objects

The Rebbe's incredible sensitivity to language extended even to objects. When a Chabad rabbi brought an armload of *lulavim* for Sukkot into the Rebbe's office and asked where to set them down, the Rebbe replied,[157] "*Oif di eitzim* (on the wood)," referring to the wooden floor. Apparently he did not want to use a word for the surface on which a ritual object was to be laid that denoted something lowly and commonly stepped on.

Before the war, the Rebbe was the editor of *Hatamim*, a scholarly journal published by Chabad, headquartered in Warsaw at that time. During a conversation with the publisher, R. Schneur Zalman Gourary, the Rebbe perplexed him by hinting, rather than saying plainly, that Rabbi Gourary didn't need to place the title and page number at the top of each page. Then, as now, that information was called a heading or header, but the Rebbe was unwilling to say that he wanted each page "without a head."[158]

A *yeshivah* student once lent the Rebbe a *sefer* (a book on a Torah topic). After some time had passed, the student approached the Rebbe after prayers one day and asked respectfully, "Rebbe, do you no longer need the *sefer* I lent you?" The Rebbe responded warmly, "When referring to a *sefer*, we don't use the expression 'don't need....'"[159]

While standing upstairs at Chabad headquarters, the Rebbe once heard one of the *gabba'im* (congregational officials) refer to the downstairs synagogue as "*unten*," which means "below." The Rebbe took the time to interject: "We don't say '*unten*' about a *shul*."[160]

The Rebbe even took issue with the term "inanimate." When he commissioned noted author R. Nissan Mangel to translate the *Tanya* into English, Rabbi Mangel used the conventional translation, "inanimate," for the Hebrew word *domeim*. The Rebbe objected, emphasizing that all existence is a continuous flow of G-dly life and energy.[161]

One of the major themes of *Tanya* (in *Shaar Hayichud VehaEmunah*) is that in truth there is no such thing as something "inanimate," because everything contains a Divine spark.... The Rebbe edited Rabbi Mangel's translation, replacing "inanimate" with "silent," meaning to say that while there is life even in *domeim*, an object in this realm is "silent" about it, concealing the inherent Divine spark it possesses. Rabbi Mangel, still wanting to maintain an elegant style, kept the word inanimate and placed the word silent nearby in brackets. When the Rebbe edited the translation for the final time, he removed the brackets around "silent" and placed them around "inanimate."

In that context, the word inanimate wasn't just a misnomer or a technical misuse of a word, it represented something more. The difference between these two words touches on the essence of reality, on its Divine root and makeup. For it is this very spark of living Divinity present in all of Creation to which we pay tribute and respect, and for which we exhibit sensitivity and consideration.

The Opposite Of...

It was common for the Rebbe to avoid negativity in speech by phrasing a condition or quality as "the opposite of" something good, rather than saying something was bad or evil. For example, there were a few occasions when instead of referring to the *yetzer hara,* the evil inclination, the Rebbe said, "The *yetzer* that is the opposite of the *yetzer hatov* (the good inclination)."

Instead of saying that things are getting worse, there were times when the Rebbe would say, in Yiddish, "*Nit-der-seder vert altz shtarker*"—the "opposite-of-order" is getting stronger. Or, "The portion that is not positive (or good) is being strengthened." The Rebbe would not describe someone whose behavior or spiritual life was declining as regressing or descending; he would use a variation of the blessing, "May you go from strength to strength," and say that the individual was "going from strength to strength in the opposite direction."

The Rebbe had many such locutions:

• When he spoke about Jews who treated each other badly, he would say they were behaving with the opposite of *ahavat Yisrael,* love of one's fellow Jew.[162]

• He would refer to an increase in sins against Divine instruction as "the opposite of increase in Torah and *mitzvot*."

• Someone who was deceptive was "the opposite of *Yaakov ish tam*"—Jacob, whom the Torah describes as honest.[163]

• Instead of referring to the *malach hamavet,* the Angel of Death, he would say, "The opposite of the *malach hachayim*," the Angel of Life.[164]

• A professed non-believer was not an apostate or an atheist to the Rebbe; he was someone expressing an idea opposite of the central Jewish statement of belief in G-d as stated in the *Shema.*[165]

• Citing a Talmudic teaching pertaining to *Parashat Noach,* the Rebbe would refer to a non-kosher animal as an animal that is not pure rather than as an animal that is impure.

There are many other such examples as well. In the Rebbe's speech and correspondence, hatred was "the opposite of love";[166] lying was "the opposite of truth";[167] curses were "the opposite of blessings";[168] arrogance "the opposite of humility";[169] sadness "the opposite of joy."[170] Even death was "the opposite of life"[171] in the Rebbe's vernacular, and the underworld "the opposite of the Garden of Eden."[172] In this way the Rebbe emphasized the Chasidic idea that evil, hatred, and other negative conditions are not entities in themselves, separate from G-dliness (which is defined as ultimate goodness); rather, they are simply the absence, and therefore the opposite, of good.

Positive Torah

The Rebbe was so committed to the use of positive language that he even refrained from quoting parts of Bible verses that cast aspersions on people.

One example is in the Book of Proverbs. King Solomon says in Proverbs,[173] *A fool believes everything, but a clever man understands his course*. The Midrash[174] explains that the *fool who believes everything* refers to none other than Moses; the Sages saw the term for fool (or simpleton) that is used here as a positive. Moses is called this because his approach to G-d involved accepting G-d's word without questioning.

The Rebbe once quoted this Midrash during a discourse to make a point about this elevated level of unquestioning faith. When the editor sent in the transcript as part of the preparation for publication, he included the full quote from the Midrash: "A fool believes everything, which refers to Moses." The Rebbe crossed out the word for fool, and rephrased it to read, "The believer of everything is Moses." He then wrote in the margin, "I intentionally omitted this word."[175] Meaning that even though the Midrash applies the term fool to Moses in a positive way, the Rebbe did not want to use a word that could mean something derogatory in reference to Moses.

In another discourse, the Rebbe quoted Psalms:[176] *Difficult in the eyes of the L-rd is the death of His pious ones*. However, in the published discourse, the Rebbe quoted only the first half of the verse, *Difficult in the eyes of the L-rd*, and then wrote "et cetera."[177] He didn't want to verbalize or print the words *the death of His pious ones*, thus applying his sensitivity to negative words even to the holy words of Psalms.

One of the Thirteen Articles of Faith is the belief in the eventual coming of Moshiach. There is a well-known melody sung to those words. However, oftentimes when the Rebbe would sing it, he did not say the words, "And even though he may tarry, I await his coming every day." The Rebbe didn't want to give any credence or vitality to the possibility that Moshiach's coming might be delayed.

Abra K'dabra / I Create as I Speak

Not only did the Rebbe believe that our language choices have a psychological impact on people—ourselves included—he also believed that words have the power to affect reality itself. It is no accident that the Hebrew word *davar*, which means "word" and is the root for the Hebrew words for "speak" and "speech," also means "thing." As mentioned previously, the relationship between words and things is very close; it can be said that words manifest real things.

The Rebbe barely escaped the Nazi horror in Europe, and lived at a time when words mattered more than ever before. Hitler, may his name be erased, gained power and galvanized the German military and people to commit horrific atrocities with the power of inflammatory words and vitriolic rhetoric. That historical milieu, in which the Rebbe's sensitivities were formulated, may have reinforced his desire to ensure that every word he or anyone else used was used consciously, compassionately, and carefully.

The Rebbe knew that words not only influence the way we think and how we react, but they also shape us spiritually and even have an impact on reality. That's why he was so adamant about excising negativity from his own words, and why he modeled a positive approach to speaking with others. This linguistic laser focus did not stem from a vague sense that we should all get along and be nice to one another. The Rebbe had seen firsthand how words can channel raw energy into concrete action. He knew deep down that if the children of G-d were to improve themselves, their language would have to reflect and demonstrate a commitment to that elevation.

CHAPTER 11

Positivity is a Choice

THE FAMED CHASIDIC MASTER, R. Levi Yitzchak of Berditchev, once met a Jew who was smoking on Shabbat. He said to him, "My friend, perhaps you forgot that today is Shabbat."

"No, Rabbi, I know that it is Shabbat," he replied.

"Ah," said R. Levi Yitzchak, "perhaps you forgot or never learned that it is forbidden to smoke on Shabbat."

"Of course I know that it is forbidden to smoke on Shabbat," the man said, cutting off his last reasonable defense.

Hearing this, R. Levi Yitzchak turned his gaze upward and called out fervently, "Master of the World, who is like Your People, Israel?! Even when I gave this Jew every opportunity to lie and mitigate his offense, he refused to do so. Where is such scrupulous honesty to be found in all the world?!"[178]

Even in the face of such a brazen, public dismissal of the dictates of Torah law, R. Levi Yitzchak made a point of finding something positive to focus on. This kind of redemptive vision, always able to find a hidden spark of goodness to build on even in the worst circumstances, is a hallmark of the Chasidic worldview in general, and the Rebbe's Positivity Bias in particular, as we will see in the following stories.

The Sincerity of a Child

On Shavuot, 5738 (1978), outside 770 Eastern Parkway, a child wandered up and took the Rebbe's hand, thinking it was his father's. The Rebbe held his hand and continued walking with him. Still not realizing his mistake, the child took the Rebbe's coat and wiped his face on it.

The child's mother was horrified to hear of this, and penned an apology to the Rebbe, exclaiming that she was pained by what had happened. She soon received her letter back, with the Rebbe's response.

The Rebbe had written "?!" after the word pained. He then added, "On the contrary: He brought me great pleasure. One cannot begin to measure the heartfulness, simplicity, innocence, and sincerity of a child—if only similar qualities could be found in adults."[179]

Rather than reprimanding or reacting negatively to the "disrespect" of the child wiping his face on his coat, the Rebbe chose to focus on the positive character traits expressed in such an act of loving familiarity.

No matter the type of embarrassment, problem, or disadvantage presented to him, the Rebbe could pinpoint some hidden fulcrum within it and flip it into an advantage or benefit.

Indeed, within almost any event or conversation, there are positive and negative elements. With practice and diligence, we too can learn to locate these inner sparks of goodness and make them glow.

Startup Pedigree

A couple once sought the Rebbe's advice regarding a possible match for their daughter. They were hesitant because they came from a very distinguished religious lineage, but their potential son-in-law did not.

"Is this not a valid reservation?" they asked.

The Rebbe responded: "Would you have refused to take Abraham, our forefather, as your son-in-law? After all, his father, Terah, worshipped idols..."[180]

The young man was not raised religiously, yet the Rebbe saw in him the glimmer of a heroic prototype. He had surely shown some level of sacrifice in departing from the environment of his upbringing—like Abraham himself. Perhaps the parents would accept him, not despite the fact that he had led an irreligious past, but *because* of it—because of the conviction and courage it took to leave the familiar behind.

A Yiddishe Mamme

R. Chaim Gutnick of Australia once reported to the Rebbe regarding a class on marriage and motherhood that he had arranged. He complained that only one woman had attended.

The Rebbe replied, "And how many mothers did Moses have?"[181]

There is no such thing as failure for a virtuosic optimist, a composer of life. For such a person, every woman or man is understood to be a potential instrument of redemption, vibrating with unsung merits that could potentially add the culminating notes to the symphony of human history.

Every situation, too, can be seen as part of a much wider picture, if we would have the eyes to see and the ears to hear.

Love Your Competitor as Yourself

A *shliach* of the Rebbe moved to an area where the Jewish institutions were winding down. Some organizations had already given up on building up Jewish life there because they didn't see any potential. The *shliach* courageously entered the fray, nonetheless. After eight years of constant efforts to seed a community, he had just begun to see a sprout emerging. Then, suddenly, other organizations began investing heavily in parallel programming, competing with his work and undermining everything he had created.

The *shliach* wrote to the Rebbe and asked permission to move to a different area where he would see greater success from his efforts.

The Rebbe replied:

> "Everything you have done there is having great success. You started from the *alef bet* [i.e., the basics] in every way. And now, through the institutions and activities you and your wife have established, your city has been transformed to the degree that other

> religious groups [are emulating you and heightening their activities]. Having raised the local profile of Torah and *mitzvot*, you have become a distinguished presence in the city, widely respected by city leaders and officials, and after all this you wonder why there are some who envy [and seek to emulate] you?[182]

With one simple gesture of confidence, the Rebbe overturned the problem: The sudden growth of competition was not a sign of the *shliach's* failure; rather, it was a sign of his "great success." The organizations were not weeds invading the *shliach's* garden. They merely had learned from his example that productivity was possible, and they had therefore renewed their own efforts.

When we fully internalize the fact that there is a hidden point of goodness and G-dliness within every person and event, we are then able to intuitively find and connect to those holy sparks, even when they are garbed in seemingly negative behavior or circumstances.

Music to G-d's Ears

The festival of Purim is delightful for children, especially when they bring their noise-makers to the synagogue in order to loudly drown out the name of the villainous Haman when it is read aloud. At one point during the reading of the Megillah in the Rebbe's synagogue, the children got very carried away in their enthusiastic noise-making. Some of the adults grew tense because they could not hear the reading properly and attempted to quiet the children.

Later, however, the Rebbe addressed those adults:[183]

> In their innocence, the children were enjoying the spirit of Purim. Of course you want to hear the reading, but we must also appreciate G-d's own great joy in seeing these children celebrate.

If we set our default mode to positive, we, too, will be able to detect divine delight within disruption and learn to celebrate the preciousness and purity of even those who appear insensitive to the spirit and inner meaning of the *mitzvot*.

A Good Sign

A young family had a private audience with the Rebbe on Chanukah. The Rebbe offered a gift of coins to their young child, as is customary on Chanukah. For whatever reason, the child rejected the Rebbe's gift. After a couple more failed attempts, the Rebbe remarked kindly, "This is a good sign! He is not someone who craves money!"[184]

Rather than seeing in the child's refusal the signs of a difficult personality, the Rebbe recast his behavior as an indication of good character.

By swiftly zeroing in on the good and revealing it with soul and warmth, the Rebbe healed, uplifted, educated, and encouraged everyone he encountered.

Truly New

A highly learned teacher once reported with pride that he was opening an educational program for Russian Jews who did not even know how to read from a *siddur*. The Rebbe responded energetically, "For them, the injunction that 'Torah should always remain new in your eyes' can be practiced literally!"[185]

This teacher, in his comment and tone, had revealed to the Rebbe that he very subtly looked down upon his students' lack of knowledge. The Rebbe, in his characteristic loving fashion, leveraged the conversation to help this teacher see his students in a different light. While unfortunate circumstances had not allowed these students the benefit of a Jewish education, these very same circumstances allowed them to approach Torah with open-eyed curiosity and creativity. They even possessed an advantage over seasoned scholars whose knowledge can paradoxically preclude or obscure novel approaches to a given subject of study.

In our final example, it is noteworthy that the Rebbe lived the same advice he gave to others, and applied his signature Positivity Bias to his own challenges, even in matters of life and death.

The Cup is Half Full

On countless occasions the Rebbe taught that optimism, reinforced by a trust in G-d, is just as important to the healing process as medicine and doctors. On Shemini Atzeret 5738 (1977), he suffered a serious heart attack. Two days later, he insisted on giving a talk, as he had done on that particular day for the previous 38 years.

"You must take care of your health," the doctor insisted. "If not, there is a 25 percent chance of a relapse." The doctor asked if the Rebbe understood what he had said. "Oh, yes," said the Rebbe with a smile. "You said that even if I don't take care of my health—which, I assure you, I will—there is a 75 percent chance that there won't be a relapse."[186]

The Rebbe's positive paraphrasing of life might seem radical to some, but it is in fact a necessary perspective for all of us to engage in to the best of our ability. If we apply some of the Rebbe's optimism to our own lives, problems would be revealed as potentials for growth, enemies would be understood as teachers, and setbacks would be seen for what they really are—springboards to the next level!

CHAPTER 12

Think Positive

THE STORY IS TOLD of a follower of R. Menachem Mendel, third Lubavitcher Rebbe, the "Tzemach Tzedek," whose son was seriously ill. He was advised to travel to the Tzemach Tzedek to ask for a blessing. With a heavy heart, he made the difficult trek to the Rebbe.

In response to his request for a blessing, the Tzemach Tzedek pronounced five Yiddish words, which have been quoted by the Chabad Rebbes ever since: "*Tracht gut vet zein gut*—Think good and it will be good."

The Chasid took these words to heart, and during the entire homeward journey he strove to strengthen his trust in G-d and visualize a good outcome for his son. When he returned home, he was shocked to see his son completely healed and back to his normal self.[187]

A Bad Plan

For many people, this kind of positive thinking is a difficult directive to take seriously. "Think positive" sounds like the naive content you'd find in a supermarket self-help book or an amateur new-age podcast peddling feel-good platitudes and banal soundbites. Besides, isn't this approach dangerous? It can set you up for great disappointment! What if you visualize an excellent result and the positive outcome doesn't materialize?

Indeed, some scientists recently have pushed back against "positive thinking," claiming that only focusing on the best outcome is not the most psychologically sound approach to life, given the high potential for failed expectations. A recent article in *Scientific American*[188] suggested that imagining the worst outcome rather than the best is a more optimal way to live life, because if you envision and plan for the worst-case scenario, you will never be let down and can only be pleasantly surprised if you end up with a positive outcome. Similarly, *Newsweek* ran a much-publicized story[189] titled "The 'Tyranny' of Positive Thinking Can Threaten Your Health and Happiness." It reported the findings of motivational scientists who said that an insistence on positivity could cause people to blame themselves for their own sadness or failure to overcome adversity.

However, the principle of "think good and it will be good" has been and continues to be an integral aspect of Chasidic philosophy in general, and a staple of the Rebbe's Positivity Bias in particular. Could it be that the psychologists in these studies are addressing the ego, whose fragility they are concerned with protecting, while the Rebbe is addressing the soul, whose only desire is to sing and soar? It would behoove us to dig a bit deeper to uncover the essence of what the Rebbes have been saying for centuries.

A Matter of Faith

In a 1963 address,[190] the Rebbe expanded on the philosophical and spiritual dynamic behind "Think good and it will be good." He began by asking the obvious question: On what basis should one believe that the outcome will be good in the face of any challenge? Isn't it presumptuous to assume that in every given situation we are always deserving of Divine grace? And what of the basic Jewish belief that there is a Divine order of reward and punishment that governs our world, making salvation dependent on righteous behavior?

The Rebbe offered these words in response:

> When a person decides to place their trust in G-d, believing that their current crisis will be resolved favorably despite facing a bleak reality, they have, in effect, risen above their own nature, which in turn elicits, reciprocally, the suspension of the Divine order, in which only the righteous are deserving of salvation. G-d understands how difficult and even "supernatural" it is for a human being to believe sincerely—to the degree that he or she no longer experiences fear and anxiety—that an unpromising and even seemingly hopeless situation will have a positive outcome. Therefore, as a result and even reward for the extraordinary act of "thinking good," G-d deems the believer, who may be otherwise un-

deserving of a positive outcome, as deserving of an extra measure of Divine generosity in this instance.

Ultimately, the efficacy of "thinking good," according to the Rebbe, is indissolubly bound up with one's faith in *G-d's ability* to manifest a positive outcome. This is the key difference between what the Rebbes are suggesting and what the studies cited above are critiquing.

Someone who doesn't place his trust in the infinite potential of a Higher Power is merely deifying their own limited thoughts. We will now explore a number of interactions in which the Rebbe further articulated this fundamental concept.

Disciplined Practice, Not Magical Thinking

While teaching in New York in 1957, a young man from Israel received a letter from home saying that his father had suffered a heart attack and was in critical condition.

At a time when overseas phone calls were rare, the young man's anxiety was deepened by the thought that his father may have already passed away. Devastated, the young man wrote a note to the Rebbe explaining the situation, ending with the words, "I don't even know what to think at this point!"

In his response, the Rebbe underlined the student's final sentence and wrote next to it, "Shocking!!! Because the instruction of our Sages in such situations is well known: 'Think good and it will be good.' I await good news."

A few tense days passed, and finally the young man reached his mother by phone.

"How is Father?" he asked.

"He's out of danger!"

"When did this happen?"

"Thursday night."

After hanging up the phone, the young man went to 770 for afternoon prayers. On his way out of the synagogue, the Rebbe turned to him and asked, "Nu, do you have good news for me?"

"Yes!" he responded. "I just phoned home and was told that my father is out of danger."

"Since when?" asked the Rebbe.

"Since Thursday night."

"And when did you begin to 'think good'?"

"When the Rebbe told me to do so," said the young man.

"And when was that?" the Rebbe pressed on.

"Thursday evening."

The Rebbe concluded, "May such things never happen again. But you must always remember to think positively."[191]

Our Thoughts Limit or Expand Our Potential

In another instance, a Chasid mentioned that he was due to have a very serious operation in a few weeks' time, and he asked the Rebbe for a blessing that the surgery be a success.

The Rebbe said pointedly, "Instead of asking that I pray that the surgery be successful, you could have asked me to pray that you not need to undergo surgery at all!"

The Chasid immediately recanted, "Rebbe, I would like to ask for a blessing that I not need surgery at all!"

The Rebbe replied:[192] "It's too late. I can only work with the faith you had when you *entered* my office."

In other words: "I can only work with the level of faith *you* have in G-d, not with the level of faith *I* have in G-d."

End of the World?

R. Yehoshua Binyomin Gordon, of blessed memory, related[193] that at a certain point in their lives, he and his wife faced a very serious challenge. At their wits' end, they decided to write to the Rebbe for guidance. They drafted a ten-page letter explaining everything. On the day their letter arrived in New York, they received a call from the Rebbe's secretary with his answer:

> Time and again in your holy work [as *shluchim*], you have imagined that the situation you find yourselves in is the end of the world, but then you saw how the situation flipped over and became visible and revealed good.... You must [in all cases] follow the command of the Tzemach Tzedek to "think optimistically, and things will turn out well."

The Rebbe's prompt response was illuminating. In Rabbi Gordon's own words: "This answer is a teaching that I try to remember every day—that as bad as things may look, they looked bad last time too, but everything turned out fine."

There are so many times in our lives when the worst outcome seemed inevitable. How many of those times took a different turn from what we anxiously expected? For many of us this is a recurring pattern of our negative thought processes. In the end, all that time spent stressing didn't do us any good, not to mention that it was actually bad for our health. Thinking good in the face of perceived adversity is helpful and healing on many levels.

Reality Begins in Your Head

In the following response[194] to someone who, it seems, had written several pessimistic letters to the Rebbe describing his life's challenges, the Rebbe elaborated on the powers of both speech and thought to impact reality for the good or its opposite.

> In response to your letter, from which it is clear that I have not yet been successful at inspiring in you a spirit of optimism, despite having told you on numerous occasions that according to Jewish teachings, one should refrain from [verbally] introducing negative and melancholy ideas into the world, which is one way of averting the actualization of [negativity].[195]
>
> And this [does not] apply [only] to verbalization—which, according to Chasidic teachings,[196] contains the power to actualize, as we learn from the behavior of the Maggid [of Mezritch], who would verbalize his novel ideas in order to bring them into the world—but even thought [itself] has the power to effect actualization, as we see from the teaching of our Rebbes, "Think good and it will be good."

In this letter, the Rebbe elucidates some of the core Kabbalistic underpinnings of "Think good and it will be good." As when the world was created, the process of actualization, where an initially spiritual idea and energy becomes manifest in physical reality, is just that—a process. The fruit of our experience and actions does not just appear out of nowhere. It is rooted in our speech (a common point made in Chasidic texts, as explored above, in Chapter 9, *Lashon Tov*), which is ultimately an expression of the seed nutrients contained within our thoughts that are planted within the soil of our souls.

Reality is Unrealistic

In our final example of the Rebbe's application and elaboration of this teaching, we get a glimpse of the integral worldview that undergirds such a faith in the power of our thoughts to impact reality.

> While I am pleased to read in your letter the quotation about G-d being the Creator of the world, Who also guides all its destinies, etc., this very good impression is weakened by the further tone of your letter, where you state that you want to be "realistic," based on the prognosis of physicians regarding your condition. I want to tell you, first, that even from the realistic point of view, we must recognize the fact that very many times, the greatest physicians have made mistakes in diagnosis. Moreover, in recent times we see that new discoveries are made daily in the medical field, with new "wonder drugs" and methods, which have revolutionized medical treatment.
>
> Secondly, observing life in general, we see so many things that are strange and unbelievable that to be

> truly realistic, one cannot consider anything as impossible.[197]
>
> ...Even medical opinion agrees that the stronger the patient's faith in cure, and the stronger his will to get better, the stronger becomes his ability to recover. Needless to say, this is not said in the way of an admonition. But, inasmuch as by individual Divine Providence you have learned of me and I of you, I think I am entitled to convey to you the above thoughts, which I was privileged to hear from my father-in-law, of saintly memory, in similar cases.[198]

If we think about the aspects of the celestial worlds that are necessary for Creation to exist at all for even a fleeting moment, not to mention all of the amazing medical and technological developments that humans are continuously discovering and putting to use, we can only marvel at the sheer unpredictable magnificence of life as a whole. Who knows what blessings are waiting to be revealed at any second?

As the Rebbe points out, there are levels of faith. A person may believe that G-d can create, but do they believe that G-d can heal? Inasmuch as the world itself is so miraculous and unpredictable, which is obvious to anyone who looks deeply into it, wouldn't an honest appraisal of reality make room for unexpected turnarounds and inexplicable interventions?

From all of the above examples we can begin to understand why the Rebbe took the concept of positive thinking so seriously.

From a psychologically practical point of view, there may

indeed be a risk or downside to thinking positive, as the person may be setting themselves up for a massive letdown if things do not work out as they had hoped. From this perspective, envisioning worst-case scenarios might actually help avoid future suffering by managing one's expectations.

However, from a spiritual perspective—and this is precisely the challenge of faith—the exact opposite is true. According to the Rebbe, it isn't that we must manage our thoughts to conform to or protect us from reality; the truth is that, whether we know it or not, we are molding reality in relation to our thoughts. It is better to think good!

CHAPTER 13

Rehearsal for Redemption

IN HIS MEMOIRS, ELIE Wiesel vividly recounts his first encounter with the Rebbe in the early 1960s. "That simple dialogue," according to Wiesel, "lasted almost an entire night," and "was a turning point in my writing."[199]

In 1964 Wiesel published his novel, *The Gates of the Forest*, whose fourth chapter, Winter, is a dramatized account of his first visit with the Rebbe.[200]

The account is grueling, heartbreaking, and painfully vulnerable. Auschwitz, of course, is the pivotal question of the conversation. "How can you believe in G-d after Auschwitz?" But as the conversation shifts from emotion to emotion, from argument to counter-argument, the Rebbe keeps pushing his visitor to reveal why he is really there, his deepest motivation for the visit. "What do you expect of me?" asks the Rebbe. To which Wiesel responds: "Nothing, absolutely nothing."

But the Rebbe is patient.

After hours of going back and forth, in a moment of epiphany, Wiesel came to realize why he had come to see the Rebbe. He confessed, "...You asked me what I expect of you, and I said I expect nothing. I was wrong. I want you to make me cry."

In the original, much longer, Yiddish version of the book that came to be called *Night*, Wiesel describes the death of his father in Buchenwald, admitting that this event was so traumatizing it had, in that moment and ever since, robbed him of his tears. "I did not cry, and this is what causes me the most grief: this inability to cry. The heart had petrified, the fountainhead of tears had dried up."

And what was the Rebbe's response? What could one possibly say to such an urgent, human request?

"That's not enough," he said lovingly. "I shall teach you to sing."

In this singular exchange, we see the Rebbe's Positivity Bias on full display in all of its redemptive sensitivity and complexity. Wiesel's tears are not denied, Heaven forbid. Facing one's pain, no matter how enormous, and feeling it deeply is essential to releasing its deadening grip on the soul. However, the Rebbe's response makes it clear that this catharsis is not the ultimate goal. It's what comes after the tears that the Rebbe remains focused on, and what he wanted to communicate to the aspiring author.

The Rebbe understood that for Wiesel to truly heal he

needed to learn not only how to cry, but how to regain his desire and ability to sing again.

And this assessment of the Rebbe, that sorrow must never swallow joy, and that tears must never drown out the song in our hearts, was not reserved for Mr. Wiesel. It was a deeper diagnosis of the Jewish soul following the wreckage of World War II. In general, as many expended their energy on memorializing the horrifying loss of Jewish life, the Rebbe consistently directed his focus and that of others to the miraculous continuation of Jewish life, in its many forms. Truly, for the Rebbe, it was never enough to just survive, we must constantly strive to thrive.

By attempting to shift the central point of national focus and self-identification away from the colossal tragedy of the Holocaust and direct it instead toward a redemptive future and a joyful present, the Rebbe chose not to devalue or trivialize such historic loss, Heaven forbid. He only worked to ensure that it not come to exclusively define and confine the way the Jewish People view their past, present, and future.

In the words of R. Jonathan Sacks: "I have read many works of post-Holocaust Jewish theology. And they all ask the same question. They ask what unites us—the Jewish people—today, with all our divisiveness and arguments. And in them I read the same answer: What unites us as Jewish people today is memories of the Holocaust, fears of anti-Semitism. What unites us as a people is that other people hate us.

"The Rebbe taught the opposite message. What unites us, he taught, is not that other people don't like us, but that G-d loves us; that every one of us is a fragment of the Divine presence and together we are the physical presence of G-d on earth. Surely that message—spiritual, mystical as it is—is so much more powerful, [and] so much more noble than the alternative."

Sing a New Song

In addition to his more wide-ranging attempts to refocus Jews on the triumphs of their heritage rather than the trauma of their history, the Rebbe also transformed the internal culture and approach to worship within his own community. Historically, Chabad Chasidut had promulgated a more austere, inwardly-focused, and cerebral form of prayer and contemplation. The boisterous singing and dancing, characteristic of numerous other Chasidic groups, particularly in the early days of the movement, was largely absent from the synagogues of Chabad.

Nevertheless, under the Rebbe's leadership, singing, clapping, dancing, and, on special occasions, even loud whistling, were introduced into the Chabad way of life. In place of private, somber, inner devotion, the Rebbe emphasized collective visceral joy and emotional exaltation as defining features of his gatherings, which often included much spiritual singing and ecstatic rejoicing.

Interestingly, this remarkable shift in Chabad culture and spiritual practice may have come about in part, not only through the vision of the Rebbe, but also through the "holy chutzpah" of a certain Chasid.

Chabad 2.0

Mr. Zalmon Jaffe, a Chabad Chasid from England, would

spend the festival of Shavuot with the Rebbe in Brooklyn.[201] At the first evening's meal in 1970, Mr. Jaffe asked the Rebbe why they did not sing a nice tune for a particular prayer in the service. The Rebbe responded that he had not heard this song being sung at his father-in-law's *shul*, and therefore according to tradition they also did not sing it.

Mr. Jaffe gathered his courage and countered, "That was the Lubavitch of yesteryear, but today we live in a modern world where we need happy *niggunim* [melodies]. I have been here now for two weeks and have not heard [the Chasidim] singing..."

"That is your fault," the Rebbe said point-blank.

"I am only a soldier," he protested.

"If so, I am 'commanding' you to sing," said the Rebbe. "Tomorrow, we should sing [during services], and those who are here now, if they will be there tomorrow, should help you."

Mr. Jaffe later related:

"I felt like Nachshon ben Aminadav, who was the first to jump into the Sea of Reeds before it split. The congregation hesitated before they joined in. Later, one fellow severely reprimanded me for singing in *shul* without the Rebbe giving the signal. I explained that the Rebbe had already given me permission previously, and he apologized profusely.

"During the meal of the first day, I thanked the Rebbe for helping me with the *niggunim*, but it was difficult. The Rebbe said that it would be much easier on the following day, and indeed it was."

The Rebbe had an uncanny ability to weigh the dictates of the past against the needs of the present, and further, to sensitively respond in an empowering way with an eye on the future. If the Rebbe's Chasidim wanted to express their spiritual yearnings and passions through song during prayer, and the Jewish world in general desperately needed to be resuscitated from the ruins of history, then sing we must! The time for quiet contemplation was past; it was now time for outright exultation.

Water from the Rock

Indeed, this outward and exuberant approach to Jewish life and practice, so different from Chabad of yesteryear, quickly came to define the general energy of Chabad gatherings, from *farbrengens* with the Rebbe in Crown Heights to Shabbat meals at Chabad Houses around the world. The impact of such a continental shift of consciousness did not go unnoticed or unappreciated. Accounts abound of people's lives being transformed while they were swept up in the swirling midst of spirited song, dance, or prayer at the Rebbe's Chasidic gatherings or synagogue services. Here is a particularly moving account[202] by author Harvey Swados, describing one of his first experiences with the Rebbe in Brooklyn.

"Looking out at the congregants, I saw what the Rebbe must have seen: A most remarkable assemblage, and one that for my part I shall never forget.

"Since I could not follow the complex line of his discourse (in Yiddish), with its parables taken from traditional Hasidic tales and homely incidents, interwoven with abstruse philosophical theory, I was free to stare at all those around me—rabbis, merchants, scholars, small businessmen, students, workmen—who were listening with an intensity I had never encountered, whether in a classroom, at the public lectern, or at a religious or political rally.... It was then that the singing began.

"At first spontaneous, [but] soon encouraged and 'conducted' by the Rebbe, who swung his forearms gaily, rhythmically to the beat of the music from his seated position, the simple song rose to a pitch of unrestrained enthusiasm, with the chorus repeated ten, fifteen times, each time wilder and faster. *A man would have had to be made of stone not to respond to this great release of joyous energy*."

Literally and figuratively, the Rebbe sought to bring the Chasidic view of joy into mainstream Jewish life; to change the soundtrack of Jewish life and history from a poignant and haunting minor melody into an exuberant and joyous major victory march. No longer should they focus on the countless persecutions and seemingly endless exiles of history. Instead, energy and attention must be invested in paving the way for the rapidly approaching light of redemption.

This new path toward outward and physical expressions of exuberance was predicated on a deep understanding of the power of joy as a motivational tool. Moreover, when coupled with his radical diagnosis of the spiritual condition and needs of the generation, it becomes clear why the Rebbe was willing to transform the former protocol of Chabad synagogues around the world. As we will see from the next story, this was all for a larger and more profound purpose.

Whistle While You Work

Whistling was originally not a common practice during

the Rebbe's life. In fact, it was considered by most to be unacceptable and even disrespectful to the serious aims and staid approach to Jewish worship that was current for most of world Jewry.

Nevertheless, at a large Chasidic gathering on Purim, 5730 (1971), the Rebbe caused quite a stir when he encouraged thousands of confused Chasidim to whistle together as a form of prayer and celebration. This norm-defying yet soul-intoxicating scene was captured beautifully by R. Dr. Meir Michel Abehsera,[203] who was present that evening:

"On the feast of Purim, I attended a Chasidic gathering with the Lubavitcher Rebbe. We were several thousand strong, all singing and clapping.

"...[Suddenly] without warning, the Rebbe turned my way and looked me straight in the eyes; he placed two fingers against his mouth and nodded in my direction, several times. I could not understand what he meant... The thought crossed my mind that he might have commanded me to whistle, but I dismissed it. Never would a man of his nobility ask for something so ludicrous!

"I looked over my shoulders to be sure that there was not someone else he was addressing, only to find that the people behind me were all looking at me. I placed two fingers over my mouth and waited.

"The Rebbe's face lit up.

"This was it! I entered an unknown dimension as I blew my first whistle. Others soon joined until we were hundreds whistling. The air caught fire with the resonance of the piercing sounds. My lower lip ached from blisters. But the

Rebbe would not let me pause. He was taking the matter quite seriously.

"He called for still more energy as I, in my abruptly unbound imagination, envisioned thick threatening black clouds shattering into dust. We discomfited darkness with our collective breath. Minds were swept clean of all indoctrination.... Every sweet seduction murmured from the other side was blown away by the stiff wind we had summoned. Fallacious arguments flew away like frightened bats as we toned the walls of our hearts to prepare for an all-out war—fairly fought, wind against wind—challenging those irrational emotions that pose as thought, but whose essence is only wind. We alienated every gaseous enemy and incurred no casualties; not even the singers hurt their throats as they sang background to our breath.

"Our final blast took off like the plaintive calls of a ram's horn...a rehearsal for redemption."

It is clear from Abehsera's description that this moment was tangibly transformative and that the experience of such ecstatic expression opened the hearts and minds of the multitudes in attendance. However, not everyone was moved in the same way.

A few years later, on Rosh Chodesh Cheshvan 5736 (1975), a photographer snapped a picture of the Rebbe encouraging whistling at a *farbrengen,* which was then published in a widely-circulated Jewish newspaper.[204]

Notwithstanding the fact that the story in the paper was written in a favorable manner, letters began pouring in from numerous people who were aghast at such a frivolous display, and by a Rebbe no less! In response, other letters came in defending the Rebbe's decision, but the detractors remained vocal and vigilant.

A few months later, on Purim of that year, the Rebbe directly addressed the controversy at a *farbrengen*:[205]

"Some months have gone by, and in the meantime I thought that someone would find a source for our whistling, but in actual fact, it hasn't happened."

The Rebbe then went on to cite numerous examples of whistling in both written and oral Torah, making a point to highlight a number of common themes present within all the different stories. For instance, whistling is a sign of uninhibited and unreserved joy. When such ecstatic expression accompanies a mitzvah, it implies the person's complete identification with the act itself, as well as with G-d, Who commanded it.

Chasidut teaches that just as when someone is overcome with joy, they cannot help but dance and sing, so too, the opportunity to connect with the Divine should evoke genuine expressions of unrestrained elation.

In the Book of Samuel,[206] King David is described as dancing and prancing in front of the nation as he returned the Ark to Jerusalem after it had been captured and then returned by the Philistines. King David was also chastised for such exuberant behavior, but he defended his actions on the basis of inspiring the masses to increased holiness. In the words of the Rebbe, "King David behaved this way specifically when it was a situation having to do with a mitzvah that elicited great joy."

The Rebbe also quoted a passage from Maimonides,[207] who states that dancing and prancing, as demonstrated in

Scripture itself, when done for the sake of a mitzvah or for spiritual ends, is not only allowed, but is an expression of spiritual greatness.

The Rebbe also pointed out that the idea of whistling is actually found in the Talmud,[208] which, in citing the verse,[209] *I will whistle for them and gather them,* teaches that whistling is a sign that Moshiach is about to arrive, when G-d will whistle and gather in the exiles, as the commentators on Scripture explain the verse.

Based on this, the Rebbe concluded:

> ...When it is a matter of increasing Jews' desire and joy in performing a mitzvah, even if there is only a [slight] chance that one person present will have a *geulah,* a "redemption" from his *yetzer hara,* then it is a mitzvah to whistle [to arouse their soul to Divine service], even if it's only a remote possibility.
>
> ...Even more so when we actually see that in certain instances, there are Jews who, through such whistling, experienced a fundamental change [in their spiritual expression] from one extreme to another!
>
> In our situation, when the whistling was going on, there were Jews present who resolved that from this very moment they would have increased enthusiasm in the fulfillment of practical *mitzvot.* In such a case, Maimonides rules that you need to behave exactly as King David did, "dancing and prancing" with all one's might!
>
> Especially when the whistling was (not a mistake,

> but) a deliberate plan that actually worked to arouse and reveal the good hidden in a number of Jews.
>
> ...Through this [whistling] we shall soon have the fulfillment of the promise,[210] *On that day G-d will whistle and gather [the Jewish People]* from the ends of the earth. [As it says[211]] *And you will be gathered one by one,* in a way that no Jew will remain in exile... May this happen with kindness and mercy, and soon.

When the Rebbe left the *farbrengen,* he met the publisher of the newspaper that ran the initial story. The Rebbe slowed down and said with a big smile, "You caused me to give this teaching."

Renew Us as in Days of Old

It is important to point out that this spiritual paradigm shift was not just a strategic decision based on a profound psychological understanding of human motivation and a change in the times. Indeed, much disengagement from Jewish life was fueled by the morose victim narrative and cloud of persecution that framed Jewish identity and engagement for so many. However, the Rebbe's emphasis on joy was primarily rooted in the radical teachings of early Chasidut, starting with the Baal Shem Tov.

Historically, Chasidim were always known for their practice of cultivated joy, long before it would have been popular or practical.

Consider the fact that before they were called Chasidim, they were referred to as the *freiliche*—the "happy ones."[212]

Prior to the 18th century, the motivational norm was

largely defined by reward-or-punishment, social pressure, ostracism, or even excommunication. This system "worked" by and large, and was considered appropriate in the general historical and cultural climate of the times. For centuries, religion was serious. G-d required constant penitence and purification from sin. And the joy of the people was simply not a spiritual priority for much of medieval Judaism. Therefore, early Chasidic emphasis on unbounded exuberance was a shock to the system.

Indeed, in 1801, when the founder of Chabad, R. Schneur Zalman of Liadi, was incarcerated due to libelous information supplied to the Czarist government by opponents of the Chasidic movement, the first complaint included in the documents presented to the government was that the Chasidim were creating a new religion, as evidenced by the fact that "in the books of the founders of Chasidism, it is stated that a person has to always be happy, not only while praying—but at all times. This idea goes against the Jewish religion...."[213]

Joy goes against Judaism? How could this be? To properly understand this controversy, as well as the novelty of Chasidic teaching, we must dig a bit deeper.

Certainly, the concept of *simchah shel mitzvah*, the "joy of a mitzvah," was always part and parcel of Jewish teachings. Moses states clearly in the Torah:[214] *Because you did not serve the L-rd, your G-d, with happiness and with gladness of heart, therefore you shall serve your enemies....* Similarly, hundreds of years later, King David exclaimed, *Serve the L-rd with joy!*[215]

Furthermore, R. Yitzchak Luria, the famed Kabbalist known as the Arizal, once said[216] that all that he achieved spiritually was a reward for his observance of *mitzvot* with limitless joy.

But the joy referred to in these earlier sources was traditionally understood as being limited to the study of Torah and fulfillment of *mitzvot*. However, when it came to activities or aspects of life not overtly linked to Divine service, joy was considered indulgent or even hedonistic.

Into this landscape entered the Baal Shem Tov and proclaimed:[217] "A Jew must strive to experience joy at all times!" *At all times,* meaning not just when performing a mitzvah. To support this seemingly radical claim, the Baal Shem Tov drew on the teaching of the Ethics of Our Fathers:[218] "All your actions should be for the sake of Heaven."

Based on this and similar verses, the Baal Shem Tov taught that whatever a person does—eating, sleeping, business, and even leisure—can all be part of the Divine service, provided that they are done with the proper intentions. As such, if a person is serving G-d in all his actions, then King David's injunction to serve G-d with joy applies at all times and in all situations.

This was the revolution of Chasidism that the Baal Shem Tov introduced and the Rebbe reinforced: Joy is essential, not just in religious matters, but in all areas of life.

Joy Annuls Harsh Decrees

R. DovBer, the Second Lubavitcher Rebbe, had a group of Chasidim who formed a *kapelye* (musical ensemble), and another group that performed on horseback on joyous occasions, such as at weddings, and so on. Among those who performed to enliven weddings and entertain the bride and groom, was R. DovBer's own son, R. Nochum. R. DovBer would observe the singing and performance from his window

It once happened that R. DovBer gave instructions for the choir and the horsemen to perform on a regular weekday. Suddenly, R. Nochum fell off of his horse. Informed that his son was in grave danger, R. DovBer nonetheless motioned with his hand to continue the festivities. After a while, R. DovBer asked them to stop and stepped away from the window into his private office. A doctor was summoned, and after examining R. Nochum, he reported that the situation proved far less severe than previously thought. He had broken a leg, which the doctor placed in a cast, but no more.

Later on, R. DovBer was asked why he had instructed the choir and the horsemen to continue with their performance while his beloved son lay injured.

He responded:

> Why don't you ask me why I asked the choir and the horsemen to perform on a simple weekday?
>
> Today was meant to be a harsh day for my son. I saw a grave accusation against him in the heavenly court. The prosecution was very powerful, and I could see only one way out. As joy sweetens the attribute of severity, I therefore called upon the choir to sing, and I asked the riders to gladden everyone's hearts with their antics.
>
> The joy they created tempered the strict decree against my son, but a small portion of the decree still remained. That is why he fell off his horse and

> hurt his leg. However, the continued revelry lessened even this residual decree. G-d willing, Nochum will recover in the very near future.[219]

The idea that joy is the most effective way to influence the upper worlds is in many ways counter-intuitive. We often think of heartfelt prayer as being filled with tears and desperation. On the surface, this makes sense, as it is in prayer that we ask for what we, our loved ones, or the world, desperately need. This story provides us with a different paradigm to consider. But how does it work?

Break on Through

Once during a private audience with a Chasid who expressed negativity and pessimism about his future, the Rebbe stood up and took out a volume of the *Zohar* from the shelf and placed it before the Chasid. It was opened to the following passage:

"*Ta Chazi*, Come and Observe! Our world is always ready to receive the spiritual flow that emanates from above.... The upper world provides in accordance with the state below. If the state below is joyous, then, correspondingly, abundance flows from above. However, if the state below is one of sadness, then, correspondingly, the flow of blessings is constricted."[220]

"Therefore," said the Rebbe, "serve G-d with joy, because human joy and optimism draws a corresponding joy above!"[221]

Heaven and earth are in constant communication. In fact, according to this teaching of the *Zohar*, what happens down here on earth sets the tone for the heavenly response to our circumstances. In other words, we can intervene and impact reality in partnership with G-d. That is the basis of prayer. But even deeper than the words that we recite in prayer is the *way in which* we recite those words. Are we filled with grief or overflowing with praise? Are we crying or singing, or are we just mindlessly muttering the words? The moods or emotions that we cultivate, both during prayer and throughout the day, become the carrier waves for our visions and dreams to manifest in our lives.

In fact, joy is seen by our Sages as the most efficacious inner state to activate when it comes to connecting our will with G-d's will. This is reflected in a popular Chasidic saying: *Simchah poretz geder*—joy breaks through all boundaries and constrictions.[222]

Nowhere is this idea more evident than in the Baal Shem Tov's approach to *teshuvah,* the process of spiritual return and realignment. Consider the following classic story, attributed to the Baal Shem Tov:

One year, the Baal Shem Tov asked R. Zev Kitzes, one of his senior disciples, to blow the *shofar* for the congregation on Rosh Hashanah. The Baal Shem Tov instructed R. Zev: "I want you to study all the *kavanot* [Kabbalistic meditations] that pertain to the *shofar* so that you should meditate upon them when you blow the ram's horn."

R. Zev applied himself to the task with joy and trepidation; joy over the great privilege that had been accorded him, and trepidation over the immensity of the responsibility. He diligently studied the mystical writings that discuss the multifaceted significance of the *shofar* and what its sounds can achieve on that holy day. Accordingly, he carefully prepared a sheet of paper on which he laid out the main points of each meditation so that he could refer to them while he blew the shofar.

Finally, the great moment arrived. It was the morning of Rosh Hashanah, and R. Zev stood on the *bimah*—the reading platform—in the center of the Baal Shem Tov's synagogue, surrounded by a sea of souls in prayer and contrition. In the southeast corner of the room stood the Baal Shem Tov, face and heart aflame. An awed silence filled the room in anticipation of the climax of the day—the piercing blasts and wailing sobs of the *shofar*.

R. Zev, quietly collecting himself, reached into his pocket for his notes. His heart froze. The paper was gone! He distinctly remembered placing it there that morning, but now it simply wasn't there. Frantically, he searched his memory for what he had learned, but his brain froze under the pressure. His mind was a total blank. Tears of frustration and embarrassment filled his eyes and wet his cheeks. He had disappointed his Rebbe, who had entrusted him with this most sacred task. He had to blow the *shofar* like a simple horn, without any deeper intentions. With a broken heart, R. Zev blew the sounds required by *halachah*, and avoiding his Rebbe's eyes, resumed his place.

At the conclusion of the day's prayers, the Baal Shem Tov made his way to the corner where R. Zev sat sobbing under his *tallit*. "*Gut Yom Tov*, R. Zev!" he called, "That was a most extraordinary *shofar*-blowing we heard today!"

"But Rebbe...Wait...What?"

"In the King's palace," said the Baal Shem Tov, "there are many gates and doors that lead to many halls and chambers.

The palace keepers have great rings holding many keys, each of which opens a different door. But there is a master key that opens all the doors. The meditations are keys—each unlocks a specific door and accesses another chamber in the supernal worlds. But there is one key that unlocks all doors and can open the innermost chambers of the Divine palace. That master key is the tears of a broken heart."[223]

This classic story is one of the most oft-cited examples of the Baal Shem Tov's privileging of the affective aspect of prayer over the intellective faculty emphasized by earlier Kabbalists. According to this view, your heart will take you deeper into the heavenly realms than your mind. Additionally, this characterization of heartfelt tears as spiritually purifying waters rather than dangerous depths to be repressed or avoided is courageous and compassionate, as we discussed at the beginning of this chapter in relation to Elie Wiesel.

However, as the Rebbe did not allow Elie Wiesel to stop at the embrace and healing release of his pain, neither (did the Baal Shem Tov nor) do the teachings of Chasidut stop at the gate of tears. For, in the words of R. Moshe Leib of Sassov, which, when juxtaposed with the story above, can be seen as its continuation, and even completion: "If tears are the master key to open up the [heavenly] gates, *joy absolutely demolishes them*!"[224]

In this spirit, the Rebbe once shared a powerful teaching that spoke directly to his lifelong dream of the redemption. In it, he applied the idea that joy breaks down all barriers to overcoming the ultimate obstacle of thousands of years of Jewish exile, as well as removing all barriers still preventing Moshiach's imminent arrival.

In the Rebbe's own words:[225]

> Throughout the years of exile, the Jewish People have longed for the redemption and prayed for it earnestly every day. Surely this applies to the *tzaddikim* and the leaders of the Jewish People, who had an overwhelmingly powerful desire for Moshiach.
>
> Nevertheless, these earlier activities cannot be compared to the storm for the coming of the redemption aroused by my father-in-law, the Rebbe, with his call: "Immediate *teshuvah*, immediate Redemption."[226]
>
> A number of decades have passed since the time of that announcement, and the array of activities he initiated to bring Moshiach. Nevertheless, Moshiach has not yet come.
>
> There is no explanation for this.
>
> Therefore, it is natural to ask: What can we do to bring Moshiach that has not already been done?
>
> In reply, it is possible to suggest, as above, that the Divine service necessary is the expression of joy *for the sake of bringing Moshiach.*
>
> In the previous generations, people surely experienced joy in connection with their observance of *mitzvot*. Nevertheless, in previous generations, the emphasis was on the service of G-d, and that service was infused with happiness. The suggestion to use *simchah* as a catalyst to bring Moshiach, by contrast, puts the emphasis on the *simchah* itself, *simchah in its pure and consummate state.*

> By meditating on the imminence of Moshiach's coming and the knowledge that at that time perfect *simchah* will spread throughout the entire world, it is possible to experience a microcosm of this *simchah* at present.
>
> And this *simchah* will surely lead to the ultimate *simchah,* the rejoicing of the redemption, when *then our mouths will be filled with joy*!

Throughout his life and teachings, the Rebbe embodied and insisted that the conscious cultivation and ecstatic experience of pure, unadulterated, and unconditional joy for its own sake is the missing link that will reopen the gates of that primordial garden we left so long ago.

CHAPTER 14

Fight Evil or Do Good?

HOW OFTEN DO WE wish we could be kinder and more loving? Who hasn't wished that they could curb their impulses to satisfy momentary needs? Who doesn't want their good deeds to outshine their selfish ones?

Everyone has the power to become the "better person" they know they are capable of being. Making positive changes is an ongoing part of spiritual growth. The question is, how?

A Jewish perspective can help answer that.

Our Sages teach[227] that we each have two *yetzers* (inclinations) within us, one that seeks to serve our soul and spiritual drive, and one that caters to our ego and physical appetites. Our highest potential is achieved when we are able to channel both of these resident energies in the direction of the greatest possible health and holiness. This requires us to actively engage the positive inclination and work to transform the negative inclination.

Toward this end, Jewish thinkers have long debated the most advantageous approach to self-refinement: Should a person better themselves by primarily fighting or fixing the negative urges within them—or by primarily focusing their efforts on doing good, serving G-d, and supporting others? Does one approach lead to the other? What are their respective benefits and logics?

The Best Defense is a Good Offense

In response to this question, two great 18th century Chasidic masters, R. Aryeh Leib of Shpole (known as the Shpoler Zeide) and R. Schneur Zalman of Liadi, founder of Chabad-Lubavitch, argued about the best way to positively shift the balance in the constant struggle between one's negative and positive inclinations.[228] Essentially, their respective approaches can be understood in classic conflict terminology: Should one invest their energy in first securing a good, solid line of defense, or in launching an early and bold offensive?

R. Aryeh Leib argued for a more defensive posture. According to this perspective, the most effective way to silence the inner voice of negativity is by ending any relationship with it. Only after expelling every impious thought, word, and deed, he said, could one devote energy to the performance of good. Paradoxically, this approach required one to focus heavily on their lower drives and negative traits in order to identify and deconstruct them.

To support his case, R. Aryeh Leib quoted King David: *Turn from evil and do good,*[229] which he explained to mean that they must be in that order—first turning from evil and only then concentrating on doing good. The scriptural proof for this opinion is commonly bolstered with a simple analogy: "Does it make sense to bring ornate furniture into a home without cleaning it first? What's the point of beautiful furnishings if they sit in filth?"[230]

R. Schneur Zalman disagreed; he argued in support of a more "offensive" strategy. He taught that by focusing and building on the good qualities already present within us, we can shift the momentum and diminish the magnetic pull of our negative feelings. Rather than putting one's ego under a microscope, which only brings us into closer contact with the evil inclination, R. Schneur Zalman suggested instead that we should go straight for the soul, so to speak. As he wrote pointedly in the *Tanya*: "One who wrestles with a dirty opponent becomes dirty himself."[231] Most political campaigners can attest to this.

Don't Focus on Yourself

The Rebbe took this approach even further. In keeping with Chabad teaching, he was unequivocally on the side of tending goodness through immersion in positivity and light, rather than on deconstructing darkness ad infinitum. He taught that by focusing your attention on others, you are able to rise above the petty claims and cravings of your ego.

When a man asked for advice on conquering a negative

impulse that preoccupied him, the Rebbe wrote him this letter:[232]

> Certainly, this is only the design of the *yetzer hara* (evil inclination). [In general,] it would be good for you to minimize your thoughts about yourself—even about those matters that appear to need correction—and exchange these thoughts for matters that involve others. How good would it be if those thoughts would focus on G-d.

This change of focus is meant to correct our natural tendency to be self-absorbed. According to the Rebbe, even when such self-centered focus is directed at positive ends, such as refining the ego, it is still fixating on the self, and the person is therefore not connecting to G-d or to others. The Rebbe sought to liberate us from the narrow confines of the isolated self by activating our higher spiritual natures in love, service, and connection with both Creator and creation for the good of all.

The Power of Doing Good

When people don't take positive action, they risk getting stuck in the mire of negative thought. Most people have experienced the frustration of desperately trying to not think about something, believing that if they ignore it, it will just go away. It doesn't; quite the opposite, actually.

However, by consciously shifting your focus from negative thoughts to the performance of good deeds, you can cause your negative urges to gradually recede or even cease altogether. Why? Because you have moved on to something better.

When you focus on the positive, there is an endless supply of good pursuits; volunteer in your community, tutor a child, donate food and clothing to people in need, study, pray, or raise money for a worthy cause. The list of ways to have a positive impact is endless.

Negative inclinations come in so many different forms: Materialism, greed, lust for power, arrogance, distractions, addictions, anger, and even just impatience with others. Working to analyze and curtail every aspect of the evil inclination can take a lifetime. Acting with loving, mindful intention can take but a moment.

When a person focuses on "doing good," they will inevitably "turn from evil" as a natural consequence.

"A little bit of light dispels much darkness."[233]

Night is banished through illumination, not elimination.

Don't Fix the Past, Build the Future

A young man once came to the Rebbe, ashamed that he had distanced himself from Jewish observance. Now he was back and sought a path of penitence for straying. The Rebbe said, "Don't focus on your past right now; rather, concern yourself with serving G-d through joy, and you'll take care of the past at a different time."[234]

Don't begin a new journey by recalling all of your previous missteps, because you may very well scare yourself away from any future progress. Begin instead with small but tangible movements in the right direction. These early successes will help you build momentum toward your goal, while at the same time whetting your soul's appetite for the spiritual fruits of goodness and positivity.

Rise Above It

The Rebbe's answer for those concerned about their negative impulses or inclinations was: "Rise above it." This was not a way of saying, "Get over it!" Rather, he meant "rise above it" quite literally, in the spiritual realm.

This, he knew, could be especially challenging for restless adolescents. As a teenager in *yeshivah,* R. Leibel Kaplan would go home after having his dinner at school. Although he had eaten, he had a habit of heading for the refrigerator when he got home. He wasn't hungry; he just wanted to see what his mother had made for dinner.

He went to the Rebbe to see if he could remove this habit. Now, on the scale of negative impulses and inclinations, this isn't high on anyone's list of "terrible sins," but it troubled him, and he was determined to rise above it. The Rebbe advised him to imagine himself as the dean of a big rabbinical seminary or as a CEO of a great operation—some position where his influence reached far and wide and commanded the respect of his peers. If this were the case, the Rebbe suggested, checking out the fridge after having already eaten would be beneath his dignity.[235]

Here the Rebbe taught the student to discontinue a negative habit by projecting himself into a realm where the negative habit was beneath him. The Rebbe didn't focus on the young man himself, nor on any lack of refinement, and as a result neither did the student. The Rebbe merely asked the student to engage with a visualization that would reveal his higher nature.

Don't Be Influenced, Be an Influencer

Dov Lent, a young student, worried that the distractions and temptations of his new university would derail him from living an observant life. The Rebbe encouraged him not to allow the secular campus environment to consume too much of his attention. "The best way to deal with the evil inclination, and with a challenging environment in particular, is not to engage in a fight with it," the Rebbe said. "Don't put yourself in an encounter with it in the first place! Rather, take your mind away from the whole temptation by saying to yourself, 'I am busy! I have no time for such things! I have learning to do, a mitzvah to fulfill, I'm helping someone.'"

Years later, R. Dov Lent reported that he'd spent his free time at university learning Torah with a similarly concerned study partner. Additionally, he helped organize campus *Shabbatons* for the whole community. "Rather than the secular environment influencing me in a negative way, I was able to spiritually influence it in a positive way."[236]

No Time for Sin

The famed Chasidic Rebbe, R. Menachem Mendel of Kotsk (1787–1859) once said, "I don't expect my Chasidim not to sin. I expect them not to have time to sin." As his advice to Dov Lent, the Rebbe was also a great believer in no time for sin.

To drive this point home, he often shared[237] a story about the great Talmudic Sage, R. Yochanan ben Zakkai. On his deathbed,[238] with his students gathered around him, he cried, saying that there were two paths before him, and he didn't know down which path he would be taken. He had been so busy in life that he'd never had time to contemplate and take stock of his spiritual state of affairs. Good deeds had literally taken up all his time.

Don't Fight, Flow

At some point, we have all found ourselves so busy and immersed in what we are doing at the moment that we enter a state of "flow." It can captivate an attorney preparing for a trial, an author eager to finish writing a novel, or a new parent bathing their child. Such intense engagement can mute our physical awareness to the point of causing us to ignore bodily needs such as hunger or fatigue. When we mobilize our energies to accomplish a higher cause, we are naturally and joyfully immersed in overwhelming positivity.

So, fight evil or do good? *Do good*! *Always and in all ways.*

CHAPTER 15

Illumination, Not Elimination

FOLLOWING THE PASSING OF his mother, a grief-stricken Mr. Charles Samuel Ramat came to see the Rebbe. Baring his soul, he shared, "Rebbe, I'm having a crisis of faith. I really do not believe. I love Judaism; I love a lot of the rituals, but they are not really part of my life."

"If I ask you to do one thing without any precondition," the Rebbe asked, "will you promise me you'll do it?"

"Yes. Anything you ask me, I promise I'll do it."

"Will you and your wife agree to light Shabbat candles every Friday night?" the Rebbe asked.

"Yes."

From that point on the Ramat family never missed a week of lighting candles to welcome Shabbat. As a result, Friday night gradually became sacrosanct for the family as a whole. Baking challah, welcoming guests, and sharing a meal all took on a special air in the holy glow of the candles.

Notably, the Rebbe asked Mr. Ramat to add something to his life, to do something new. On the surface, lighting Shabbat candles is a single, seemingly simple mitzvah, but for the Ramats it was life-changing. This weekly practice of coming together as a family for something sacred added a whole new layer of depth and meaning to their lives, while also exponentially enhancing their appreciation and connection to Judaism.

According to Mr. Ramat, a child of Holocaust survivors, this one small request of the Rebbe's "kept my family on a Jewish path throughout our lives, and my daughters have followed suit."[239]

Instead of dwelling on the areas of Jewish practice that were lacking in their lives, the Rebbe simply asked the Ramat family to add more light to their life. And that made all the difference.

The story above is indicative of the Rebbe's approach to influencing people in a positive manner. Whether in relation to Jewish identity or observance, or ideological differences and disagreements, the Rebbe consistently chose to add more light and introduce more love to a given situation rather than struggling with the darkness head-on.

Whereas the message of many other religious leaders to non-religious Jews was that they must curtail certain behaviors, the Rebbe's approach was different. He sought to inspire people to introduce new sparks of holiness into their lives, believing firmly that light begets more light.

This interpersonal aspect of the Rebbe's Positivity Bias often yielded surprising, exponential results.

If You Grasp a Part, You Grasp the Whole

In 1958, Mr. Jacques Lipchitz, a well-known and influential modern artist and sculptor, came to see the Rebbe.

During their meeting, recalls Lipchitz, "I told him everything about my doings, about my sins; I'm not kosher, I do not pray, I do not go to synagogue. I even told him about my sculptures that were standing in churches."

The Rebbe listened to everything the artist said and then made two requests: First, he asked Lipchitz to put on *tefillin* and pray every morning. Second, he urged him to marry his current wife according to Jewish law.

When Lipchitz emerged from the Rebbe's office, he was clearly deeply moved by their exchange.

Years later, Lipchitz related in an interview that "a few days later [the Rebbe] sent a man with *tefillin*. Since then, I *daven* [pray] every morning. It is of great help to me. He really did something for me by advising me to do that…."

When asked why he felt it was so important for him to pray and put on *tefillin* every day, he said, "It puts me together with my people. I am with them. And I am near to my L-rd, to the Almighty. I speak with Him…He gives me strength for the day…. It did something very important for me. I could not live anymore without it."[240]

Here we see a man who had drifted from traditional Jewish life warmly embraced by the Rebbe, whose only request was that he add more light to his morning—which in turn illuminated his whole life.

Don't Debate, Dance!

Chaim Cohen grew up as a staunchly Orthodox Jew. For many years he was even a member of the religious advocacy organization Agudat Yisroel.

However, for reasons unknown he began to break away, until at some point he left religious Judaism altogether. After a long and successful career as a judge, Cohen was eventually appointed to Israel's Supreme Court, where, much to the consternation of the Orthodox establishment, he consistently used his position to push his secularizing agenda.

In fact, it was during this time that Chaim Cohen became infamous throughout the religious world, as he signed into law the proposal that one did not need to be halachically Jewish in order to qualify for the Law of Return, which grants any Jew from around the world automatic citizenship.

This was an issue that caused the Rebbe much pain, and he felt compelled to take a harder-line public stance than he was usually wont to do. The ripples of this conflict reverberated throughout Israel and the wider religious Jewish world.

Therefore, when Chaim Cohen arrived at the Central Lubavitch Synagogue at 770 Eastern Parkway during the celebration of Simchat Torah in 5736 (1975), you can imagine the shock of those gathered when the Rebbe decided to honor him with the recitation of a verse of the *Atah Hareita* prayer, as well as with holding a Torah during the *Hakafot*.

Not only were many of those present likely to be

uncomfortable with extending such an olive branch to a professed enemy of the religious community, but the rest of the Orthodox establishment would certainly look upon this gesture with harsh judgment.

Nevertheless, the Rebbe applied his signature Positivity Bias and chose to respond to a difficult situation with love, and the commitment to always add more light no matter how dark the situation may appear on the surface.

Indeed, when his personal aide nervously asked the Rebbe how to handle the sensitive situation, the Rebbe responded forcefully: "A Jew is here with a desire to reconnect, and you don't want to give him a Torah scroll?!"

And so give him a Torah they did! Following which the Rebbe encouraged the dancing of Mr. Cohen and the thousands in attendance for 45 minutes straight, with his spirited clapping and constant encouragement. Throughout the entire time the Rebbe kept his eyes locked on Judge Cohen, who tightly held and ecstatically danced with the Torah.

Years later, one of the Chabad *shluchim* in Manhattan met a very close friend of Judge Cohen and invited him to meet the Rebbe. The friend stubbornly refused, saying: "Ever since Chaim Cohen attended that Simchat Torah with the Rebbe he changed many of his views and opinions. I [for one] am not yet ready to change my opinions. Now I am the one who has to suffer as a result of Chaim Cohen's Simchat Torah spent with the Rebbe!"[241]

In addition to religious matters, the Rebbe also applied this positive approach to influencing people or organizations who held different and even diametrically opposed points of view. As we will see in the following stories, the

Rebbe's spiritually-based strategy to spread light, love, truth, and peace in the world simply did not leave any room for running away, shutting down, or writing off any adversary or opponent.

A Lighthouse Shows the Way

A Jewish executive who ran a South African ad agency accepted the African National Congress as a client to help them project a better public image. One day, while visiting the ANC headquarters, he walked out of an elevator and was shocked to see a large poster of Yasser Arafat on the wall. Disturbed and disillusioned to learn of the ANC's affiliation with terrorists, his friends advised him to ask the Rebbe for guidance.

"Although I have strong liberal and anti-Apartheid leanings, I feel like I'm working for the wrong people," he wrote. "Should I continue to work for them or not?"

"Don't stop," the Rebbe replied. "To the contrary, continue working with them, but make every effort to influence them for the good."[242]

In a place of darkness, we must become a beacon of light. If all good people were to abandon every space of conflict or challenging conversation, there would be no counterbalance to the prevailing negativity and chaos would reign. Cutting off contact almost never achieves the desired transformation of the "other side." Isolating and alienating forces of darkness creates more fuel for those destructive fires to burn. Confronting darkness and reflecting light is the only way to reveal the truth—not by argument, but by shining example.

The Way to Someone Else's Heart is Through Your Own Heart

Throughout his career as a well-known, politically-active and outspoken lawyer, author, and Harvard professor, Alan Dershowitz had numerous occasions to discuss with the Rebbe various issues and cases concerning the Jewish community.

One such correspondence provides another example of the Rebbe's Positivity Bias as applied to dealing with people with whom one disagrees. In Dershowitz's own words:[243]

"[A number of] years ago, I had the chutzpah—in the worst sense of the word—to write an arrogant letter to the Lubavitcher Rebbe. I had read in the newspaper that the Lubavitch movement was honoring Jesse Helms as part of the annual 'Education Day' gala, and there was no man in America I despised more than Jesse Helms. As chairman of the Senate Foreign Relations Committee, he absolutely stood for everything that I was opposed to in those days, including being strongly anti-Israel.

"I wrote a letter saying, in essence, 'How can you honor a man who stands for everything that is opposed to Jewish values in America?' And I received a letter back from the Rebbe, a very respectful letter; a letter that I cherish for its content.

"He lectured me, but in the nicest way, telling me that you never, ever give up on anybody. Today Jesse Helms may be against Israel, but tomorrow, if we know how to approach him and speak to him, maybe he will turn out to be a champion of Israel.

"At the end of the letter, the Rebbe included a very

significant P.S. in which he explained his approach to influencing others for the good.

"He wrote that people—but especially politicians, who often act out of expediency more than conviction—should be engaged in a positive way. [In] that way, we can try to influence them.

"And I have to tell you, I had my doubts about it, but as they say, the rest is history.

"Although I still disagree with Jesse Helms on many issues, *when it comes to Israel, he has become our champion.*

"I believe that he became a champion of Israel because the Lubavitcher Rebbe understood something that most of us didn't understand: How to communicate with people of different backgrounds and cultures in a way that lets the light in."

Don't Argue, Inspire!

Jewish youth in a certain community were being targeted aggressively by missionaries. A concerned community activist asked the Rebbe, "How should we approach the young Jews who have become involved with Christianity?"

The Rebbe responded, "Don't argue with them about the claims of Christianity. Offer them something new to think about. Inspire them with the beauty and joy of Judaism that they have not yet had a chance to experience."[244]

Don't delegitimize. Open their eyes.

A Candle of Truth

On September 24, 2009, one day after Gaddafi and

Ahmadinejad held court at the UN advocating hatred and lies about Israel, Prime Minister Benjamin Netanyahu addressed the UN and opened with a personal story from the podium.

In 1984, Netanyahu, then serving as Israel's ambassador to the UN, was asked to meet with the Rebbe in Brooklyn. He came to 770 for the holiday of Simchat Torah, a night of spirited singing and dancing with the Torah. Thousands were gathered, waiting for the festivities to begin. As the Rebbe entered and took his place at the head of the gathering, Netanyahu was pushed to approach him. While the throngs of Chasidim waited impatiently, the Rebbe spoke candidly with Netanyahu about various matters and pressing concerns relating to Israel and the international community.

"The Rebbe told me, 'You are going to a house of lies. Remember that in a hall of perfect darkness, if you light one small candle, its light will be seen from afar, by everyone. Your mission is to light a candle for truth and the Jewish People.' This is what I have tried to do ever since. This is what we are all asked to do."[245]

According to the Rebbe, we are here to light a candle of truth, every day and in every way.

Pray for Your Enemies to Change

It goes without saying that the Rebbe took matters of Israeli national security extremely seriously, meeting regularly with Israeli officials at the highest levels to address and solve security issues.

Additionally, the Rebbe was not against war when it was

necessary for survival and protection. However, the Rebbe never condoned outright hatred of the other, even an enemy.

Based on his Positivity Bias, the Rebbe believed that there was always a good point within each and every person that, if connected to and supported, could illuminate even the darkest personalities and their perspectives.

In 1982, during the bitter Lebanon war, the Rebbe made a seemingly shocking statement to the effect of: *You do not have to pray that the fighters and members of the PLO should die, pray instead that they should have a change of heart.*[246]

This radical approach to combative antagonists is a powerful, even challenging, expression of the Rebbe's strategy of "fighting" darkness—not by stamping it out of existence, but by working to transform it into light; in this case, transforming sworn enemies into supportive allies.

This idea is actually rooted in ancient Jewish tradition.

The Talmud[247] relates the story of R. Meir and his brilliant wife Beruriah: "There were certain lawless men in R. Meir's vicinity who used to cause him constant suffering. In response he prayed that they should die. On hearing his prayer, Beruriah pointed out to her husband that undoubtedly his prayer was justified on the basis of the verse: *Let sins cease.*[248] But, Beruriah argued, the verse does not say that sinners should cease; rather, it says *Let sins cease*. Furthermore, she argued, the verse goes on to say, *and let the wicked be no more*. Meaning that when sins have ceased from the world, there will no longer be any wicked men. Based on this, Beruriah suggested to her husband, he should pray that the sinners repent and then they will no longer be wicked." The story concludes by stating that R. Meir acted on Beruriah's advice and the lawless men did in fact repent.

The Rebbe elaborated:[249]

> Yes, there are violent people and terrorists in the world. But there is nothing that says the only way to deal with them is through taking their lives. Even when we speak of "the enemy and the avenger," our actions must be "to stop the enemy and the avenger." Meaning, to stop and to annul the fact that he is an enemy and avenger. In the language of the Talmud, "The sins should cease—not the sinners themselves." To the point that they will become our friends and assist us.

Each of the stories above demonstrates a consistent thread running through the Rebbe's advice and interactions when confronted with adversarial people and perspectives.

If a person calls upon their own dark forces to combat the darkness of others, even if they win, they still remain in the dark. Abolishing negativity without introducing any positive alternative just creates a vacuum likely to be filled with even more ignorance and animosity.

Indeed, "A little bit of light dispels much darkness."[250]

Only through the introduction of light does darkness lose its dominion and a new day is able to shine. Put differently: *The way to fight evil is through the process of illumination, not elimination.*

CHAPTER 16

On Youth and Rebellion

BEFORE ALMOST ANY OTHER Jewish leader, the Rebbe acknowledged the positive spirit of youthful rebellion that characterized much of Western culture during the 1960s. To the dismay of their elders, young Jewish men and women were becoming increasingly distrustful of parents and teachers, leading them to turn from the values and traditions with which they had been reared. But the Rebbe saw that by rejecting their parents' teachings, these young people were beginning a search for something deeper.

From a conservative perspective, the burgeoning counterculture appeared as a threat to traditional Judaism. But according to the Rebbe's Positivity Bias, it had the potential to engage and uplift the restless spirit of the generation. If the hippies were truly devoted to the ideals of peace and love, then with the proper exposure, many could surely find spiritual avenues to express their ideals within a Jewish context. Undoubtedly, Jewish thought and practice had much light to shed on the pressing social and spiritual issues of the day—the compassion of G-d, freedom, a spirituality of love, revolution, community, and global unity—it was all in the Torah, prophecies, and mystical tradition. The warming flames of Judaism were waiting to further ignite these impassioned souls, if unpacked and presented sincerely and sensitively.

The challenge was in how, on a large scale, to connect Jews in the counterculture with the study of Torah and the observance of *mitzvot,* and how to uncover and amplify the Divine essence in their souls through the prism of Torah Judaism.

Degeneration or Regeneration

In the 1960s, Chabad Lubavitch began holding "Encounter with Chabad" weekends for students at its Brooklyn headquarters, introducing young men and women to the rich world of Torah and Chasidism. By 1970, Chabad was opening campus-based outreach programs at universities across the United States, bringing a new spiritual dimension to young Jews who had lost touch with their religious traditions.

As early as 1963, the Rebbe was writing encouragingly about the American youth movement. Here is a freely translated excerpt from a letter to R. Pinchos Mordechai Teitz:[251]

> Every generation has its particular quality, unique

to its time. In our generation, particularly in the last few years, we are witnessing a spiritual awakening, which is being called—though those who have called it so are unaware of the true significance of the term they have coined—"a return to roots." Regardless of how it is being currently understood, the quest to "return to roots" is, in essence, the soul's quest for *teshuvah,* for reunion with its source in G-d.

We are seeing this awakening primarily among the youth, who experience everything with a greater depth and a greater intensity. Young people also have no fear of changing their lifestyle, as long as they are convinced that they are being given the truth, without compromise and equivocation.

This is particularly the case with the youth of our country. In other countries, there is a double hurdle to be overcome: First one must uproot the false ideologies that have become ingrained in certain circles among the younger generation, and only afterward is it possible to implant the proper ideas in their minds. This is not the case in this country, where [because of their rebellion against what they have been taught] the youth is virgin soil, if only they are given the truth in its purity. We have witnessed in actuality that those who are not intimidated and present the truth without equivocation have been met with a true response among the youth.

I don't want to be critical, but I am forced to note that, to our great misfortune, this awakening has

> not been utilized, thus far, by those who purport to be the leaders and spiritual guides of their communities, certainly not to the extent that it could have been utilized.
>
> Our sages have taught that "the deed is the primary thing." It therefore goes without saying that the purpose of my writing all this is not for the sake of discussion, but in the hope that you and your colleagues will launch a broad and spirited effort to encourage this awakening and—most importantly—to have it translate into concrete changes in the day-to-day life of all those to whom this call can reach.

The emerging youth movement and culture were not impending crises, but golden opportunities for spiritual connection and growth. What appeared to many on the surface as brazen rebellion was actually an expression of a principled generation willing to commit to higher, meaningful ideas. From the Rebbe's perspective, it was incumbent on Jewish leadership to recognize and respond authentically to the needs and challenges of the youth; to engage them, not enrage them by writing them off.

Dare to Be Different

Unlike many traditionalists, the Rebbe was not put off by the long hair, beads, and eye-catching clothing of 1960s youth. He once[252] received a visit from Yosef Dov Krupnik, a young man at a Lithuanian-style *yeshivah* who had grown out his beard. His teachers didn't like it because they thought it looked too much like the style of the hippies, but the Rebbe urged him to keep it and said it wasn't such a bad thing to look different from others, stressing that:

> Our Sages tell us that the Jewish People were saved from Egypt because they stood out from the Egyptians in three important ways. They had unique clothing, they spoke a unique language, and they had unique names.

A similar idea holds true for the Jewish hippies, the Rebbe explained, many of whom were prominent leaders of the entire movement. They had Jewish-sounding last names [the Rebbe mentioned Abbie Hoffman, Allen Ginsberg, and Mark Rudd, née Rudnitsky]. They wore distinctive clothing (such as beads, bell-bottoms, and ponchos). And while they didn't speak Hebrew, they did have their own jargon within English, which was different from the English spoken by the masses. Indeed, who says these "rebels" are any less worthy of redemption than the rest of the Jewish People?

Between Parents and Children

While the Rebbe held young adults to the commandment to honor their parents, he also recognized that there was something refreshing and positive about youth having the courage to think for themselves and even to influence their parents and teachers. In this spirit, he cited a Talmudic passage[253] stating, "It is taught in a *Baraita* that R. Nehorai says, 'During the generation in which the Son of David [Moshiach] comes, youths will humiliate elders and elders will stand in deference before youths, a daughter will rebel against her mother, and a bride against her mother-in-law, the face of the generation will be like the face of a dog, and a son will not be ashamed before his father.'"

While the Sages were no doubt criticizing the degeneration of society that would occur just before the Messianic era begins, the Rebbe saw something positive in this passage, namely, the ability for young people to serve as positive agents of change.

The Rebbe also suggested, in 1970, that if young people were rebelling against the established system, the defenders of that system had better examine what they were defending and how they were defending it:

> The complaints that people have against the younger generation, that they are destroying...the so-called establishment, should be addressed to their educators. When parents and teachers taught the younger generation proper behavior, they explained it as the means to be able to afford a nice home, have a large bank account, own two Cadillacs ("his" and "hers"), and to be honorees and seated at the head table at banquets.... When this constitutes the reason for choosing between good and evil...it is understandable why the youth will ultimately lose all patience for such falsehood.... The youngsters are in the process of a spiritual journey. We cannot allow them to drift and get lost. We must educate them according to their needs, in a pleasant and kind manner, and lead them to a proper understanding of right and wrong.[254]

It is always much easier to place the blame on someone else in a given situation. But here we see the Rebbe admonishing not the rebellious youths, but the very system in which they were raised. If the younger generation is rejecting the ways of their elders, this is above all a call to the parents and teachers to reflect on their own values that they are attempting to pass on. Indeed, it is often our children who teach us the deepest lessons, such as how to love and support each individual in the unique way they require.

Hear O Israel

Ultimately, according to the Rebbe, the counterculture's tendency to rebel and disobey was akin to the age-old Jewish tradition of questioning authority, as can be seen in the actions of Abraham, Moses, and many other leaders in the Torah. The Rebbe also seemed to admire young people for their adherence to principle and their dismissal of the creature comforts offered by society. He realized that the youth yearned for something more meaningful than what they saw as the norm, and in some ways similar to the Rebbe himself, they were willing to turn the world upside down to achieve it.

"We've seen already that in times of emergency, a crisis, when a fire is raging, our youth are ready for real selflessness and sacrifice," the Rebbe told a newspaper reporter. "By nature, the Jew is not afraid of hardships. By nature, the Jew is defiant. We're a 'stiff-necked people,' a people of self-sacrifice, a nation of habitual rebels."[255]

Through the redemptive lens of his Positivity Bias, the Rebbe saw that the Jewish youth who made up so much of the counterculture could be, and perhaps in some cases already were, directed toward serving G-d and giving priority to the life of the soul.

"In our era, there prevails, in certain circles, a strong tendency toward self-assertion and independence, not only in material spheres, but also in the ideological," the Rebbe wrote[256] just before Rosh Hashanah in 1967.

> For one who is not accustomed to subordinate himself, but is consistently independent in his thinking—should such a person come to the conviction that he must acknowledge a Supreme Authority, it permeates him deeply and fundamentally, and he finds the strength to reorient himself completely and permanently.

The qualities exhibited by the youth in their full-scale cultural rebellion were exactly those that would inspire and sustain the spirit in a meaningful life of religious devotion and community. The Rebbe saw this clearly.

The following summer, following youth protests in New York, Chicago, and Paris, the Rebbe made a direct connection[257] between the audacity and passion of Jewish adherents to the counterculture and their potential as leaders in Torah-true Judaism:

> The youth are brazen, have chutzpah, and are not deterred by anything—not by world opinion, not by their parents or families, not even by the opinions they themselves entertained a day earlier.... Instead, they proudly proclaim their absolute freedom to do

> as they wish. Specifically because of their chutzpah, it is easier to draw them to the true path of Torah and *mitzvot*! ...When we successfully inspire the youth, they will not suffice with personal Torah observance, but—due to their fierce indomitable spirit—they will also inspire others to do the same. They will be an unstoppable force that will transform the entire world and bring it in alignment with integrity and justice.

Prescient as always, the Rebbe saw in the rebellious Jewish youth of the 1960s the beginnings of the *baal teshuvah* movement that exploded beginning in the early 1970s. He understood that eventually many young Jews would trade their love beads for *tefillin,* their hand-knitted poncho for a *tallit,* and their desire for revolution into revelation. They would take the passion they had poured into social activism and the perusal of political tracts and channel it into Torah study and the bringing of fresh energy and spirit to American Judaism and beyond.

This particular expression of the Rebbe's Positivity Bias—seeing the redemptive spark in the youth challenging the ways of their elders—is one of the most potentially impactful. It can be applied not just socially and on a large scale, but also personally, for parents struggling to understand what their children are trying to say beneath the surface of their "acting out." According to the Rebbe, there is no such thing as "just acting out." There is always something deeper being expressed, a need or a lesson, if we would but open our eyes, ears, and hearts to what our children are trying to tell us.

CHAPTER 17

Channeling

"He who is born under [the mazal or constellation of] Mars will be a shedder of blood. R. Ashi observed, [he can channel that aggression by becoming]: Either a surgeon, a shochet (kosher-slaughterer), or a mohel (circumciser)." –Shabbat 156a

IN THE EARLY 1950S, a couple and their young daughter had a private audience with the Rebbe. After the wife and husband had asked for advice on various issues, the Rebbe turned to the girl and asked if she had any questions. Her parents tried to quiet her as she began to speak, so as not to take more of the Rebbe's valuable time, but the Rebbe encouraged her to go ahead. With a concerned look on her face, the girl asked the Rebbe whether he thought that atomic energy was good or bad. "In your kitchen at home, there is a knife. Is the knife good or bad?" the Rebbe asked.

The girl replied, "It depends on what it is used for. If it is used to cut food, then it is good. If it is used to hurt someone, then it is bad."

"That is a good and true answer," the Rebbe told her, "and the same could be said for atomic energy or any other technology that man has developed."[258]

Although the above story, which occurred during the nuclear standoff of the Cold War, is focused on how we relate to emergent technologies, the Rebbe also applied this same "neutral" approach as a general principle to numerous areas in our lives.

In fact, a fundamental aspect of the Rebbe's Positivity Bias was that (as long as permissible according to the Torah) anything and everything has the potential to be illuminated and elevated, if channeled in the right way. This "permissive" approach of the Rebbe, albeit with a halachic caveat, stood in stark contrast to many of his rabbinic contemporaries.

For example, many Orthodox Jewish leaders of the time viewed new media technologies such as radio, television, and the first iterations of the Internet as spiritually dangerous, and therefore to be avoided at all costs.

The Rebbe, however, saw them as neutral instruments with immense potential for good.

Similarly, the Rebbe turned our perception of numerous psychological attributes upside down, revealing positive spiritual potentials cloaked within seemingly superficial, shallow, or self-centered personality traits and behaviors.

Simply put: *The Rebbe sought to channel and spread Divine consciousness by any means necessary.*

Based on his spiritual calculus, the redemptive rewards almost always outweighed the regressive risks. It was just a matter of locating and amplifying the G-dly spark within.

What follows are numerous stories in which the Rebbe can be seen offering a counterintuitive view on what are commonly considered as deleterious character traits and behaviors. The Rebbe encouraged elevating these toward positive ends.

Beauty: Not Just Skin Deep

One Sunday morning, a winner of the Miss Israel competition visited the Rebbe for a blessing.

The Rebbe blessed her and then said:

> The Torah says, *Beauty is false,* but the verse continues, *a G-d-fearing woman is to be praised.*[259] The commentaries explain that if a woman is G-d-fearing, she uses her [physical] beauty for beautiful [spiritual] endeavors.... Good tidings, and please relay this message to your friends and the organizers of the event.[260]

What's remarkable about the Rebbe's message is that it turns the literal meaning of the verse on its head. Instead of reading the second half of the verse as a rebuke or negation of the first, i.e. that the only thing laudable is one's inner character, the Rebbe sees the second half of the verse as qualifying the first, meaning that beauty is naught unless a woman is righteous and G-d fearing. If she is, her external beauty is no longer empty or deceptive but reflects and expresses an inner spiritual beauty. If utilized appropriately, such beauty can be used as a means to inspire grace, faith, and kindness in others.

Prestige, Titles, and Status

Philanthropists Count and Countess Maklouf Elkaim were reluctant to use their inherited titles, deeming it pretentious to do so.

The Rebbe once addressed their hesitation in a private audience:

> Since, by Divine Providence, you possess these prestigious titles, don't hesitate to use them to open doors for Jewish causes. People will take you more seriously if you introduce yourselves as Count and Countess. Others may use their titles egotistically, but you should use this unique privilege to positively impact the people you meet.[261]

A lust for lofty titles or status can often bring out the worst in a person as they seek to climb the social ladder at the expense of anyone who stands in their way. Additionally, once such status has been attained, it can easily seduce them into thinking that they are better than others or above the law. However, here we see the Rebbe encouraging those privileged with such a position not to shy away from it, but to own it and use it for the good of others.

In our next story, the Rebbe encourages someone to work toward attaining a professional title in order to be more effective in their spiritual pursuits.

As a physics student at Penn State University, Dr. Yaakov Hanoka took a year's break from pursuing his PhD to study Judaism in a *yeshivah*. He became so enamored with Torah-true Judaism that he wanted to remain in the *yeshivah* instead of continuing with his doctorate. Toward the end of his first year, he had an audience with the Rebbe, during which he brought up his plans for the future. Much to his surprise, the Rebbe said, "I want you to go back to the university to get your PhD." "But Rebbe," Dr. Hanoka countered respectfully, "if I stay on in *yeshivah*, perhaps I can become a campus rabbi and go on to share my experience and religious passion with Jewish students, inspiring them to learn more about their heritage."

The Rebbe answered with a smile: "You will accomplish more for *Yiddishkeit* with three initials after your name."[262]

The Rebbe understood the social psychology of titles, brands, and packaging. Rather than scoffing at the wider culture's obsession with mere labels, the Rebbe sought to employ it to spread a positive spiritual message to the largest possible audience.

After Dr. Naftali Loewenthal completed his PhD thesis on "The Concept of Mesiras Nefesh, Self-Sacrifice, in the Teachings of R. DovBer, the Mitteler Rebbe," he wanted to have it published as a book to reach a wider audience. He asked the Rebbe whether he should send it to a general Jewish publisher, to the Kehot Publication Society—which specializes in specifically Chabad topics—or to an academic publisher. The Rebbe replied, "You should try to get it published by the most famous academic publisher."[263]

Publicity

It is accepted as a general principle in Judaism that the most spiritually refined way to go about performing *mitzvot* is to do them discreetly and for their own sake rather than for public acknowledgment or personal reward.

The qualities of inwardness and discretion in regard to a person's own merits are highly valued in Chasidism, as they serve to mute or nullify our pernicious ego, which constantly craves affirmation.

Maimonides spells this out clearly when he writes:[264] "The highest form of charity is that the giver doesn't know to whom he gave nor the recipient from whom he received."

Nevertheless, the Rebbe sought and encouraged people to publicize their spiritual achievements and positive accomplishments in as loud a voice as possible. Commenting on the nature of contemporary media, which focuses on scandals and cynicism, the Rebbe taught, "If noise could be used to spread the message of negativity, why can't we use noise for the good!?"[265]

On a different occasion the Rebbe told a public figure, "It would be good for you to study Torah regularly, even if only a few minutes every day. And if you do this without keeping it a secret, you would be a shining example for others!"[266]

In our current media climate, saturated as it is with news of people's flaws and failings, the Rebbe clearly understood the importance of publicizing good deeds and positive qualities. Faith and hope need fuel for their spiritual fires. Stories of small but meaningful victories can swell other people's sails.

Indeed, the Rebbe once told a *shliach*, "We do not hear

anything from you." The *shliach* sent the Rebbe a detailed report. The Rebbe responded and said, "*Mitzvah l'farseim osei mitzvah* (It is a mitzvah to publicize those who do a mitzvah)."[267] Based on this comment, the *shliach* took upon himself to write an article about his latest successful activities and published it in numerous local newspapers.

Similarly, in answer to a philanthropist who wished to give charity anonymously, so as not to be motivated by the desire for honor and recognition, the Rebbe suggested a different perspective: "If a building is dedicated in your name, and your name on its wall is visible to all who walk by, others will also want to give. More people will thus benefit."

Arrogance

The Rebbe told the story[268] of a Chasid of R. Schneur Zalman of Liadi, R. Mordechai Liepler, who claimed that his arrogance was responsible for keeping him on the right path. He said that when his *yetzer hara* (negative inclination) would confront him and say: "Mottel, come on, commit a sin," he would face it resolutely and respond: "I am a Chasid, not to mention I am wealthy, well-respected, and learned—and you are attempting to convince me to transgress?!"

A high self-estimation, if related to properly, may actually serve as a safeguard. In this way even arrogance can be used for positive spiritual means—as a deterrent against lowering one's spiritual or moral bar.

Ego

A man asked the Rebbe: "Rebbe, what should I do to get rid

of my inflated ego?" "Why get rid of it?" the Rebbe replied. "Why not live up to your own great expectation of yourself? Be the amazing person whom you believe you are."

Classical Chasidic thought emphasizes and values *bittul*, the nullification and negation of ego or entitled self. In fact, *yeshut*, the strong sense of selfhood, which is predicated on a skewed sense of self-importance, is considered by the Chasidic masters to be the nemesis of holiness.

However, according to the Rebbe, ego too can be channeled for holiness; in fact, it must. From this perspective, the ego is not inherently negative. Furthermore, if integrated within a broader spiritual structure, it can play a catalyzing role in our attempts to serve a greater good.

In a related story: A prolific lecturer on Chasidism visited the Rebbe to discuss a personal struggle. "Rebbe," he said, "I don't know if I have enough *ahavat Yisrael* to be doing what I do. Teaching sometimes makes me feel superior to my audiences, and I feel like my ego has become inflated as a result of my lectures. Perhaps others are better suited for this work, as they would not allow it to go to their heads." "Do not hesitate because of these feelings," the Rebbe responded. "When it comes to doing good, action is what's most important."[269]

Never let a little ego scare you away from doing good for others. The initial motivation of the gesture does not matter to the recipient of kindness. This activist's sentiment is expressed beautifully in a quote from R. Schneur Zalman of Liadi when speaking to a student troubled by the presence of his ego in the performance of what were meant to be selfless deeds: "Though your charitable donation may lack sincerity, *I can assure you, the poor man eats with sincerity.*"[270]

Self-Centered

While self-centeredness often has negative implications, the Rebbe, while commenting on the spiritual purity and presence of children, emphasized its positive essence:[271] The sense that we each play an absolutely central role in the purpose of Creation. When we direct this innate conviction toward its most elevated expression, we do so in the faith that nothing is without significance and everything has a real, even cosmic effect.

Instead of a tyrannical sense of absolute entitlement, holy self-centeredness can ground us in a loving stance of absolute responsibility. As our Sages state,[272] "Every person is obligated to say: For my sake was the world created." *Therefore, its health and vitality is up to you, too!*

This matter of our perceived impact on the world is essential in the Chasidic understanding and approach to the service of G-d.

What you do matters! The world needs you! Live like it all depends on you!

Insecurity or Inspiration

A Chasid went to the Rebbe for a private audience and complained that his outwardly righteous behavior was frequently prompted by inner thoughts and concerns about his public image. "I am often consumed and motivated by thoughts of what others will say or think about me," he said.

The Rebbe replied:

> That's not a bad way to think if used as a motivator. Next time you are debating whether to stay and study longer, think to yourself, "What will people say about me?" and this will cause you to study for longer.[273]

In an ideal world, our positive behavior would be motivated by an inner identification with our core values rather than by the way we may or may not be perceived by others. However, the Rebbe's view was that our flawed inner intentions should never get in the way of doing a mitzvah or helping someone in need. According to this view, we can harness our seemingly shallow hunger for status and attention to inspire us to go beyond where we might have reached based on our "pure" motivations.

Transform insecurity into inspiration.

Dissatisfaction

Yitzhak Rabin, the late prime minister of Israel, was in a private audience with the Rebbe. "How are you?" the Rebbe asked him warmly. "I can't complain," Rabin replied, "life is good."

The Rebbe replied, "It's true that our Sages teach,[274] 'Who is rich? One who is satisfied with what he has,' but this applies only to material wealth.

"When it comes to spiritual matters, however, a person must never be content with his current state. No matter how much he has achieved, he must strive for more the next day."[275]

A cultivated sense of *perpetual dissatisfaction* is not in vogue these days, to say the least.

We live in an era of "be here now," in which everyone is working on "accepting what is," in a constant search for fulfillment. But the Rebbe points out that, although positive in relation to material riches, this kind of enlightened contentment is not productive spiritually. In relation to the soul, we must constantly strive to dive deeper and climb higher.

A Chasid would constantly update the Rebbe with news of his communal activities. He asked whether the Rebbe was happy with his report.

The Rebbe smiled and replied: "Happy, I most certainly am—but by nature, I'm never satisfied with what has already been done in an area where even more can be achieved."

The Rebbe continued softly, "Somehow, I feel this is a part of my nature that I needn't change."[276]

Envy

Jealousy and envy are not character traits often cast in a good light; indeed, "Do not covet"[277] is one of the Ten Commandments. Petty, vindictive, judgmental, possessive—these are but a few of the descriptions of someone in the grip of jealousy. In spiritual traditions across the globe these traits are identified in order to be avoided.

Our Sages, however, thought and taught differently: "The jealousy of scribes increases wisdom."[278]

Along these lines, the Rebbe would often say that if you see a person who is better than you in a particular field, don't give up or be dejected. See it as an indication that you can learn from him and become better yourself.

We can see this dynamic at play in a letter addressed to Professor Velvel Greene,[279] in which the Rebbe says he is envious of the recipient due to his unique ability and work in spreading Torah to the most far-flung places.

After sharing a story he heard from his father-in-law, the Rebbe, about his grandfather, R. Shmuel, the fourth Lubavitcher Rebbe, in which similar envious sentiments were expressed to one of his followers, the Rebbe wrote, "I will only add the obvious, that envy in matters of Torah and *mitzvot* is quite in order."

In a world of social networking where we are bombarded with other people's success stories, it is especially relevant for us to learn how to react to others' accomplishments not with resentment but with motivation to reach higher.

Stubbornness

The L-rd said to Moses: "I have seen this people and behold! they are a stiff necked people."[280]

In a conversation with the Rebbe, a young student recounted her difficulties in adjusting to a new program she was enrolled in. Although she was following her dreams by immersing herself in this new field of study, she felt out of her element and lacking in prior learning.

The Rebbe replied:

> You can do it. You have a strong will. And not only that, we are a stiff-necked people; we are stubborn about wanting to achieve....[281]

This classic description of the Jewish People, used in the Torah to describe their penchant for endless complaining, is used here by the Rebbe to describe a positive spiritual trait—the stubbornness necessary to stay the course, to never give up, to achieve and to excel.

Lack of Trust

A student of R. Levi Yitzchak of Berditchev knocked on his door one day. He said, "You say that you can and must elevate everything; everything has a divine spark, and it's our job to find it and bring it out. I have a question: What is there to elevate in a lack of trust in G-d?"

R. Levi Yitzchak calmly replied:

> When someone knocks on your door and asks for your help, it is best not to trust that G-d will help this person, but instead to act as if their well-being depended on *you*. At such a moment, it is good not to be so trusting.

The well-known Israeli journalist Shlomo Shamir once scheduled a private audience with the Rebbe. During the discussion, which revolved around faith in the contemporary world, the Rebbe said:[282]

> There are many among us who are living in despair. They've despaired of our spiritual condition; they don't believe that anything can be changed. Some raise their eyes to the heavens, saying, "Only G-d in heaven can help." This is dangerous.

> It's very dangerous nowadays to walk around in despair, relying on help from heaven alone.
>
> My father-in-law, the Rebbe, once told me: "The Talmud says that before the arrival of Moshiach, insolence will rise, the wisdom of sages will be used for lowly things, truth will be absent, the face of the generation will resemble the face of a dog, and so on. And the Talmud concludes: 'Upon whom can we lean [rely]? On our Father in Heaven.' Leaning [solely] on our Father in heaven is another one of the 'calamities' the Talmud is enumerating."

In another instance of turning a well-known Torah dictum inside-out, both Rebbes read the end of this passage not as an admonition against what was previously stated, but as another proof of the generation's depravity. By relying on G-d alone, we relinquish our agency, the very power that endows us with G-d's image and blessing.

Similar to the story of R. Levi Yitzchak of Berditchev cited above, the Rebbe suggests that such "complete faith" may stand in the way of our own, and the world's, eventual redemption. Claiming that "it's all in G-d's hands," can be merely seeking to absolve oneself of responsibility. In such a way we turn our faith into a theological sleight-of-hand, a kind of existential vanishing act, to let ourselves off the hook regarding the state of the world or our own souls.

"If not you, who? If not now, when?" —Hillel the Elder[283]

Melancholy

A Chasid living in London had a son named Yaakov, who

was always very melancholy. He was withdrawn and did not seem to get excited about anything. The Rebbe said[284] that he should use this melancholy for learning. Introversion is actually good for study, and the penchant for critical judgment is beneficial for locating what is lacking and articulating what is necessary for progress.

The Rebbe suggests that melancholy is also a sign of exceptional talent in potential, and needs to be channeled properly. In fact, its general qualities—introversion and critical judgment—are especially well-suited to excel in Torah study, contemplation, and self-refinement.[285]

Bitterness

In 1982, on the anniversary of his father's passing, the Rebbe spoke of the difference between sadness and bitterness.[286] Sadness is a feeling that depletes the person's energy and leaves him feeling progressively lower and increasingly lost. Bitterness, on the other hand, has more of a bite or sting. It therefore stimulates the person to action. Its concentrated pain presents us with a direction forward.

The feeling of hitting rock-bottom leaves us with few options but to rise. It is our responsibility to transform our sadness into bitterness. This requires us to feel our sadness in order to incorporate it into our soul's purpose, rather than become comfortably numb and relinquishing ourselves to the depressive rhythms of a disoriented existence.

It is certainly no coincidence that the Rebbe brought up such emotional concepts on the anniversary of his father's passing:

> Reflecting on the passing of a loved one is seldom joyous and often brings up feelings of sadness and even bitterness. Regarding sadness, the *Tanya* states that it must be avoided at all costs, while a sense of bitterness is permitted. In fact, R. Schneur Zalman of Liadi writes that the latter can actually lead to positive results—not only for those commemorating the event, but also for the soul of the departed.

By giving ourselves the time and space to deeply feel our sadness and losses, we can concentrate their essence into a potent force of growth and inspiration in our lives, and in the lives of others, for the good.

Channeling Popular Culture and New Technologies

"Everything G-d created in His world, He created to express His glory."[287]

The Rebbe sought to consciously incorporate every possible advancement and expression of the modern age into his redemptive mission. This approach was based on a firm belief in the Kabbalistic concept that everything in Creation has a Divine spark waiting to be released and reconnected to its source. Everything has its purpose, and there is no darkness that does not harbor the potential for light.

This predilection for holy appropriation expressed itself practically in the Rebbe's sophisticated use of every newly emergent medium of communication during the last century. Where other religious leaders found fear and danger in the new developments, the Rebbe found faith and motivation in the Chasidic belief that literally anything could be utilized for holiness.

In fact, during many of his discourses, broadcast around the world via telephone, cable, and satellite, the Rebbe would encourage the use of modern communications to unite mankind. He explained how people across the globe, normally divided by space and time, now had an opportunity to study, pray, and resolve together to do one more good deed, thereby forming a universal wave of unity.[288]

Through the radio, classes on the *Tanya* could be made available to those who could not otherwise make it to a Torah class; through his televised talks, he could communicate with many who would never think to attend a spiritual gathering; and through satellite technology, Chanukah events could be organized to bring together Jewish People from around the world.[289]

"One might think, 'What can I possibly accomplish sitting in this tiny corner of this huge planet of billions of people?'" the Rebbe said. "Today, we see how one person lighting a candle in his tiny corner can illuminate the entire world."[290]

In addition to new technologies and means of communication, the Rebbe also sought to inspire successful secular artists to utilize their craft as a vehicle to transmit the Torah's light to a world often shrouded in darkness but inwardly yearning for illumination.

For example, the Rebbe asked R. Moshe Feller, the Chabad *shliach* to Minnesota, to encourage singer-songwriter Bob Dylan, with whom he had a warm relationship, to write a song conveying the importance of the Seven Noahide Laws, the universal code of morality for all of humankind.[291]

There are numerous accounts of the Rebbe not only not discouraging, but emphatically encouraging the creative kosher use of film, music, graphic novels,[292] non-religious forms of meditation, and modern art as creative mediums through which the redemptive messages of Judaism may be effectively broadcast.

It is not the covering but what is contained within that truly counts. As we have seen throughout Jewish history, Torah and redemption can emerge from the most unexpected people and unlikely places. In fact, G-dliness is often right in front of our face, hiding in plain sight. Sometimes we just need a Rebbe to open our eyes to see the true potential of the world—and ourselves.

CHAPTER 18

Disabled or Differently-abled?

THE REBBE'S PREDISPOSITION OF positivity was especially present in relation to people who were perceived to be lacking in some way. He would address individuals in challenging situations in a way that, rather than reinforcing their perceived limitations, illuminated their inherent positive potential.

In this chapter, we will explore the Rebbe's interactions with, and correspondences concerning, people with mental or physical disabilities, including soldiers injured in the course of duty.

Special Children

In 1979, there was a heated debate among public health professionals and politicians regarding the housing and handling of children and adults diagnosed with various mental disabilities. Whereas previously such people had been essentially removed from the public sphere and placed in large, state-run institutions, often functioning in reportedly negligent conditions, a new proposal was being circulated to reintegrate these individuals into their family's and community's neighborhoods in a new type of group-home environment.

As a result of this new proposal, there was a large amount of public dialogue surrounding this issue. In the midst of this debate, Robert Wilkes, the director of the Child Development Center at the Coney Island Hospital, wrote to the Rebbe:[293] "As a Jewish social worker and the chairman of Region II Council For Mental Retardation in Brooklyn, I would be most interested in learning what your views are regarding 'the care and education of Jewish retarded individuals'—those persons who, from birth, are slow in thinking, speaking, and learning." Specifically, Wilkes wanted to know how he (and we) might "view this issue—that is, caring for individuals who have a disability that requires lifelong care and supervision—from a Jewish perspective."

This initial query led to a fascinating exchange between Wilkes and the Rebbe. Impressed and inspired by the depth of the Rebbe's responses to him, Wilkes received approval to invite the Rebbe to address a conference of Jewish health-care, social work, and communal professionals focused specifically on the issues and needs of Jewish children with disabilities. This was possibly, at this point in time according to Wilkes, the first conference of its kind.

The Rebbe was moved by the invitation, and supportive of the goals of the conference. Although he was unable to attend due to the demands of his schedule, he took the time to write an official statement to be shared with the conference.

In this statement, the Rebbe thoughtfully reveals his positive view and approach to the lives and education of people with disabilities. As we will see, these ideas were revolutionary in their time, and despite the advances that have been made in society's relationship to people with different abilities, they still retain an edge and urgency.

In the late 1970s and into the 80s it was standard to refer to people with disabilities as handicapped or retarded. In fact, the conference itself, organized by leaders in various fields, was officially called, Conference for the Jewish Community on Issues and Needs of Jewish Retarded. Within this context, we must view a tangential sentence in the Rebbe's letter in order to grasp its paradigm-shifting sensitivity and importance.

After a few introductory remarks, the Rebbe writes:

> With regard to "Jewish retarded"—parenthetically, I prefer some such term as "special" people, not simply as a euphemism, but because it would more accurately reflect their situation, especially in view of the fact that in many cases the retardation is limited to the capacity to absorb and assimilate knowledge, while in other areas they may be quite normal or even above average....

Many years later, Wilkes recalled: "It was a fantastic letter. And astoundingly forward thinking. Today we use the terms 'special education,' 'special needs,' and so forth, but back then the terminology was unheard of.... To the best of my knowledge, 'special' was a term the Rebbe coined. I certainly hadn't heard it before." Whether the Rebbe actually coined the term "special" or was an exceptionally early adopter is beside the point. This comment, when understood within its historical context, gives us a glimpse into the Rebbe's ultimate concern and care for the human condition.[294]

This, in fact, is a direct subversion of the common definition of a disability—a lack. In this single aside, the Rebbe flips this popular misconception on its head: A perceived lack in one capacity suggests a higher capacity in another. A seeming lack in mental acuity or social sensitivity, for example, may imply a heightened spiritual or imaginative capacity.

In another letter, the Rebbe addresses this very point:

> To return to the subject of the correspondence, namely, the needs of the special children (or the so-called retarded or developmentally limited, as often spoken of), they are, to be sure, limited in certain areas (and who is not?), but...human experience is replete with examples of individuals who have been severely limited in some aspects, yet they subsequently excelled...in other aspects.

This was the Rebbe's underlying logic in his viewpoint as revealed in this correspondence—everyone has a unique gift. We should be defined by our personal strengths. It is up to us to recognize and help reveal each individual's dormant blessings and potential for the good of the world. This applies to everyone.

At the end of this letter, the Rebbe, in characteristic

fashion, made one last suggestion to further evolve the overall situation toward the most positive outcome:

> I am quite convinced that if a proper system of aptitude tests were instituted to determine the particular skills of our special children at an early age, and if appropriate classes were established to enable them to develop these skills, the results would be enormously gratifying, if not astounding. Needless to say, such an educational method would greatly enhance their self-confidence and general development, not to mention also the fact that it would enable them to make an important contribution to society.

In this last directive, the Rebbe reveals an even deeper level of his vision: We (society) need them (people with disabilities) as much as, if not more, than they need us.

This reversal of social roles and perceived values regarding people with mental disabilities is also echoed in the Rebbe's interactions with Israeli soldiers who were injured in the line of duty.

Special Forces

In 1976, Joseph Cabiliv joined a group of disabled soldiers on their IDF sponsored tour to America. Since being confined to a wheelchair as a result of the injuries he sustained in the Golan Heights, Joseph had a very difficult time adjusting and reintegrating into society, including in his own community and family.

Whether it was in the awkward or painful visits from friends and family in the hospital following surgery or the uncomfortable avoidance by random people on the street, Joseph was constantly being confronted with society's inability to deal with the handicapped, even when they were national heroes. In fact, when Joseph encountered other disabled veterans, he found that they shared his experience of alienation and shame as a result of the way people treated them after their disabling injuries. They were viewed as less-than, in constant need of assistance, as no longer useful or capable. The abyss that opened up between them and the rest of society only added insult to their injuries.

Now here they were in New York City, alone together. Upon hearing of their arrival, a Lubavitcher promptly made his way to their hotel to invite them to meet with the Rebbe. The group accepted the invitation, and arrangements were quickly made to transport them to the Rebbe's headquarters. Soon they found themselves in the large synagogue in the basement of 770 Eastern Parkway.

After they were all seated, the Rebbe entered and greeted them one by one, looking each of them in the eye. According to Joseph,[295] "From that terrible day on which I had woken without my legs, I have seen all sorts of things in the eyes of those who looked at me: pain, pity, revulsion, anger. But this was the first time in all those years that I encountered true empathy." After apologizing to the Israeli group for his Ashkenazic-accented Hebrew, the Rebbe proceeded to deliver a short address, in which he said:[296] "If a person has been deprived of a limb or a faculty, this itself indicates that G-d has given him special powers to overcome the limitations this entails and to surpass the achievements of ordinary people." He then emphatically added: "You are not 'disabled' or 'handicapped;' rather, you are special and unique, as you have potential that the rest of us do not possess."

As the Rebbe made clear on numerous occasions, the idea that G-d does not give human beings greater challenges than they can handle applies to all of life's challenges, not just moral and religious ones. Therefore, the greater the challenge one is faced with, the more confidence and support G-d offers them.

In this case, the Rebbe again turns society's perceptions upside-down, insisting that far from being "disabled," these soldiers, *as a result of their injuries*, were blessed with near super-powers to overcome their obstacles and rise above their seeming limitations. Of course, ultimately, it was up to them to access and activate these energies.

Like Jacob who, after wrestling with the angel, walked away with an injury as well as a new name and mission, these soldiers, according to the Rebbe, were now being called upon—and were given the requisite inner resources—to not just survive their injuries, but to thrive, inspire, and contribute to life in their own way.

"I therefore suggest," the Rebbe continued, adding with a smile, "—of course it is none of my business, but Jews are famous for voicing opinions on matters that do not concern them—that you should no longer be called *Nechei Yisrael* ('the disabled of Israel,' their official designation by the IDF) but *Metzuyanei Yisrael*, 'the Exceptional of Israel.'"

We see here yet again the Rebbe finding in someone's apparent lack or challenge a unique ability, gift, and opportunity to grow and become more than they, or anyone else, ever thought possible.

This is a clear and moving lesson for each of us, whether we are struggling with disabilities or relating to someone with disabilities. The way you view yourself and others can either reinforce a fixed set of limitations or open up new vistas of limitless potential. Therefore, do not define yourself or others based on your or their lacks or challenges. Each of us is so much more powerful and capable than we could ever imagine. Always choose to see the good and unique potential in everyone, no matter their situation or condition.

CHAPTER 19

Moral Struggles: Vice or Virtue?

A TRADITIONAL JEW WHO FOUND himself in a relationship that is discouraged by the Torah once visited the Rebbe to discuss his religious quandary. He desperately wanted to live his life according to the letter of Jewish law, and yet his heart was persistently leading him in a different direction.

After presenting his situation to the Rebbe, the man fell silent. He braced himself for a strong rebuke, expecting to be told in no uncertain terms how grave a transgression he was committing.

The Rebbe, too, remained silent for a while.

"I envy you," he finally said. Caught off guard, the young man did not quite grasp the meaning.

The Rebbe continued: "There are many ladders in life;

each person is given his or her own. The ladders present themselves as life's challenges and difficult choices. The tests you face are the ladders that elevate you to great heights—*the greater the challenge, the higher the ladder*. G-d has given you this difficult test because He believes you can overcome it, and He has endowed you with the ability to do so. Only the strongest are presented a ladder as challenging as yours. Don't you see, then, why I envy you?"[297]

Not only did the Rebbe not chastise this young man, he even went so far as to completely upend his perception of the situation he found himself in. No longer was the young man "cursed" as a victim of circumstances outside of his control; rather, he was now blessed with a golden opportunity to ascend a spiritual ladder whose upper rungs reached higher than most.

His unique challenge was no longer a source of shame and suffering; it was a sign of G-d's special faith and favor.

To more deeply appreciate what the Rebbe meant, we must first understand the basic sources of such an outlook in Jewish thought. Only then will we be able to clearly recognize the profundity of this particular expression of the Rebbe's Positivity Bias.

While Torah is undoubtedly an organic whole, with each concept being interdependent on every other concept, it is possible to isolate a handful of core teachings that form the basis of the Rebbe's radical approach to challenges.

First, it is a basic premise that *struggles reflect strength, not weakness*. This idea is expressed in the Talmud, which states, "G-d does not make impossible demands of his creations."[298]

Just as it is inconceivable that loving parents would

knowingly give their child a task that is beyond their capabilities, G-d, our loving Parent, does not present us with a challenge that is beyond our capacity to meet.

From this perspective, each of our individual tests are actually signs of G-d's confidence in our dormant potential; they are, in effect, proof of our unexpressed superpowers just waiting to be revealed.

Secondly, and this is key, *G-d is good and wants nothing other than to provide us with the ultimate good.* To receive this ultimate good, we have to work for it and earn it; otherwise it is what our Sages refer to as "bread of shame."[299]

Bread of shame is everything that we have been given in our lives without honest effort on our part. It may be good, but it is not the ultimate good, and we therefore do not fully appreciate it.

From this perspective we can understand each one of our individual life challenges as another opportunity to "earn" and enjoy a higher level of goodness, as we will, through our efforts, "own" what we have achieved.[300]

Thirdly, and this idea may be the most counter-intuitive: *The holier or greater the person, the more vulnerable they are to base temptations.* This, too, is expressed in the Talmud, which states,[301] "The more righteous one is, the more powerful is their negative inclination."

On one level, this reminds us that even those who are spiritually advanced always remain susceptible to error. But on a deeper level, this teaching forces us to never lose sight of the potential saint within every sinner. For it is precisely those who have the highest spiritual potential who are confronted with the strongest temptations.

With these three core concepts in mind, let's now explore a handful of different areas in which the Rebbe expressed his unwavering optimism in people's abilities to overcome their particular challenges and reveal new light from within their perceived darkness.

Transitioning into the Mundane World

In response to an individual who was struggling with making the adjustment from the world of the *yeshivah*—where Jewish life is supported on every level—into the mundane world, where distraction and deviation are so much more readily available, the Rebbe penned the following powerful response.[302]

> If anyone wishes to attain any worthwhile objective, the road is not an easy one, and one must be prepared to make certain sacrifices. As a matter of fact, the more ambitious and worthy the objective, the greater must be the effort and sacrifice, which in themselves are criteria as to how important the objective is.

In this case, the Rebbe actually interprets the existence of a challenge as a metric to determine value in the spiritual domain.

Another point made by the Rebbe is that only through facing up to challenges is a person's highest self made manifest. This reveals an even deeper purpose to the challenges we experience—that of an existential exfoliant.

As a final point, the Rebbe adds:

> Looking back into Jewish history, you have surely noted that the Jewish People became worthy of re-

> ceiving the Torah only after going through the crucible of Egyptian bondage, after they had proven themselves able to retain their identity and not be assimilated in a culture that in those days was regarded as the highest and most advanced. And so it is in the personal experience of an individual....

Meeting Business Challenges

The following example demonstrates the Rebbe's Positivity Bias in relation to business challenges.

A certain individual once wrote to the Rebbe seeking guidance and support as his business—the profits of which had been earmarked for various charitable donations—had taken a severe downturn.

After acknowledging the individual's understandable feelings of anger and confusion at having experienced such a loss immediately after pledging to donate his proceeds to support Jewish education, the Rebbe drew an encouraging connection between his current challenge and the "trials and tests of the first Jew, our Father Abraham":

> Abraham was told to go to a land unknown to him (Canaan, later to become Eretz Yisrael), where, he was promised, he would become great and a source of blessing for all.
>
> Yet, no sooner did he arrive there, than a famine broke out in that particular land with such severity that he had to leave at once and go to Egypt, which undoubtedly was with G-d's approval.

> Under these circumstances, one might have expected that Abraham could very seriously question Divine Providence, which seemed so inconsistent and contradictory.... Yet, Abraham not only did not complain, but did everything with joy and gladness of heart, taking his whole family with him, etc.
>
> Of course, it all turned out only as a test of his Bitachon [trust] in G-d, for soon afterward Abraham was richly rewarded, and he returned to Canaan laden with cattle, silver, and gold, as the Torah tells us.... In light of the above, you ought to consider yourself very privileged to have the *zechut* (merit) to be considered worthy of *nisyonot* (tests) similar to the above, and the similarity surely requires no elaboration.[303]

In this fascinating letter, the Rebbe boldly draws a symbolic comparison between this businessman experiencing a test of faith to none other than Abraham, the father of the Jewish People. Not only was he not alone in his struggles, but due to his financial hardships and the ensuing challenge to his faith, he now had the opportunity to follow in the footsteps of our most revered spiritual forefather.

In this particular scenario, we see that the ability to deal gracefully with business difficulties has definite *spiritual* repercussions. In fact, the way a person acts in relation to their livelihood is one of the primary proving grounds in which their faith is reflected and revealed most clearly.

Even the Incarcerated Can Focus on the Positive

For our final example, we will follow the Rebbe all the way down into the veritable pit of prison. Let us look at how the Rebbe responds to individuals who find themselves in jail, where their personal freedoms and dignity are often severely limited and compromised.

One weekend, an organization that services the needs of Jewish inmates organized an extended Torah study program in Crown Heights for Jews in federal prisons. The program included participation in the Lubavitcher Rebbe's *farbrengen* (public gathering) on a Shabbat afternoon. During this gathering the Rebbe taught the following:[304]

> The entire concept of prison as a punishment is not in accordance with the Torah... We do find that Joseph was placed in prison...but that was only in reference to the conduct of the Egyptians. Although there are two instances in the Torah where people were placed in "custody," those were not punishments. Rather, as the verses in both instances continue, they were only kept there until they would be taught the correct punishment. The same applies to other instances in Jewish law—they are only meant as a precursor to other punishments.
>
> The reason for this is simple: The mission of every person on earth is to make for G-d a dwelling place in this lowest of worlds. Therefore, there is no reason to put a person in prison behind lock and key, because to do so is to negate the possibility for him to carry out his mission—contrary to the purpose of his creation on this earth.

However, for the nations of the world incarceration is both simple and accepted, and, as stated, earlier, this conduct dates back to ancient Egypt and has continued through the ages to this day.

Nevertheless, even for them, in the enlightened countries that act justly, there has been a change for the good when it comes to the concept of prison—it is no longer simply to cause pain and suffering; rather, it is to bring benefit. First and foremost, so that the person doesn't present a danger to society. Furthermore, they use the prisoner's time spent in the prison to return him to the right path and teach him the truth so they can prepare him for a new life—a life based on the foundations of integrity and justness—upon being released from prison.... The main point for them is to return them to the right path and to bring them to a place where they can turn over a new leaf so they can conduct their lives according to integrity and justness. And furthermore, they themselves can help others change for the better by relating their personal life-stories and the consequences they had to deal with....

We can learn from this a lesson in the way we serve G-d:

The general concept of exile is similar to that of a prison, because the fact that a Jew is incapable of fulfilling the *mitzvot* that are connected with the Holy Temple is similar to a prisoner who isn't free to do what he desires. And this is aside from the

> fact that he was exiled from his home and proper place—the land of Israel. As our Sages say, we are "sons who were exiled from the table of their father."
>
> However, the intent in this is that of a descent that leads to an ascent. Therefore, even as we are in exile, we must utilize this opportunity to draw down and reveal G-dliness even in the dark place and existence of exile...and through this we can attain an unbelievable ascent, which would not have been possible without the preceding descent.

In another address,[305] the Rebbe pointed out that the intent of prison in enlightened countries is to educate the prisoner to change his ways and to be able to live a proper life when he is released. Furthermore, the goal is to magnify his good qualities and to remove "the unwanted" things by explaining to him that they aren't worthwhile. The Rebbe then went on to say that prisoners should realize that since they have the power to be released early through good conduct, they should consider the keys to their prison in their own hands and therefore not feel that they are truly imprisoned. And even those who have too many years left for that to be a consideration should at least realize that, as Maimonides states, each person has the power to tip the scales for the entire world with a single positive action. Therefore, by adding in good deeds, they have the ability to hasten the coming of Moshiach, at which time they will be released not only from the general exile but from their personal exile as well.

The Rebbe, in characteristic fashion, turned on its head

a fate that others naturally curse, presenting it instead as a powerful source of potential blessing.

It is clear from all of these stories that the Rebbe firmly believed that everything could and should be related to as being for the ultimate good.

It is only natural for repeated moral and spiritual challenges to chip away at our self-perception of being good and holy in essence. This corroded self-image often only serves to further undermine our efforts to overcome the vicious and self-defeating cycle of sin, failing, and depression.

In the midst of any challenge, it is very easy to give up or to blame ourselves. This defeatist tendency only keeps us stuck in our own suffering, or worse, drags us down into even worse circumstances.

Furthermore, it is very easy for us to judge others who have made what we consider to be poor decisions. Always the exemplar of a higher perspective, the Rebbe saw the potential in every person and tirelessly sought to activate their dormant energies and resources for positive change. He often taught that from a spiritual standpoint, life's tests and challenges, *by definition,* indicate inner strength, not weakness, as well as G-d's faith in us and our ability to overcome and excel.

Indeed, Chasidut teaches that the Hebrew word for test, *nisayon,* is etymologically linked to the Hebrew word for elevate and miracle (the latter being the elevation of the supernatural over the natural)—*nes*. This highlights the fact that from the Divine point of view, a test provides the means for elevation and ascent, as well as the conditions for us to perform higher and better and to create personal miracles.

As such, no situation should be seen as impossible to deal with in a constructive manner. There is always the possibility for free choice and hard work in response to any circumstance.

All challenges, if related to positively, may therefore serve to strengthen our self-image in that they communicate G-d's ultimate faith in our abilities to overcome them.

From this perspective, a personal struggle may even be seen as a sign of favor, for *G-d loves those whom he chastises.*[306] Every test of our faith or character is a potential portal of transformation for the good; it all depends on how we approach and pass through it.

CHAPTER 20

Setback or Springboard?

MORDECHAI (MEL) LANDOW WAS a successful businessman with close ties to the Lubavitch community who had recently come upon hard times. After hearing about Mr. Landow's troubles through a mutual friend, the Rebbe reached out and wrote him a letter.[307]

Rather than comforting or merely commiserating with Mr. Landow on account of his downturn, the Rebbe took the opportunity to encourage him to capitalize on it:

> I surely do not have to emphasize to you that the true businessman is not the person who can [only] manage his affairs when conditions are favorable and things run smoothly and successfully, but also, and even more so, when he shows that he knows how to cope with an occasional setback. Indeed, fac-

> ing up to the challenge of adversity makes one a stronger and more effective executive than before, with an added dimension of experience and a keener acumen, to put to good use when things begin to turn upward. Sometimes, a temporary setback is just what is needed for the resumption of the advance with [even] greater vigor, as in the case of an athlete having to negotiate a hurdle, when stepping back is the means to a higher leap.... In plain words, I trust that you are taking the present difficulty well in your stride...and that the setback has indeed served as a springboard for the great upturn in the days ahead.

In this inspiring letter, the Rebbe deftly applies one of the most important principles in Chasidic thought, known as *yeridah l'tzorech aliyah* (descent for the sake of ascent).[308]

This profoundly paradoxical concept is based on the premise that G-d is the ultimate good, and thus wants only good for his creations. Therefore, at the core of every event or experience, including those that appear wholly negative, there lies a divine spark of purpose. This idea gives birth to the notion that every fall has within it the potential for a subsequent rise.

The Rebbe regularly referred to and invoked this principle of descent for the sake of ascent in response to people's struggles and conflicts. This was one of the strongest expressions of the Rebbe's Positivity Bias, as we will see in the examples below.

A Running Start

Shortly after the Rebbe assumed his position of leadership, several young American men from secular backgrounds began studying in the Lubavitcher *yeshivah* in Brooklyn. One of them, a student from Chicago named Mendel Greenbaum, received his draft notice a few short months after he had begun studying.

He was very upset. "While I was not observant," he explained to his friends, "I had all the time in the world and I misused it. Now, when I've begun to appreciate the importance of time and have begun using it productively, I am no longer my own master. How could G-d do this to me?"

Afraid that his practice of Torah and *mitzvot* would suffer at the army base, he went to the Rebbe seeking guidance.[309]

The Rebbe responded, "Sometimes in life one must take a step backward in order to be able to go forward in the future." The young man remained silent, with a puzzled look on his face.

When the Rebbe saw his bewilderment, he got up from behind his desk to illustrate his point. The Rebbe took a chair and said, "If I wanted to jump over this chair I couldn't do it, because I'm right in front of it. But if I would just take a few steps back and get a running start, I could gain the momentum required to clear the obstacle.

With the Rebbe's blessing, Mendel enlisted and spent two years in the army, serving in various posts across Western Europe. Throughout this period, he continued to faithfully observe the *mitzvot,* finding time to pray and study in even the most difficult of circumstances. Following the Rebbe's advice, Mendel began reaching out to the dozens of other

Jewish servicemen he encountered throughout his tour of duty. From wrapping *tefillin* to preparing for Pesach and learning the weekly *parshah*, Mendel went from being a self-interested student of Torah to becoming a leader of sorts, teaching and tending to others as the circumstances required.

This story demonstrates an important dimension of *yeridah l'tzorech aliyah*, namely that it is the experience of descent itself that provides the very momentum to break through prior limitations. Far away from any communal or religious support system to rely on, Mendel had to activate the Divine point within himself, which empowered him to become a spiritual support system for others.

By contextualizing our temporary isolation within a wider process, *yeridah l'tzorech aliyah* revolutionizes the way we understand our falls. We are then able to see how being distant can bring us even closer to our goal than we were before.

Elevating Exile

The Rebbe further applied the concept of *yeridah l'tzorech aliyah* to the most devastating and disorienting event in Jewish history, namely *galut*—the exile and dispersion of the Jewish People from the Holy Land, the epicenter of Jewish spirituality.

Exile has played, and continues to play, an enormous role in the fashioning of Jewish identity and spiritual expression. After more than 2,400 years punctuated by numerous national exiles, the trauma and vulnerability of our collective homelessness is indelibly stamped upon our psyche and expresses itself in countless ways.

Beginning with the expulsion from the Garden of Eden to the numerous displacements of the Jewish People from the Land of Israel, including the most recent Roman exile, the motifs of eviction and wandering have in many ways defined the diasporic Jewish worldview.

The most common interpretation of this painful history offered by the Sages very early on is that exile expresses G-d's harsh judgment of our national shortcomings. However, when seen through the Chasidic lens of *yeridah l'tzorech aliyah,* exile itself takes on a positive connotation.

As the Rebbe wrote in response to an existential letter he received requesting his insight into the meaning of *galut*:[310]

> To be sure, we recognize *galut* as a punishment and rectification for failures to live up to our obligations in the past as, indeed, we acknowledge in our prayers: "For our sins we were banished from our land." But punishment, according to our Torah, called *Torat Chesed* (a Torah of loving kindness), must also essentially be *chesed,* loving kindness. Since G-d has ordained the Jewish People to carry the difficult and challenging task of spreading—in all parts and remotest corners of the world—the Unity of G-d through living and spreading the light of Torah and *mitzvot,* the greatest reward is the fulfillment of this destiny, or, as our Sages put it, "The reward of a mitzvah is the mitzvah itself."[311] Thus the ultimate purpose of *galut* is linked with our destiny to help bring humanity to a state of universal recognition of G-d.

Here we see the Rebbe applying his signature Positivity Bias to one of the most negatively perceived events in all of Jewish history. According to this view, despite the immense suffering it brought on, *galut* was ultimately a positive development, because it provided the necessary conditions for the Jewish People to evolve spiritually. It also brought them into fruitful encounters with an array of host cultures across the many lands they inhabited and influenced throughout their stay.

In the words of John Adams, the second president of the United States: "I will insist that the Hebrews have done more to civilize men than any other nation. If I was an atheist and believed in blind eternal fate, I should still believe that fate had ordained the Jews to be the most essential instrument for civilizing the nations....[312]

In another letter, Adams wrote, "They have given religion to three-quarters of the globe and have influenced the affairs of mankind more and more happily than any other nation, ancient or modern."[313]

From this perspective, the archetypal descent from the Holy Land is but a necessary step in the ultimate ascent—the redemptive process of history that will ultimately unite the Jewish People and all of humanity in peace and holiness with G-d.

Saving Sin

One may have noticed in the above teaching that, along with the first archetypal exile from the Garden, the Jews' historical exile from the Holy Land was initiated through moral or spiritual failure. This holds true for our individual experience as well. Our shortcomings are what ultimately push us to progress, if processed properly. This is perhaps the most radical expression of the idea of *yeridah l'tzorech aliyah,* finding the positive potential in the lowest point of human behavior—in the experience of sin itself. Obviously this does not condone sinful behavior as a strategy for spiritual growth.[314] It is only meant to contextualize our sins and falls, both national and individual, within a larger[315] constructive process.[316]

The Rebbe once explained at a *farbrengen*[317] that the deteriorations that the world and an individual suffer as a result of human actions and free choice are also in accordance with G-d's plan, and therefore must also lead to a productive goal. As such, these diminishments are also part of G-d's intended goal. Although the sinful act is certainly contrary to G-d's will, the decline of the state of the world or the individual that results from the sin is not contrary to His will. It follows then that the decline is not a true descent, but a necessary component of the ascent to which it leads.

In the Rebbe's own words:

> Since the deterioration was enabled by G-d, the quintessence of goodness, and it is the nature of the good to bestow goodness, it must be that there was no other way to arrive at an ascent of this magnitude. For if there was an easier and straighter path to the destination, one that does not involve hardship and painful plunges, why would G-d allow for the more difficult path?

Like a rubber band whose reach, when released, depends on how far back it was pulled in the opposite direction, so is the powerful yearning for closeness that is created by temporary distance and deviation. A break, when mended, can create an even deeper bond and more lasting cohesion; the temporary separation of partners can lead to even greater closeness. There is greater profundity and passion in *re*union than in a static state of unceasing union.

Filling the Void

Thus far we have explored positive dynamics present within experiences of descent, deviation, and distance. In our final story, we will uncover the hidden fullness within emptiness.

In 1977, the Rebbe suffered a serious heart attack during the joyous festival of Shemini Atzeret. While a doctor was drawing his blood during his treatment, the Rebbe asked: "What is it that draws the blood from the veins, the needle itself or the vacuum of the syringe?" The doctor answered that it was the vacuum.

"That reminds me of a troubled man who once came to see me," the Rebbe said to his secretary, who was standing nearby. "He complained that he was 'empty' inside and unfit for anything. I told him that, in fact, the opposite was true—an empty vessel can draw in with much greater intensity than a vessel that is full, so he is actually full of potential."[318]

The Rebbe then applied this idea to the general sadness that his absence at the holiday gathering had created among the Chasidim.

"Since I will not be able to speak in public on account

of my health," he said to his secretary, "I ask you to repeat this teaching. Just as a vacuum draws in more forcefully than something that is filled, at the gathering tonight, even though the person usually sitting in my chair will be absent, the spirit of the festival should not be dampened. On the contrary—the vacuum will evoke all good things from heaven."

Similar to a syringe whose emptiness is what pulls substance into it, the Rebbe encouraged the Chasidim to harness the void created by his absence in order to draw forth deeper spiritual energies from within themselves. This would give them the momentum to reach greater spiritual heights than they might even have achieved with the Rebbe in attendance. Remarkably and redemptively, the Rebbe was able to find greater presence in his own absence.

In all of the above stories and teachings, the Rebbe consistently challenges us to not only see the silver lining within each cloud, but to remember the joyful harvest contained within each drop of rain. Within each setback there is a hidden springboard to a more fully revealed and redeemed future.

In the poignant words of R. Jonathan Sacks,[319] reflecting on his time spent intensively studying the teachings of the Rebbe: "I began to see how one theme ran like a connecting thread through many of his talks—the idea of *yeridah l'tzorech aliyah*, a descent for the sake of an ascent. Yes, the Jewish People had undergone a monumental tragedy during the Holocaust; yes, Jewish life as he found it in America when he became the Rebbe was in a weakened state. But the Rebbe, with his profound belief in Divine Providence, was convinced that descent is the beginning of ascent, disconnection is a call to reconnection, and tragedy itself is the prelude to redemption."

CHAPTER 21

Obstacle or Opportunity?

THE REBBE'S POSITIVITY BIAS helped him see every obstacle as an opportunity waiting to be realized. This mode of thinking infused his advice and guidance to people of all backgrounds and circumstances.

Crisis or Challenge

Mr. Benzion Rader, a businessman from London who faced a financial crisis visited the Rebbe for his counsel and blessing. "I had hoped to meet under different circumstances," he said to the Rebbe, handing him several papers outlining his business problems.

After reading through the report, the Rebbe asked him, "Do you know what the difference between *emunah* and *bitachon* is?"

"No," he replied.

"Let me explain it to you," said the Rebbe. "*Bitachon,* trust in G-d, is not simply a higher form of *emunah,* faith. *Bitachon* is a whole different way of relating to G-d. If one is faced with a problem and one has *emunah,* then one has faith that G-d will help him overcome his problems. But if one has *bitachon,* one doesn't think there is a problem at all, for he understands that G-d doesn't send problems, only challenges."[320]

Someone who truly trusts in G-d's goodness does not see obstacles, only opportunities.

Rebel with a Cause

In the 1960s, many Jewish leaders bemoaned the counterculture of the younger generation, blaming it for leading the youth away from Jewish communal life and tradition.

The Rebbe, on the other hand, saw that generation as revolutionizing the way we relate to change and ultimate authority, even going so far as to compare them to the generation that left Egypt and received the Torah.

A leader who was invited to speak in a symposium on "the future of the American Jewish community" wrote to the Rebbe for advice regarding how to address the disaffection of the younger generation, and the corresponding bleak predictions for the future of Jewish life in America. The Rebbe answered in a detailed letter, dated 15 Iyar 5724 (1964)[321] in which he alludes to a phenomenon that paralleled the counterculture, namely the nascent *baal teshuvah* ("master of return") movement, which saw waves of disaffected and unaffiliated young Jews embark on a spiritual journey and return to their roots.

> It is customary to find fault with the present generation by comparison with the preceding one. Whatever conclusions one may arrive at from this comparison, one thing is unquestionably true, namely that the new generation is not afraid to face a challenge. I have in mind not only the kind of challenge which would place them at variance with the majority, but even the kind of challenge which calls for sacrifices and changes in their personal life.

Here, the Rebbe refers to the challenges inherent in adopting the structures and strictures of traditional life from amid a more permissive secular society. To do so seemingly places one at variance with the ideals of freedom and progress. On the other side of it, the open-minded enthusiasm and insight of the newly religious could place them at odds with the habituated world of the religious establishment they were trying to enter. The sacrifices and social consequences could thus be a heavy load. Yet the spiritual drive of this generation allowed them to bear such a burden:

> Some of our contemporary young people are quite prepared to accept such a challenge even with all its consequences. This is quite different from olden days, when it took a great deal of courage to challenge prevailing popular opinions and ideas, and a person who had the courage to do so was often branded as an impractical individual or a dreamer, etc.
>
> In my opinion, it is also an advantage that many of our young people do not rest content with taking up a challenge which has to do only with a beauti-

ful theory, or even deep thinking, but want to hear about the practical application of such a theory, not only as an occasional experience, but as a daily experience; and that is the kind of idea which appeals to them most.

Furthermore, nowadays, we are used to seeing quick and radical changes at every level in the physical world. If this is possible in the physical world, it is certainly possible in the spiritual world, as our Sages of old had declared, "A person may sometimes acquire eternity in a single instant."

...You will surely gather that the preceding paragraphs are in reference to the beginning of your letter, in which you express your discontent at the younger generation's lack of deeper knowledge of the various aspects of the Torah. But as you are well aware, just prior to the departure from Egypt, the Jews were in a state of slavery in its lowest form.... Indeed, anyone familiar with the conditions in Egypt in those days knows how depraved the [culture was], and much of this had tarnished the character of the Jews enslaved there. Yet, in the course of only fifty days, the Jews rose to the sublimest height of spirituality and true freedom, both physical and spiritual.

If the conditions would be similar to those which existed at the time when the Children of Israel left Egypt, with complete faith in G-d, following the Divine call into the desert, leaving behind them the fleshpots of Egypt and the fat of the land, not even

> taking any provisions with them, but relying entirely on G-d, and in this state of dedication to the truth they followed the Pillar of Light by (day and by) night—should these conditions be duplicated, or even approximated today, then one may well expect a most radical change, not only over a period of years, but in the course of a number of days.

The Rebbe takes a seemingly insurmountable obstacle, the breakdown of Jewish community and continuity, and in a stroke of redemptive genius sees a bright and bold opportunity for spiritual breakthrough and Jewish renewal.

Traditional religious leadership looked at the explosive questioning of authority by the youth as the blatant beginnings of deterioration and degeneration, while the Rebbe recognized in this disruptive turn of events the signs and seeds of renewal and regeneration.

Historical adherence to a traditional mold always provided a certain measure of certainty for Jewish continuity; however, it also limited any progress beyond that mold. Just as tradition defines, it can sometimes confine. One of the potential downsides of any traditional system of authority is that its regimented nature can limit authentic individual spiritual expression and creativity, desensitizing its adherents to the marvel and mystery hidden within the tradition's core.

On the other hand, Jews who left or were raised outside of traditional structures, when introduced to the living wisdom at its core, can become a powerful force of inspiration and revitalization. They can utilize their newfound passion and perspective to illuminate the very structures that seemed limiting, revealing their inner vitality and light.

In truth, Judaism does rely heavily on transmission and tradition, so the Jewish establishment was right to fear that everything of value could be wiped away in one fell swoop. However, the Rebbe asserted the opposite. With no boxes, the sky was the limit. Thanks to the probing questions and justified challenges of the youth, the ground was now laid for a massive rebirth of authentic Jewish exploration, emotion, experience, and elevation.

With the benefit of hindsight, the Rebbe's predictions were certainly borne out. The widespread socio-spiritual phenomenon of the 1960s, based on questioning authority and returning to one's roots, is in fact what started the *baal teshuvah* movement, carrying along unprecedented levels of freshness and insight with each new returnee. This massive wave of spiritual creativity has successfully touched hundreds of thousands of people's lives and continues to impact every corner of the Jewish world today.

A Tree Grows in Brooklyn

Sometimes the more difficult an obstacle the greater the opportunity that lies within. In the next story, the Rebbe helps a political leader see a blessing where she had formerly seen a curse, and to turn insult into inspiration.

When Shirley Chisholm was elected in 1968 to represent New York's 12th Congressional District, which included her own neighborhood of Crown Heights, she made headlines as the first African-American woman elected to Congress. However, she soon found her Congressional career stunted at its start by race-related politics. Bowing to political pressures from Southern politicians, the House's leadership assigned Chisholm to the Agriculture Committee, a place where it was assumed she could have little influence.

At the time, some in the New York media questioned the appointment and expressed doubt as to Chisholm's ability to affect the legislative agenda.

She was committed to taking care of the issues in the inner city, but her committee didn't have the power to do so. She felt depressed and angry.

But then came a phone call from the Rebbe's secretary: "The Lubavitcher Rebbe wants to see you." During the meeting, the Rebbe told the congresswoman, "I know you're very upset."

"Yes," she answered, "I'm deeply insulted. What should I do?"

"What a blessing G-d has given you!" the Rebbe told the stunned Chisholm. "This country has so much surplus food, and there are so many hungry people. You can use this gift that G-d gave you, your current position, to feed hungry people. Find a creative way to do it."

Tasked with this charge, Chisholm happened to meet Senator Bob Dole on her first day in Washington. He was looking for help for Midwestern farmers who were losing money on their crops. "Americans have started purchasing produce from Cuba," the senator told her, "and as a result of those imports, our farmers are losing business. Now they have a huge surplus of unsold food, and we don't know what to do with it."

"Aha!" Chisholm thought, "the Rebbe's advice!"

During the next few years, and for the duration of the

1970s, Chisholm worked to expand the national Food Stamp Program, which allowed poor Americans to buy subsidized food from Midwestern farmers. Finally, in 1973, the Agriculture and Consumer Protection Act mandated that Food Stamps be made available in every jurisdiction in the United States. She and Senator Dole went on to co-create the Special Supplemental Nutrition Program for Women, Infants, and Children (WIC), which today benefits more than eight million people each month.

The ultimate impact of the Rebbe's Positivity Bias, on display throughout this book, is movingly summarized in Shirley Chisholm's words at her retirement party: "I owe all of this to a rabbi who was an optimist, who taught me that what you may think is a challenge is actually a gift from G-d. And if poor babies have milk, and poor children have food today, it's because this rabbi in Crown Heights had vision!"[322]

We cannot control what happens to us or what life throws our way, but we can control the way we relate and respond to it. Is your life a never-ending parade of aggravating obstacles, or a non-stop flow of amazing opportunities? The choice is yours!

CHAPTER 22

Optimizing Turbulence, Transition and Transience

HOW DO YOU HANDLE situations that disrupt your schedule? How do you deal with obstacles on your path? What about sudden illness or other emergencies that force you to put your life on hold? When plans do not go your way, what then?

Many of us become disoriented when our lives take an unexpected turn. We know where we are going, and anything that veers from that course is met with resistance and even rejection. We are supposed to be in control and we know best.

But what if we saw life in a different light? What if we weren't necessarily in charge all the time? What if there is more going on in our lives and in the world than we are aware of? By cultivating an appreciation for the role of

Divine Providence in our lives, we can discover the hidden meaning and opportunity within any situation we find ourselves in.

No Such Thing as "Stuck"

In 1979, Mrs. Miriam Swerdlov attended a Chabad-sponsored convention for women and girls in Detroit. After the inspiring event, while waiting to board the plane for home, Miriam and about 20 other women learned that the flight was canceled due to a snowstorm.

The group rushed to a payphone and called the Chabad headquarters in New York to ask the Rebbe what to do. The leader of the group, Mrs. Miriam Popack, spoke with the Rebbe's secretary and told him that they were stuck in Detroit. "He put us on hold, and a minute later came back on the line: 'The Rebbe doesn't understand the word "stuck,"' he said." Mrs. Popack proceeded to explain what the word stuck meant, to which the secretary replied, "The Rebbe knows what stuck means. The Rebbe says that a Jew is never stuck."

Caught off guard by the Rebbe's response, the women immediately got the message and rose to the occasion. They spread throughout the airport and began handing out Shabbat candles to the Jewish women they met. As a result: "There are women and families today all over the United States lighting Shabbat candles because we got 'stuck' in Detroit."[323]

As far as the Rebbe was concerned, there is no such thing as being stuck. Wherever you are, it's where you are supposed to be. The art of living purposefully is to figure out why you are supposed to be there, and to accomplish that mission.

No Such Thing as a Detour

Each day, Rebbetzin Chaya Mushka Schneerson, the Rebbe's wife, would go out with a driver for fresh air at a park in Long Island. One day, as they neared the park, they found their regular route closed off due to road work and were forced to take an alternate route. As they drove along trying to find their way, they passed a woman on the side of the road crying and protesting. When they stopped at the traffic light, the Rebbetzin turned to the driver and said: "I heard a woman crying. Can you go back and see what that was about?"

They turned around and drove back to the beginning of the street, where they saw a woman standing on the curb weeping, while workers were carrying furniture from a house and loading them onto the truck of the county marshal. The Rebbetzin asked the driver to find out what was happening. The marshal explained that the woman had not paid her rent for many months and was now being evicted from her home.

The Rebbetzin then inquired how much the woman owed, and if the marshal would accept a personal check. The sum that the family owed was approximately $6,700. The marshal said that he had no problem accepting a personal check, as long as he confirmed with the bank that the check was covered. He also said that if he received the payment, his men would carry everything back into the house. Then, to the driver's surprise, "She took out her checkbook, wrote out a check for the full amount, and asked me to give it to the marshal." The Rebbetzin then urged the driver to quickly drive away before the woman realized what had transpired.

Amazed by what he had seen, the Rebbetzin's driver

could not contain himself and asked the Rebbetzin what had prompted her to give such a large sum to a total stranger.

"Once, when I was a young girl, my father[324] took me for a walk in the park. He sat me down on a bench and began telling me about Divine Providence.[325] 'Every time'—said Father—'something causes us to deviate from our normal routine, there is a Divinely ordained reason for this; every time we see something unusual, there is a purpose in why we've been shown this sight.'

"Today," continued the Rebbetzin, "when I saw the detour sign instructing us to deviate from our regular route, I remembered my father's words and immediately thought to myself: every day we drive by this street; suddenly the street's closed off, and we're sent to a different street. What is the purpose of this? How is this connected to me? Then I heard the sound of a woman crying and screaming. I realized that we had been sent along this route for a purpose."[326]

The above story demonstrates the Chasidic perspective that there is no place devoid of G-d.

Every phase of our journey, even our detours, is meant to bring us exactly where we need to be, if we would but remain present. This is the essence of Divine Providence, which effectively sanctifies each moment by granting it ultimate significance.

Every step is a destination of its own. This perspective is especially helpful when we find ourselves lost or knocked off course. It is then that we are most tempted to overlook our immediate surroundings, as our mind can be elsewhere.

The following teaching of the Rebbe, based on the Torah's description of the journeys of the Jewish People through the desert, highlights this process-oriented, providential aspect of the Rebbe's Positivity Bias.

All Part of the Journey

Toward the end of the Book of Numbers, the Torah lists the 42 different journeys the Jewish People undertook along their path from Egypt to the Promised Land.

During a Chasidic gathering, the Rebbe once posed the following question:

> Chapter 33 of the Book of Numbers opens with the words, *These are the journeys of the Children of Israel.*
>
> However, it then proceeds to recount not the journeys themselves, but the 42 encampments at which they *stopped* during their sojourn in the Sinai Desert!
>
> This is because these encampments were not seen as ends unto themselves but as way-stations and stepping-stones in the larger journey of the Jewish People to attain their goal of entering the Promised Land. Therefore, the stops themselves are referred to as journeys, because they were part of what brought about the ultimate objective.
>
> The same is true of our journey through life. Pauses, interruptions, and setbacks are an inadvertent part of a person's sojourn on earth. But when everything a person does is toward the goal of attaining the "Holy Land"—the sanctification of the material world—these, too, become journeys of their own. Ultimately, these unplanned stops are shown to have

> been the true motors of progression, each a catalyst propelling us further toward the realization of our mission and purpose in life.[327]

Even when we are stationary, we can still be moving toward our goal. Steps and stops are part of a larger process that transcends and includes them both. From this perspective, even when we are moving away, we can be coming closer.

Thus far we have explored some of the Rebbe's redemptive responses to delays and detours on the path. The following two stories demonstrate how even during times of crisis and tragedy, there is a deeper purpose and potential for positive impact waiting to be actualized.

What's Your Mission?

The son of a Chasid who was hospitalized just before the High Holidays visited the Rebbe before Yom Kippur to receive a piece of honey cake, as per Jewish custom. Smiling, the Rebbe handed him a piece of cake and said, "Give this to your father, and may G-d bless him with a sweet and healthy year." The Rebbe continued earnestly, "Tell your father that when he finishes the mission for which he was sent to the hospital, G-d will set him free from there."

Inspired by the Rebbe's message relayed by his son, the man proceeded to initiate conversations with his doctors and fellow patients regarding their spiritual well-being. The day after Yom Kippur, the Rebbe sent his personal secretary to visit the man in the hospital. His first question was: "The

Rebbe wants to know, have you completed your mission here yet?"

Years later, after the father had passed, the family heard from one of his doctors who said that he had been deeply touched by him, and that his spiritual life had deepened and been redirected as a result of their conversations during his time in the hospital.[328]

We can imagine the Chasid initially thinking that what brought him to the hospital was a medical condition, and that the people around him were merely fellow patients, doctors, and nurses. Upon receiving the Rebbe's message, he began to see others not as patients and doctors but as individuals brought together by destiny and Providence, co-travelers on a journey, waiting to be elevated through a spiritual interaction. The medical condition was simply the pretext for the real mission waiting to be accomplished—an illuminating encounter between souls.

Every Moment is Part of Your Purpose

In the mid-1970s, during the early years of R. Yisroel and Vivi Deren's *shlichut* in Stamford, Connecticut, one of their children became ill and was in the hospital for an extended period. With other children to care for, including a baby, one parent had to always be at the hospital while the other remained at home. It was a trying time for everyone, and getting anything done beyond taking care of the family was very difficult.

At a certain point, Rabbi Deren called the Rebbe's secretary to issue the regular report of his activities. He humbly reported that because of his son's condition, he had spent almost all of his time at the hospital, to the neglect of his numerous other projects.

The line went quiet. A short while later, the secretary returned and said: "The Rebbe says that certainly the *Eibershter* (G-d) didn't make such a thing happen so that you should suffer or be anguished because of it. Surely you have a *shlichut* to do there; go find it and do it."

Rabbi Deren got the message and began reaching out to Jews throughout the hospital—wrapping *tefillin*, giving inspiration, and providing comfort for those in need. In that one conversation, his view of his situation was transformed and he truly understood that "'every moment is a part of your *shlichut*; your Divine purpose,' which is something that the Rebbe had said on more than one occasion."[329]

It's Always Right Now

Our final story speaks to those times in life when we find ourselves in between assignments or in transition, neither here nor there.

R. Avrohom Glick, a young rabbinic student from Melbourne, married a teacher from Worcester, Massachusetts, and on the Rebbe's instructions joined his wife there, assuming the role of organizing youth activities in the community. After a few years, a position opened up in Australia and he was invited to relocate to Melbourne by the Chabad emissary there. He asked for and received the Rebbe's approval and blessings.

However, once he began preparing for the move to

Australia, he began to feel as if he were just treading water in Worcester. He had already wound up his activities there, but as he had not yet moved to Australia, he felt neither fully here nor there. He had yet to depart, but his mind was elsewhere.

During a personal audience, he confided his state of mind to the Rebbe, who responded,

> In the Torah we find that during the forty years the Jews were wandering in the wilderness, they would sometimes set up the Tabernacle—the Tent of Meeting—just for one day and then take it apart, which was obviously a very difficult job. However, for that day, it was considered permanent—they were in that place as though they were going to be there permanently. This was pertinent to many laws.
>
> Therefore, when a Jew finds himself in a place—even for only one day—he must treat it as though he were there permanently, and not as if he is there with a packed suitcase, ready to go.[330]

On another occasion, a young man wrote to the Rebbe that he planned on making a short trip to a certain city. The Rebbe replied:

> ...The Tabernacle was a formidable structure, consisting of hundreds of foundation sockets, wall sections, pillars, tapestries, and furnishings; a work crew of several thousand Levites assembled the Tabernacle at each camp, and dismantled and transported it when the Divine command would come to move on... Yet even at their shortest encampment,

> the entire Sanctuary was set up—down to its every last component and fixture—to serve as the "meeting point" with the Almighty, if only for a single day.
>
> When you arrive at your destination, you should also utilize every free moment to reach out to our fellow Jews and to bring to them the wellsprings of Torah, regardless of the length of time that you plan to stay.[331]

We should always make the most out of exactly where we are, no matter how fleeting that moment may be. As the following chapter illustrates, throughout the Rebbe's life he embodied the advice he would give to others and manifested the principle of Positivity even in the most harrowing of situations.

CHAPTER 23

From the Front Lines: A Rebbe Revealed

IN 1941, WITH AN increasingly dark and dangerous cloud forming over the Jewish People, particularly those within reach of Hitler and his advancing army, the Rebbe escaped Europe to join his father-in-law, R. Yosef Yitzchak Schneersohn, in America.

Prior to their immigration, the Rebbe and the Rebbetzin lived in France as the German expansion across the continent was taking place, experiencing mortal anxieties of a people under siege.

During this tense and turbulent time, the Rebbe had many encounters and experiences that left an indelible mark on others, as well as on himself, as we can see from the following episode.

On the third night of Chanukah, 1944, the Rebbe sat down to write a revealing letter[332] in response to a former wartime acquaintance from his new home in Brooklyn, NY. In it, we are given a view into the mind of the Rebbe, as he describes the spiritual impact of his experience as a displaced person in Europe during World War II:

> Your letter awakened memories of the time we were together in Vichy and Nice, under difficult and alien conditions.
>
> From the time when a person is uprooted from his habitual environment until he grows accustomed to the demands and conditions of his new place, in this interim, there come to light certain traits of his inner character as they are in their purity, undistorted by the expectations of society.
>
> Often, these traits reveal hidden virtues of this person—virtues that may have been hidden even from himself under the layers of "manners" and social conventions. Fortunate is the person who does not allow these traits to disappear when he subsequently settles down and finds tranquility.

Unexpected obstacles and emergencies have the potential to bring out the best or worst in a person. When all of their stabilizing support systems, including the ever-present pressure of their peers, are stripped away, they are presented with a golden opportunity—a litmus test to see who they really are and what they really believe.

The paragraph above is the kind of statement that can be very difficult to say or hear, depending on the nature of the situation. The worse the situation, the harder it is to offer or accept such a "silver-lining" interpretation, unless the one offering it has actually lived through that same situation. Then their testimony serves to bear miraculous witness to the potential strength of the human spirit and cannot be dismissed as just another hollow platitude to assuage someone else's suffering, of which they know nothing.

This is precisely what we have in the case of this letter—a revelatory report from the frontlines of the battle between life and death, good and evil, order and chaos, soul-devotion and self-preservation. The person who emerges from this letter is defined by a steadfast commitment to higher values, a profound faith in Divine Providence, and unflinching self-reflection, even in the worst of circumstances. They are also willing to learn from and find the positive in any situation, no matter how bad. This is the essence of the Rebbe.

In heart-breaking story after heart-warming story from this unfathomable period in the Rebbe's life, we consistently encounter the same thing: A man on a mission to help his fellow Jews and to stay connected to G-d and Torah on the deepest level, no matter what stood in his way. We are thus able to learn not just from what the Rebbe said, but from how he lived and what he did.

The First "Dollars" Campaign

Along with millions of other frightened Jews across Europe, the Rebbe and the Rebbetzin were uprooted from their home during World War II. First, in 1933, shortly after the Nazis assumed power in Germany, they moved from Berlin to

Paris. Then, in June, 1940, they fled Paris upon the German invasion, arriving safely in Vichy.

Nevertheless, it was only relatively safe; life anywhere in Nazi-occupied Europe was extremely unpredictable and dangerous for Jews. The hotels in Vichy did not welcome the influx of helpless refugees with open arms. In fact, to even walk through the door of a hotel, a guest had to prove that he or she possessed at least 100 dollars; a sum far beyond the scant means of most refugees.

The Rebbe had a single 100 dollar bill, which he did not hesitate to put to good use in service of others in need. He would venture out to the teeming streets seeking unmoored refugees and families with nowhere to go. Happily handing over the bill of "admittance," he would then direct them to the hotel where he was staying. After they were admitted, they would stealthily slip the bill back to the Rebbe unnoticed, only for the Rebbe to hastily return to the streets filled with souls in transit, seeking safety from the storm.[333]

This story is an example of *mesirat nefesh*, "putting one's life on the line" for a holy cause. Not satisfied with securing his own safety, the Rebbe repeatedly risked his life and freedom for the sake of other Jews. The Rebbe's inspired practice of sacred activism in the face of imminent danger certainly provided people with a glimmer of hope, as well as a shining example of what the human spirit can accomplish when motivated by love.

Always a Jew

Here is yet another instance[334] where the Rebbe exhibited an exceptional degree of *mesirat nefesh*—this time for the sake of remaining proudly Jewish, even in the face of danger and intimidation. This is a quality the Rebbe sought to impress upon others throughout the rest of his life.

While in Southern France during the war, R. Yehuda Aryeh Lieberman befriended the Rebbe and would often walk with him to *shul*. As mentioned, Southern France was then ruled by the Vichy government—a Nazi puppet government, which was, for the time being, tolerant of Jews at best. Eventually, a law was passed that required every person to register with the new government and disclose his or her religion. Essentially, this was a law intended to make it easier for the Nazis to locate every Jew.

Shortly after the rule was enacted, Rabbi Lieberman and the Rebbe went together to register at the government office. According to Rabbi Lieberman, when the officer saw the Rebbe, he simply wrote down "religious." Ever attentive, the Rebbe noticed this and insisted that they list him as a "Religious Jew," even though he put himself in great danger by doing so, because it would make it easier for the Nazis to, G-d forbid, locate and identify him.

Rabbi Lieberman couldn't believe it. The Rebbe refused to be disassociated from his Jewish identity, the plight of his people, and from G-d for even an instant, even at the expense of his own life and safety.

We Called Him Monsieur

R. Dovid Aaron Neuman currently lives with his family in the Williamsburg section of Brooklyn. He was interviewed in November, 2013, and shared the following remarkable story which happened during the war.

"...In the midst of all this chaos and upheaval, my family was forced to split up.... I was sent to an orphanage in Marseilles. The orphanage housed some forty or maybe fifty children, many of them as young as three and four years old. Some of them knew that their parents had been killed; others didn't know what became of them. Often, you would hear children crying, calling out for their parents who were not there to answer. As the days wore on, the situation grew more and more desperate, and food became more and more scarce. Many a day we went hungry.

"And then, in the beginning of the summer of 1941, a man came to the rescue. We did not know his name; we just called him "Monsieur," which is French for "Mister." Every day, Monsieur would arrive with bags of bread—the long French baguettes—and tuna or sardines, sometimes potatoes as well. He would stay until every child had eaten.

Some of the kids were so despondent that they didn't want to eat. He used to put those children on his lap, tell them a story, sing to them, and feed them by hand. He made sure everyone was fed. With some of the kids, he'd sit next to them on the floor and cajole them to eat, even feeding them with a spoon, if need be. He was like a father to these sad little children.

He knew every child by name, even though we didn't know his. We loved him and looked forward to his coming.

Monsieur came back day after day for several weeks. And I would say that many of the children who lived in the orphanage at that time owe their lives to him. If not for him, I, for one, wouldn't be here.

Eventually the war ended, and I was reunited with my family. We left Europe and began our lives anew. In 1957, I came to live in New York, and that's when my uncle suggested that I meet the Lubavitcher Rebbe. Of course I agreed and scheduled a time for an audience with the Rebbe's secretary.

At the appointed date, I came to the Chabad Headquarters at 770 Eastern Parkway and sat down to wait. I read some Psalms and watched the parade of men and women from all walks of life who had come to see the Rebbe. Finally, I was told it was my turn, and I walked into the Rebbe's office.

He was smiling, and immediately greeted me: "*Dos iz Dovidele*!—It's Dovidele!"

I thought, "How does he know my name?" And then I nearly fainted. I was looking at Monsieur. The Rebbe was Monsieur! And he had recognized me before I had recognized him. It was unbelievable."[335]

In such acts of care and consolation we are able to see signs of the Rebbe's emerging role as a spiritual provider and protector of the Jewish People

Was it character traits like these that the Rebbe was referring to in his letter above that revealed themselves in the midst of such madness?

The fact that the Rebbe recognized this boy, now a man, over 15 years later immediately upon introduction, speaks volumes for the Rebbe's unfailing presence of mind and profundity of heart. To keep the face and name of a single orphaned child alive in one's memory over years of war and across oceans of history is nothing short of breathtaking.

Journey to Calabria

The Rebbe was not only concerned with caring for Jewish bodies during this time, he was just as concerned for Jewish souls. As we will see, he was willing to risk his life to uphold the Torah and *mitzvot* at the highest possible level, no matter the cost. Even while in imminent danger, the Rebbe refused to diminish his spiritual integrity and religious observance even one iota.

R. Menachem Tiechtel was originally from Belgium. With the onset of the war, at the age of 18, he fled to Vichy, France, where he worried and waited alongside so many other desperate Jews. It was there that he crossed paths with the Rebbe and witnessed this story.

Chabad Chasidim are very particular about the kind of *etrog* they use for the mitzvah of the four species during the festival of Sukkot. Specifically, they prefer *etrogim* from Calabria, Italy. As the festival approached, the Rebbe expressed interest in crossing the border to procure one of these special fruits.

During this tumultuous time, every Jew had to be "invisible," for fear of arrest, abduction, or worse. Under such circumstances, crossing the border was an unthinkable danger; being caught by border guards would mean certain death.

Suddenly, the Rebbe disappeared. When he just as suddenly returned a few days later, his face was beaming. He had, against all odds and advice, crossed the border and made it back with an *etrog* in hand! Not only did the Rebbe himself get to fulfill the mitzvah at the highest possible level, he was very happy to enable a multitude of Jews in Vichy to do the same.[336]

The Rebbe's Notebooks

Throughout the Rebbe's voluminous correspondences and personal annotations to various Chasidic texts, there may be found occasional references to what he referred to as his *reshimot*—"journals" or "notebooks." For many years, no one knew exactly what *reshimot* the Rebbe was referring to. A month after the Rebbe's passing, the mystery was solved when three such notebooks were discovered in a drawer in his room.[337]

The entries in these journals date between the years 1928, the year of the Rebbe's marriage, and 1950, the year of his father-in-law's passing, which was followed by his assumption of the leadership of the Chabad-Lubavitch movement. These 22 years were certainly formative for the Rebbe. Additionally, as this was a time before he took on his public role, these notebooks provide us with an intimate window into the Rebbe's inner life and worldview.

During this period, the Rebbe kept these notebooks with him at all times, jotting down the scholarly and sublime products of his mind, even in the most precarious of circumstances—including his evacuation from Berlin in 1933, his escape from Nazi-occupied Paris in 1940, and his subsequent wanderings as a refugee in Vichy France and Fascist

Spain. One entry, for example, is dated the evening before he boarded the ship that was to rescue him from Nazi-occupied Europe in Lisbon, in June of 1941.

It is mind-boggling and truly humbling to consider that the Rebbe remained so consciously committed and creatively connected to Torah study throughout such terrifying and turbulent times. This story gives new urgency and meaning to the oft-quoted verse: *She (Torah) is a tree of life to those who grasp onto her.*[338]

Each of the above stories offers a different example of the Rebbe's living response to his own very human struggles, transitions, emergencies, and unrest. Rooted in his belief in the Divine purpose and goodness behind every event and experience, no matter how unsettling, the Rebbe saw in every moment a Divine calling and opportunity, and thus an ability to make a difference.

It is up to each of us to strive toward living these truths in our own lives.

CHAPTER 24

The Power of Reframing

AFTER COMPLETING HIS EDUCATION in Montreal, R. Mendel Lipskar went to study at the Chabad *yeshivah* in New York. As was the custom, students would have a short audience with the Rebbe on the occasion of their birthday; the Rebbe would offer a blessing, and the student could ask for guidance.

That year, Mendel was having difficulty with his study partner—they couldn't stop arguing. Whatever he would say, his partner would contradict; whatever his partner would say, Mendel would contradict. When his birthday arrived and he spoke with the Rebbe, Mendel expressed his frustration with the situation: "Rebbe, there must be something wrong with me. I find myself constantly arguing with my study partner...." He then asked for guidance in this regard.

Rabbi Lipskar recalled:[339]

"The Rebbe said to me, 'It would appear that you have a gift for *pilpul*.' By *pilpul*, he meant the ability to engage in critical Talmudic debate in an attempt to clarify the meaning of difficult texts. He encouraged me to perfect this method. And suddenly, a situation that had seemed to be quite negative appeared before me as a tremendous opportunity for self-improvement.

"After that, when I studied with my partner, I had a completely different sense of what our argument was all about. It was something positive—we were arguing because we were dissatisfied with a shallow reading of the text; we each wanted to find a deeper meaning!"

This is a classic example of what therapists and coaches call "reframing," a technique used to help people look at a particular situation, person, or relationship from a different perspective. Also referred to as cognitive restructuring, the idea is that a person's point of view depends on the frame through which it is viewed, and defines the focus and limits of their purview. When that frame is shifted, the meaning changes, and the person's thinking and behavior often change as well.

As evidenced in his response to the *yeshivah* student's complaint, the Rebbe was a master of redemptive reframing. Through a brief encounter or even just a word, the Rebbe could reframe an entire worldview, relationship, event, or path of life.

Stories of such profound spontaneous shifts in perspective in dialogue with the Rebbe provide a revealing frame that show the Rebbe's Positivity Bias at work in real time.

Guinea Pig or Pioneer

When Sheindel Itkin was 14, a new advanced Lubavitch girls' high school opened in the neighborhood, which her father encouraged her to attend. Willfully asserting her independence and not wanting to feel like a "test-case" for the new program, Sheindel adamantly refused, desiring instead to attend the more established school in the district. Disappointed, her father urged her to write a letter to the Rebbe requesting insight and direction.

Sheindel did in fact pen a bold letter to the Rebbe, which she concluded with the following provocative words: "I do not want to be a guinea pig."

Reflecting on this years later, she admitted: "Maybe it was a little bit inappropriate to write this, maybe I had no right to. But I was a teenager, and I was very independent in my thinking. And I was so adamant about not going to [the new school]."

A few days later, Sheindel received a response from the Rebbe that completely changed her perspective. Her original letter had been returned to her, with a slight modification, made in the Rebbe's hand. The Rebbe had simply crossed out the term 'guinea pig', and had written: "*chalutzah*," in its place, which means, "pioneer."

"*Chalutzah*? You're telling me to be a pioneer? I'll climb the mountain, I'll forge the river, I'll do anything!"

"The Rebbe knew how to reach a teenager with one word. One simple word that understood the essence of who I was. My need to be unique, to be special, to be different, and to forge new paths.... So of course, I went to [the new] high school. We were the 'pioneer' class."[340]

Following that inaugural year, Sheindel maintained a lifelong involvement with Beis Rivkah High School in Crown Heights, and is currently serving as its principal. The Rebbe reframed her situation and shifted the course of her entire life with a single word.

Invest in the Future

Bobby Vogel, a businessman in London, was instrumental in establishing a renowned Lubavitch boys' high school. During what was to be his last audience with the Rebbe, Bobby expressed remorse that he could not continue to financially maintain the school. The burden, he said, was for the most part resting on his shoulders, and it felt like too much for one person.

The Rebbe smiled and said, "I will speak to you in the language of a businessman. Imagine you are dealing in diamonds. If you had a bag full of diamonds, and I placed some additional blue-white diamonds in there, would you complain?"

The Rebbe concluded warmly, "You are carrying diamonds. Never put them down; carry on."[341]

In this deceptively simple metaphor, the Rebbe turned Bobby's frame inside-out. What was initially perceived as a burden was revealed to be a blessing. Each student is a precious gem to be polished and prepared for a life that illuminates and enriches its environment. From this perspective, a child's education is not a costly obligation but a golden opportunity.

As a lasting result of the Rebbe's "reframe," Bobby

continued his financial support of multiple schools and educational projects over the next 40 years.

Second Class Citizen

A young *yeshivah* student who was, despite his best efforts, only academically average, felt badly about not achieving the level of scholastic excellence he aspired to based on the expectations of his family and community.

This caused him to fall into a depression. When one of his peers asked him what happened, he explained that he had gone to the *rosh yeshivah*, the dean, to discuss his gnawing feelings of inadequacy, failure, and fear that he would never achieve the Torah renown he so desperately hoped for.

Trying to comfort him, the *rosh yeshivah* explained that even if he never became a Torah scholar or teacher himself, he could always go into business and use his success to support other Torah scholars and institutions.

Although well intentioned, these "comforting words" caused the young student to fall even deeper into despair. He had been raised with the belief that the highest achievement attainable was to be a great Torah scholar. Now he was being told that this childhood aspiration and dream was beyond his abilities, and at most he could support the achievements of others.

The friend to whom he had unburdened himself advised him to write a letter to the Rebbe to express his bitter feelings, which he did.

The Rebbe wrote back the following:

> There is a Mishnah that clearly articulates the mis-

sion statement of human existence: "I was created to serve my Creator."[342]

According to this simple but profound teaching, the goal of all human existence, our raison d'être, is to serve G-d. There are numerous pathways to do so. One of them is the study of Torah, but another, just as important, is the support of Torah study.

Some personalities and abilities are well suited for one particular path, and others are better suited for another path, but the end goal for all human beings is the same, no matter the path.

Our unique abilities are G-d's way of teaching us which pathway toward that universal goal is right for us.

The Rebbe's letter completely reframed the young student's understanding of his life's purpose and redirected his life's aspirations and ambitions.[343]

As a result, his spirits were lifted and his sense of dignity and purpose were restored. In the Rebbe's explanation, it is not that there are first-class citizens (i.e., Torah scholars) and second-class citizens (business and lay-people) who serve and support the first class citizens. Neither the scholar nor the supporter is superior nor inferior. They merely have different ways to achieve the same goal, which is service of G-d. *In all your ways, acknowledge G-d, and He will direct your paths.*[344]

Plowing is Part of the Process

When R. Avrohom Glick began teaching at the Chabad *yeshivah* day school in Melbourne, he coordinated various youth activities. After three years, his role became more administrative as the Jewish Studies coordinator. A significant portion of his day was now spent on disciplining students sent to him from the study hall. According to Rabbi Glick: "I began to feel that I was not using my time in the most productive way. Instead of being an educator, I had become a policeman."

On his next trip to the US, while meeting with the Rebbe, Rabbi Glick mentioned these negative feelings about his current role. Without skipping a beat, the Rebbe replied:

> Plowing is one of the thirty-nine categories of work that are forbidden on Shabbat. This, however, raises a question. The general rule is that an activity that is destructive is not considered "work" and is not forbidden by the Torah. Plowing a field, which involves breaking up the earth, seems to be a destructive act, and should therefore not be forbidden on Shabbat.
>
> The answer is that plowing is an essential prerequisite to planting. Seeds won't grow if the ground is not prepared properly. And if seeds won't grow, there will not be any wheat, and in turn there will not be any bread. Discipline in school works the same way. It's a necessary prerequisite for teaching, and without it, proper learning cannot take place. You are not wasting your time in maintaining discipline. Far from it, as you are actually facilitating real teaching and learning.[345]

This reframe refocused Rabbi Glick's view on the full arc of the educational process.[346]

In just a few words, the Rebbe reassured Rabbi Glick

and at the same time taught him a profound lesson. What might seem like a negative task when looked at in isolation is actually serving a positive end and higher purpose when viewed in the wider context of a larger process.

Such is the power of reframing!

CHAPTER 25

Reframing and Redeeming the Past

THE STORIES IN THE previous chapter focused on encounters people had with the Rebbe where he helped them reframe their *current* experience in order to move toward a more positive future. In this chapter, we turn our attention to a more sensitive aspect of the Rebbe's Positivity Bias—reframing the *past*.

The Best Way to Lose Money

Once, in an audience with the Rebbe, R. Bentzion Wiener mentioned something that had been bothering him for a long time. A while back, he had lent his friend a large sum of money, which his friend had never paid back.

Deeply frustrated by this betrayal, he asked, "How could

it be that after performing a good deed and helping another person I should lose so much? How could G-d allow this to happen?"

The Rebbe answered:

> Sometimes it is ordained from heaven that a person should "lose" his money by paying doctor bills, parking tickets, or some other kind of misfortune. Yet, when such a decree is in place but has not been enforced yet, we get a chance to lose the same amount in a different, kinder way—by performing a good deed, such as helping out a friend in need.[347]

With the help of the Rebbe's reframing, Rabbi Wiener was able to view his misfortune in a different light, and to grasp the bigger picture and process of which he was a part. In his own words: "Instead of losing money with tears, I could lose it with a smile."

Although the above story makes a strong point, it is admittedly on the lighter side of life. The following incident wades into deeper waters, and addresses a darker aspect of Jewish history.

Reframing the Holocaust

The following public address by the Rebbe poignantly expresses a very deep point of view that may be hard for many to digest emotionally, even if it is intellectually sound. I chose to include it, because it reframes the way most of us relate to personal loss in particular, and the tragedies of Jewish history in general.

Delivered on 11 Nissan 5733 (1973), the Rebbe, who

rarely spoke about the Holocaust publicly, shared the following perspective:[348]

> A fundamental principle to consider: If you ask a thinking person, "Can a spear or sword harm something spiritual?" they would laugh at the question, because the two have no connection. What ability does a sword or spear have—or fire or water, for that matter—to damage something spiritual?
>
> Everyone knows that fire can injure only the body, and [though it] may sever the connection between body and soul, it can burn the soul no more than water can drown it.... And if you were to ask a rational individual, "What is a person's essence?" If they took a moment to consider persons whom they love, whom they are close with, such as their father or mother, and ask themselves, "What are they truly, body or soul?" they will surely answer that a person is their soul! For even though they are made of flesh and blood, and they connect with them physically through touching and speaking with them—with whom are they really connected? Who [or what] is it that is [really] precious to them? Whom do they defend? Whose pain are they alarmed about? It is indeed the soul of the beloved person with whom they have a connection....
>
> This soul, even when it was sent to Auschwitz, and it gave his or her life for being a Jew, [only] the body was taken, but the soul remains. The connection between body and soul may have been broken, but the

soul lives on. The soul remains [whole] a day after Auschwitz, a year after Auschwitz, and a generation after Auschwitz.... How long does it remain whole?

There is no reason to say that any [physical] changes in this world affect the soul. There is no reason to say that the soul ever ceases to exist. What does this principle tell us?

If someone were to come and report, "I met a person once for a moment, and that person was crying; it must be that their entire life was full of incredible and unbearable pain! How do I know this? Because at the moment that I saw them, they were crying and screaming in terrible pain!" Or, if they report the opposite, "I met someone at one time, and they were full of great elation, so their life must be one long story of joy and happiness, without any pain whatsoever!" Such a person would be called a fool. The fact that [they] observed one moment out of a person's 120 years of life does not indicate in any way the story [or quality] of that person's entire life, past or future.

Likewise, those who perished in Auschwitz lived a certain number of years up to that point, and thereafter, their souls [continue to] live on for thousands of years to come.... [It's true that] we saw the person for a [terrible pain-filled] moment, [but] compared to the soul's eternal life, [it] was less than a passing moment in 120 years. [Therefore,] it is illogical to conclude by observing one minute of a soul's eternal

> life that this unequivocally proves what that soul is feeling for eternity.
>
> As pertains to us regarding all the questions that are asked about the Second World War, how it could happen and how it reflects on the eternal existence of the Jewish People, it is similar to observing a person's life for a single moment and judging from this how their life must have been and always will be....

It is crucial to put things into perspective when analyzing the quality of our personal lives or Jewish history in its entirety. One can get trapped or frozen in a particular moment of the past, especially if it was filled with trauma and loss. When this happens, we define ourselves through a lens of pain. However, when we take a step back and reflect on what preceded our trauma, as well as what will follow our immediate lifespan, we are able to see such pain and suffering as but a fleeting and finite point within an infinitely vast panorama. Our timeless souls are not bound or defined by any one moment.

On an individual level, the Rebbe speaks to those who upon experiencing loss and sorrow cease to see the world as they did before—who have come to define themselves by their pain. Worse yet, their life story is seen and experienced through a frame of grief, which holds them back from fully living and loving again.

On the collective level of Jewish history, the Rebbe's words address the typical post-Holocaust victim-narrative, which emphasizes the many persecutions Jews have suffered at the hands of their enemies—highlighting how Jews have lost, rather than lived, their lives throughout history. By reframing our national focus and self-definition, the Rebbe did not devalue or trivialize the colossal loss and destruction of Jewish life brought about by the Holocaust, Heaven forbid. Instead he attempted to ensure that it not confine the way the Jewish People view their past, present, and future—which are *also* filled with joy, abundance, faith, and beauty.

The instances above explore loss on different levels. By expanding the scope of our vision to include the spiritual dimension, the Rebbe reminds us that every single event in our lives, no matter how painful, occurs within an infinitely larger field of significance and meaning. If time heals all wounds, as they say, than imagine what eternity can do.

CHAPTER 26

Silver Linings and Spiritual Upcycling

IN 1977, DURING THE *Shemini Atzeret* celebrations taking place in the Rebbe's synagogue at 770 Eastern Parkway, the Rebbe began to experience sharp and severe chest pains.

The spirited singing and ecstatic dancing came to a grinding halt as the thousands in attendance filed hurriedly out the door into the crisp fall night air, deeply worried about the Rebbe's health and anxious for answers. Medical attention arrived on the scene to assess the situation and determined that the Rebbe had suffered a massive heart attack.

As soon as the Rebbe's physical condition stabilized somewhat, he requested his doctor's permission to attend the following day's festivities in order to deliver his annual Simchat Torah address.

Dr. Ira Weiss, his primary cardiologist, would not hear of it. In fact, according to Dr. Weiss, "The Rebbe had a heart attack that involved such extensive damage that in anyone's normal medical experience, one would worry about the possibility of survival." Instead he let the Rebbe broadcast a twenty minute *farbrengen* from his office following the festival's conclusion.

Regardless of the fact that he was physically removed from the thousands of concerned Chasidim gathered to hear him speak, the Rebbe highlighted the positive spiritual outcome of these seemingly unfortunate circumstances.

"For a certain reason," the Rebbe began, "[rather than speaking during the festival, when such technologies are forbidden] we speak after its conclusion, which allows us to use media to communicate what we say in distant places. [This goes to show that even though we may be] physically far apart, we are obviously spiritually very close, which is the main thing among Jews..... A [special] bond is formed by this, a unity, among all who hear this speech...."[349]

The Rebbe went on to further emphasize the power of this special kind of non-local connection, illuminating the various ways that Jews are spiritually unified across time and space through Torah values and shared religious practice.

Here we see the Rebbe applying his uncanny ability to pierce through all negative appearances in order to reveal the unique blessings contained within each set of circumstances, no matter how precarious or perilous, even in respect to his own life and mortal experience.

Finding the silver lining in every ominous cloud doesn't just happen. It depends upon a person's willingness to consciously curate their worldview and condition themselves to seek out the good in every situation.

The Rebbe believed unshakably in Divine Providence, meaning that G-d does not do anything that is not for our ultimate benefit, no matter how painful a particular experience may be in the moment.

This is the redemptive lens through which the Rebbe viewed the world. It is the cornerstone of his Positivity Bias, which he communicated to all he encountered.

The more we internalize this radical perspective, the more likely we will be able to find the hidden rays of light, even within the darkest of nights.

The moving stories throughout this chapter vividly demonstrate the Rebbe's constant quest to reveal the good concealed within every event and circumstance—and, just as important, to inspire others to do so as well.

All Is Not Lost

In his letter addressed "To the Sons and Daughters of Our People Israel," dated "In the Days of Teshuvah, 5732" (1971), the Rebbe wrote the following:

> Inasmuch as G-d Himself has prescribed and enjoined upon each and every Jew the manner of Jewish conduct in the daily life—how is it altogether possible that there could be a situation wherein a Jew does not have the possibility of conducting himself, in all details of his daily life, in accord with

the Will of G-d, the Master of the whole world. Yet, as we all know and see it, in certain parts of the world, there is such a situation where Jews, with all their desire, and even Mesiras Nefesh (self-sacrifice), are actually precluded from adhering in every detail to the Will of G-d, because of circumstances beyond their control. To cite a well-known analogy: Self-sacrifice can spur a person to jump from the roof, but it cannot make him leap from the ground to the roof.

The answer to the above questions—at any rate, briefly—is as follows:

To be sure, the essential thing is the actual deed. On the other hand, feeling and devotion are also of supreme importance. Thus, when a situation sometimes arises wherein a Jew finds it impossible, even with Mesiras Nefesh, to carry out a Divine commandment in actual deed, it evokes in him a distress and anguish at being unable to perform the particular mitzvah; a true and profound anguish that pervades him through and through to the core of his soul. This brings him to such a close attachment to G-d, and to Torah and *mitzvot* and Yiddishkeit in general, the like of which he could not have attained without the said distressing experience. In such a case, not only is he deemed quite guiltless for not having actually fulfilled the mitzvah—since he had no possibility whatever of doing it, but he is rewarded for his intense desire to fulfill it: and what is

> even more important: His soul-life henceforth gains a profundity and completeness to which he might possibly never have reached in any other way.
>
> Also in regard to actual performance, it becomes evident that when G-d eventually takes him out of that situation and places him in circumstances where he is able to carry out also the mitzvah, or *mitzvot*, which he was previously unable to fulfill, he now carries them out with a depth, enthusiasm and sincerity which he had not had before.[350]

In this powerful response to a pointed psycho-theological question, the Rebbe turned normative Jewish thought inside-out to reveal its deeper dimensions. Not by undercutting the importance of deeds and actions in Jewish life and spiritual practice in favor of a purely spiritualized or philosophical Judaism, but by opening our eyes to the many levels of experience that comprise a single mitzvah.

The fruit of action does not just appear out of nowhere, it grows out of the branches, trunk, and roots of our internal emotions, intentions, and intuitions. Our inability to physically manifest intention generates a corresponding emotional response of yearning to connect and consummate our faith and devotion.

In our own lives, despite our best efforts and intentions, we each experience moments of unrealized connection and communion. Instead of writing off these un-actualized moments in disappointment, we can learn to embrace and elevate the deep waves of emotion swelling and emerging from within the ocean of absence and longing.

Through highlighting the multi-dimensional inner world of our experience, the Rebbe revealed a positive outcome within a negative situation.

When Tragedy Strikes

The Rebbe once received a letter describing a particularly distressing series of events. A man had sponsored the writing of a Torah scroll, a costly and time-consuming endeavor. After a full year of work, he had invited members of his community to a festive meal in his home on the festival of Shavuot to celebrate the completion of the scroll, which was scheduled to be presented to the synagogue in the days following the festival.

During the course of the celebration, a young woman suddenly fell ill and died. The host was shocked and devastated, to say the least. Unsurprisingly, as a result of this tragic event, he had some gnawing existential and spiritual questions that would not go away.

The distraught host wrote to the Rebbe, posing the following questions:

1. How can it be that a mitzvah such as the writing of a Torah scroll should be the cause of such a tragedy?

2. What lesson must he, the host, derive from the fact that something like this occurred in his own home?

The Rebbe's response is an astonishing expression of his Positivity Bias, constantly striving to find and elevate the fallen sparks of Divine light:

> It is impossible for man, a finite *creation*, to comprehend all the reasons of the Infinite *Creator*. Indeed,

we would not have a way of knowing even some of G-d's reasons were it not for the fact that G-d, Himself, told us to seek them out in His holy Torah.

Furthermore, each and every individual has been granted a set amount of years of life on earth....

Based on these points, one can *perhaps* venture to say that had the departed one (peace be upon her) not been invited to the celebration, she would have found herself at the *onset* of her attack in completely different surroundings: On the street, in the company of strangers, without the presence of a doctor who is both a friend and a co-religionist, and without hearing words of encouragement and seeing the faces of friends and family in her final moments.

Can one imagine: a) The difference between the two possibilities? b) What a person experiences in each second of her final moments, especially a young religious woman on the festival in which we celebrate and re-experience our receiving the Torah from the Almighty?!

According to the teaching of the Baal Shem Tov—that every event, and its every detail, is by Divine Providence—it is *possible* that one of the true reasons why *you* were inspired from Above to donate the Torah scroll, etc., was in order that, ultimately, the *ascent* of the young woman's soul should be accompanied with an *inner tranquility*, occurring in a Jewish home—whose symbol and protection is the

> *mezuzah*, which opens with the words, *Hear O Israel, the L-rd is our G-d, the L-rd is one.*[351]
>
> Obviously, you and your wife, may you live long, have many merits. Without having sought it, you were granted the opportunity from Above to perform a [selfless] mitzvah of the highest order: a) To ease the final moments of a fellow human being; b) to take care of a *met mitzvah* (a dead body with no one to care for it) until the ambulance arrived.
>
> The extreme merit of the latter can be derived from the fact that Torah law obligates a High Priest to leave the Holy of Holies,[352] even on Yom Kippur, to take care of a *met mitzvah*!
>
> Such special merits come with special obligations. In your case, these would include explaining the above to those who might have questions identical or similar to those posed in your letter, until they see the event in its true light—a tremendous instance of Divine Providence.[353]

One can hardly think of a more inauspicious event—a woman dies in a house in which the completion of a Torah scroll is being celebrated on Shavuot, the very festival that commemorates the giving and receiving of the Torah on Mt. Sinai.

Even from within this tragedy, the Rebbe was able to identify and compassionately communicate the positive benefit of the events, as painful and confusing as they were. Not only that, he asked that others spread that communication, using the events to illuminate G-d's ultimate goodness even in the most shattering experiences.

Redemption from Within Destruction

A woman was happily preparing to celebrate the wedding of her beloved daughter. However, tragedy struck less than a week before the wedding, and the woman's own mother suddenly passed away. Beside herself with grief, and harboring questions about the foreboding timing of these two matrilineal events, the woman reached out to the Rebbe for consolation and insight.

The Rebbe responded by citing an ancient Jewish teaching that states that Israel's redeemer was born immediately after the destruction of the Holy Temple. This juxtaposition of destruction and redemption is certainly not coincidence; rather, it reflects G-d's intimate involvement in the human and cosmic process of redemption. Even when seemingly random suffering or hardship occurs, G-d always provides a hidden blessing or potential benefit within that painful experience—if we would but seek it out and kindle its miraculous light to guide us on our path forward.

In the case of this Midrash, when the Jewish People learned that Moshiach was born amid such profound brokenness, it gave them the spiritual strength to survive the loss of the Temple and weather the long storm of exile.

Thus, we can see that even in periods of terrible suffering, there is always a concealed expression of goodness; this is G-d's garden beneath the ruins of history.

We all have our own *churbans* (destructions), which are,

according to the Rebbe, accompanied by our very own redeemers or redemptive potentials. While it would only be natural for the woman in the story to think that the joy of her daughter's wedding was ruined on account of the loss, and to feel devastated that her mother wouldn't be physically present at the wedding, the Rebbe suggests that she might see it differently. The Rebbe explains that since death is certainly tragic, and we often need a boost to overcome this loss, therefore, one could say that G-d orchestrated her daughter's wedding to be in proximity to her mother's passing to make it easier for her to cope with the loss, seeing the growth of her family and the perpetuation of her mother's legacy.[354]

The timing of her daughter's wedding was not a tragedy; rather, it was a blessing and source of comfort—if seen through redemptive eyes!

This is the essence of the Rebbe's Positivity Bias: To believe in G-d's ultimate goodness, to know that blessings await us beneath the surface of our experience, no matter how bleak, to actively seek those blessings out, and to spread their light to the world beyond.

These core principles require our active internalization and integration into the ways we encounter, interpret, and interface with the world.

Through such interactions, the Rebbe role-modeled this redemptive way of life to us—not just for our own benefit in a particular circumstance, but also for the benefit of all those with whom we might come into contact, who might themselves need a spark of this miraculous light.

CHAPTER 27

A Positive Approach to Loss

Nowhere is the Rebbe's Positivity Bias as pronounced as in his approach to loss and tragedy. Simply put, the Rebbe's perspectives on the catastrophe of death are nothing short of redemptive.[355]

In his communications with people who were grieving, the Rebbe consistently emphasized that from a spiritual perspective, the loss of a loved one is not the complete loss we often consider it to be.

After Life Is...

In 1960, a group of college students came to see the Rebbe. One of the topics they discussed was the Jewish understanding of death.

The Rebbe explained:

> The word [used to describe death in Judaism is] *histalkut*[, which] does not mean death in the sense of coming to an end but rather an elevation from one level to another on a higher plane. When one has accomplished his mission in life, he is elevated to a higher plane....
>
> Death is not a cessation of life, but rather, one's spiritual life takes on new dimensions or is, as we said, elevated to a higher plane. This is logical and follows also from the principles of science which are considered to be the "absolute truth." In science, the principle of the conservation of matter states that nothing physical can be annihilated. This table or a piece of iron can be cut up, burned etc., but in no case could the matter of the table or the iron be destroyed. It only takes on a different form.
>
> Likewise, on the spiritual level, our spiritual being — the soul — can never be destroyed. It only changes its form, or is elevated to a different plane....
>
> [Accordingly,] the term "after-life" is inappropriate. Rather, it is a continuation of life. Until 120, life is experienced at one level, and at 121, 122 and 123, etc., it is carried on at another level, and thus we go higher and higher in the realm of spirit.[356]

According to the Rebbe, death is not an abrupt end to life; rather, it is a continuation of the soul's journey on its path to completion and reunification with G-d.

Spiritual Bliss

In a letter written by the Rebbe in 1978 to a family in Milan who had experienced a death in the family, the Rebbe writes:

> The only thing that an illness or a fatal accident can do is cause a weakening or termination of the bond that holds the body and soul together, whereupon the soul departs from its temporary abode in this world and returns to its original world of pure spirit in the eternal world.[357]

Further on in this letter, the Rebbe describes the soul's experience when it departs this world:

> Needless to say, insofar as the soul is concerned, it [death] is a release from its "imprisonment" in the body. While [the soul] is bound up with the body, it suffers from the physical limitations of the body, which necessarily constrain the soul and involve it in physical activities that are essentially alien to its purely spiritual nature.... In other words, the departure of the soul from the body is a great advantage and ascent for the soul.[358]

Elsewhere, the Rebbe clarifies this theme even further:

> Henceforth [after death], the soul is free to enjoy the spiritual bliss of being near to G-d in the fullest measure. That is surely a comforting thought![359]

Far from being the traumatic erasure that many people imagine it to be, death actually liberates the soul from its physical limitations, allowing it to soar freely, without its prior earthly constraints.

Eternal Connection

Throughout his correspondence with those in mourning, the Rebbe insisted that there remains an ongoing, spiritual connection between the living and the deceased, and that this relationship is not merely theoretical—it is also tangible. In fact, it is a dynamic relationship that can be developed and enhanced.

In a letter written to a war widow, the Rebbe writes:

> The ties between two people, and certainly those between a husband and wife or between parents and children, are chiefly of a spiritual, not of a material, nature. That means that a bullet, a grenade, or a disease can affect the body, but not the spirit or the soul. The physical bond between two persons can be broken...but not their spiritual relationship.[360]

The Rebbe's teachings in this regard come to life in the following story, related by R. Nachum Rabinowitz, a Chasid from Jerusalem. He was once waiting for a private audience with the Rebbe. Among those waiting with him was a man, obviously wealthy, who looked utterly despondent. But when the man emerged from the Rebbe's room, he looked like a different person; his face radiated vitality and optimism.

Curious about this radical change of mood, Rabbi Rabinowitz inquired about the man's identity from the Rebbe's secretaries and arranged to see him. When the two men met, Rabbi Rabinowitz asked if the man could share with him what had transpired in the Rebbe's room.

"Recently," the man related, "my only son died. At that point, I felt that my life no longer had any purpose. I saw no value in my wealth and status. I went to see the Rebbe in search of consolation and advice. The Rebbe asked me what my feelings would be if my son went overseas and were living in a foreign country from which he could not communicate with me; however, I could be assured that all his needs were being met and that he wasn't suffering at all. I answered that, although the separation would be difficult to bear, I would be happy for my son."

The Rebbe continued: "And although he could not respond, if you could communicate to him and send him packages, would you do so?"

The man answered, "Of course."

"This is precisely your present situation," the Rebbe concluded. "With every prayer you recite, you are sending a message to your son. And with every gift you make to charity or institution you fund, you are sending a 'package' to him. He cannot respond, but he appreciates your words and your gifts."[361]

Continued Impact

In a related letter, written to the grieving teenage daughter of Mrs. Rasha Gansbourg, who had passed away suddenly on the second day of Sukkot in 1969, the Rebbe elaborates further on this idea. He explained that through performing good deeds in her mother's merit, especially those inspired by her mother's influence, she and her siblings were not only reaching out to their mother in the next world, or "sending her packages," so to speak, but they were actually enabling her to have a continued presence and impact in the physical world:

> The bond between the living and the soul that has ascended endures, for the soul is enduring and eternal and sees and observes what is taking place with those connected with her and close to her. Every good deed they do causes her spiritual pleasure, specifically the accomplishments of those she has educated and raised in the manner that brings about the said good deeds. That is to say, she has a part in the deeds that result from the education she provided her children and those whom she influenced.[362]

In another letter to someone grieving the loss of a loved one, the Rebbe continues developing this theme:

> The departure of the soul from the body is a great advantage and ascent for the soul…the loss is only for the bereaved, and to that extent it is also painful for the soul, of course.
>
> [However], there is yet another point that causes pain to the soul after departing from the body. While the soul is "clothed" in the body, it can actively participate with the body in all matters of Torah, *mitzvot,* and good deeds practiced in the daily life here on earth. But since all this involves physical action and tangible objects, the soul can no longer engage in these activities when it returns to its heavenly abode, where it can only enjoy the fruits of the Torah, *mitzvot,* and good deeds performed by it in its sojourn on earth. Henceforth, the soul must depend on its relatives and friends to do *mitzvot* and good deeds also on its behalf, and this is the source of

> true gratification for the soul and helps it ascend to even greater heights.[363]

Therefore, the good deeds performed by those in mourning can certainly be a source of comfort to the bereaved, filling the void left by death with positive action. But they also provide comfort and pleasure to the departed soul, providing them with a way to maintain an ongoing, even active, relationship with their loved ones.

Life is the Best Commemoration

When the Rebbe's cousin, Yitzchak Schneerson, wrote to him in 1952, telling him of his involvement in the creation of The Tomb of the Unknown Jewish Martyr in Paris, today called Memorial of the Shoah, memorializing the victims of the Holocaust, the Rebbe wrote back politely but forcefully:

> Forgive me if my view is not in accordance with yours.... Now at a time when there are hundreds of thousands of living martyrs, not "unknown" by any stretch, who live in abject need of physical bread, and many more in need of spiritual sustenance, the main impediment to meeting their needs is simply lack of funds. Therefore, whenever funds can be procured, this immediately creates a dilemma: Should the monies be used to erect a stone [memoriam] in a large square in Paris to remind passersby of the millions of Jews who died sanctifying G-d's Name, or should these monies sustain the living who are starving, either literally or figuratively, to hear the

word of G-d? The solution to your dilemma is, I believe, not in doubt.[364]

It is only natural to want some tangible way to hold on to the memory of our departed loved ones. However, throughout his talks and correspondences, the Rebbe continually encouraged people to take positive action to create a living legacy rather than a static one, even when the legacy proposed was a holy one. In this spirit, the Rebbe taught that the best way to do this is not just by creating memorials of bricks and stone, but by pursuing positive deeds that will tangibly impact those still living, while simultaneously also benefiting the souls of the departed.

Consolation Through Activity

This was an important and consistent theme throughout the Rebbe's teachings: Intensifying positive activities after a loss helps foster a heightened sense of purpose and can be an effective means of achieving comfort.

In 1956, after a vicious terrorist attack at a school in the Israeli village of Kfar Chabad had claimed six lives, the local inhabitants were completely devastated.

In the words of a newspaper article that appeared at the time, "Despair and dejection pervaded the village and began to eat away at its foundations. Some officials in town wanted to close the school. Others saw what happened as a sign that their dream of a peaceful life in the Holy Land was premature. Perhaps we should disband, seek refuge in safer havens? The village was slowly dying."

The Rebbe's reaction? While Judaism does not provide

explanations for tragedy, it does have a response. Thus, the Rebbe's reply to the stricken village was: "I strongly hope that, with G-d's help..., you will overcome all hindrance, you will strengthen private and public construction, you will expand all the institutions in quantity and quality, and you will intensify Torah study—our protection—and mitzvah fulfillment with joy..."[365]

The doubts the residents of Kfar Chabad had begun to harbor regarding their communal project of establishing a village were being exponentially exacerbated by their preoccupation with grave thoughts and pessimistic conversations. Only by immersing themselves in positive activities to further growth would they begin to see their mission in a better light, and their faith in its future would blossom again.

By choosing to intensify forward movement in the face of loss—especially in the face of terrorism and acts of hatred—we quietly claim a victory for peace and hope over violence and fear. In effect, our actions become living proof that evil does not prevail, and that ultimately life triumphs over death. Conversely, reducing positive efforts and activities on the heels of tragedy only contributes to promoting the ideological goals of the perpetrators.

The Hidden Yield Within Destruction

In fact, through the redemptive lens of the Rebbe's Positivity Bias, disaster can be seen as paving the way for even greater regeneration and blessing than ever before.

An incredible demonstration of transforming a void left by the loss of life into a positive force for life was illustrated by the Rebbe himself when on 25 Adar 5748 (1988), only one month after his wife's passing, the Rebbe inaugurated a global Jewish birthday campaign on the day that would have been her 87th birthday, saying:

> Here is a suggestion, and it would be of great merit to her soul, that in connection with the ascent of her soul, the following custom should be established: Jews should begin to [publicly] celebrate their birthdays, [even though] in previous generations this was observed only by certain individuals and in a discreet manner....[366]

To the Rebbe, the most appropriate and noble way to commemorate the loss of life was through the enhancement and celebration of birth.

As the above story illustrates, on each occasion that the Rebbe experienced personal loss, he channeled and redirected the pain and grief into building and expanding opportunities for growth and affirmations of life.

There are, in fact, numerous examples of this approach. During a gathering in 1980 marking the passing of his father, the Rebbe announced that Jewish seniors should be assisted in using their time to continue to learn and grow. He went on to establish a network of educational institutions for the elderly, named after his father, of righteous memory. Similarly, when the Rebbe's mother passed away, the Rebbe created and dedicated a series of weekly talks in her honor. Understandably, the loss of his wife was very difficult for the Rebbe. Soon, however, in addition to the Birthday Campaign mentioned above, he also began requesting that her legacy be memorialized through other positive actions. Toward this end, he bestowed special blessings on those who initiated projects in her name, such as the building of a girls' school, for instance.

Resurrection

In conclusion, one of the most uplifting expressions of the Rebbe's Positivity Bias in the context of loss was the emphasis he placed on a basic article of Jewish faith: One day, all souls in history will return to earthly life and physical body, with the coming of Moshiach. The Rebbe would emphasize again and again that not only is death not an ending, and not only does the soul live forever, but an element of bodily existence itself is eternal. The following story demonstrates this powerful conviction.

In October of 1967, a few months after the Six-Day War, a terrible tragedy struck the home of Ariel Sharon, the famous Israeli army general and subsequent prime minister. Sharon's eleven-year-old son Gur was playing outdoors with an old gun and was killed.

The Rebbe immediately reached out to Sharon with a letter, which included the following message:

> I was deeply grieved to read in the newspaper about the tragic loss of your tender, young son, may he rest in peace....
>
> At first glance, it would appear that we are distant from one another, not only geographically, but also—or even more so—in terms of having been unfamiliar, indeed, unaware of each other, until the

> Six-Day War... But on the basis of a fundamental, deeply rooted, age-old Jewish principle, namely, that all Jews are kindred...it is this interconnectedness that has spurred me to write these words to you and your family....
>
> An element of solace even in so great a tragedy is expressed in the traditional text [of the words spoken to a mourner], hallowed by scores of generations of Torah and tradition among our People: "May the Omnipresent comfort you among the mourners of Zion and Jerusalem."
>
> On the face of it, the connection [between the individual mourner and the mourners of the destruction of Jerusalem and the Holy Temple] appears to be quite puzzling. In truth, however, the main consolation embodied by this phrase is in its inner content... Just as we have complete confidence that G-d will certainly rebuild the ruins of Zion and Jerusalem, so do we trust that regarding the loss of the individual mourner, G-d will fulfill his promise: *Awake and rejoice, you who repose in the dust,*[367] and we will experience true joy when all are reunited with the future resurrection of the dead.[368]

There is no greater loss in this world than death, yet the Rebbe tirelessly worked to reveal the hidden light within this realm of profound darkness, balancing empathy with elevation, pain with perspective, and dignity with deeds of loving kindness.

It is truly a testament to the strength of the Rebbe's

Positivity Bias that he continued to apply its redemptive perspective even in such sensitive and painful circumstances. Through his compassionate example, we can learn to transform grief into growth, loss into life, and ultimately, tragedy into triumph.

CHAPTER 28

On a Positive Note

IN 1993, NOBEL PRIZE-WINNING psychologist Daniel Kahneman performed a fascinating experiment to explore the veracity of the peak-end rule. Kahneman exposed two groups of people to ice cold water for varying periods of time. The first group was exposed to 60 seconds of 14-degree water. The second group was exposed to 60 seconds of 14-degree water followed by an additional 30 seconds of 15-degree water. That final 30 seconds of slightly warmer water made all the difference.

Although the second group was exposed to equally cold water for an even longer amount of time, they overwhelmingly rated the experience as less painful than the first group of people, simply because their exposure ended with a slightly warmer temperature. This experiment is often cited as a classic example, among many subsequent studies, supporting the peak-end rule.

Simply put, a person is most likely to remember an event or experience as positive or negative based on its ending. This insight has profound ramifications for understanding the connection between our experiences in the moment and our future memories of those experiences, which may not necessarily concur. What's more, there may even be ways for us to positively influence our memories for the better. In fact, according to the peak-end rule, one of those ways is to consciously aim for a positive ending.

But why would anyone want to pay so much attention to the way they remember things before they've even experienced them? According to Dr. Susan Krauss Whitbourne: "There are many advantages to remembering the past in a positive way. In my research on personality and aging, I've found that the older adults with higher levels of self-esteem and wellbeing are the ones who tend to focus on the positive events from their lives. Long-term happiness often depends on your forming a favorable narrative of your life. Those who ruminate over their failures, disappointments, and mistakes are not only less happy in the moment, but also risk experiencing chronic depression."[369]

Unsurprisingly, a similar sensitivity to the "power of the end" is found throughout Jewish thought and practice. A few examples, from among many, will suffice. For instance, the Talmud states that "a dream follows its interpretation."[370] Based on this teaching, our Sages crafted a ritual and script for one to recite in front of three witnesses following the occurrence of a bad dream. The person describes the dream and the witnesses then repeat in no uncertain terms that this was a *good* dream. By extending the arc of a dream into waking consciousness, this practice creates an opportunity for the dreamer to craft a positive ending to an unsettling dream. In other words, a dream does not simply end when the dreamer wakes up; the real end of a dream is arrived at in its interpretation. We thus give it a positive spin.

Another example is found in the Talmud[371] in the context of how a person should ideally end a conversation. The Talmud states that we should be careful not to end an interaction while discussing frivolous or meaningless matters; rather, we should make sure to end conversations on topics related to spiritual or communal concerns.

Interestingly, as a source for this social sensitivity, the Talmud brings the example of the early prophets, "who would conclude their talks with words of praise and consolation." Our social interactions with others often determine, or at least punctuate, our experience or memory of a given day. A single conversation can make or break our mood in the moment, as well as our feelings about life in general. Paying close attention to the way we end and imprint those exchanges can positively impact our lives and the lives of those we cross paths with as well.

One more relevant example appears in Rashi's comment on the very last verse of the Book of Lamentations, one of the most profound meditations on existential exile and suffering.

The book itself, consistent with most of the rest of the text, ends on a dark and dismal note: *For if You have utterly rejected us, You have [already] acted exceedingly harsh against us.*[372] In response to this despondent finale, Rashi refers to the custom of repeating the second-to-last line of Lamentations upon concluding the book: *Return us to You, L-rd, that we may be restored. Renew our days as of old.*[373]

His comment reads: "Since he [the reader] concludes with words of reproof, he has to repeat the preceding verse again."

We see in Rashi's comment a clear expression of our Sages' sensitivity to the power of endings. For had they not instituted the practice of repeating and thereby re-emphasizing a positive line from the previous verse, the community would be left in a state of disarray following such a deep reflection on the most painful chapters of its past, the destruction of the Holy Temples. In order to imbue the Jewish People with a more positive and hopeful message for the future, our Sages took the initiative to create a new ending that is focused on the eventual healing of all our wounds.

The Rebbe picked up on such ideas scattered throughout Torah and rabbinic literature and wove them together into a cohesive worldview and strategy for life based on the power of endings. This heightened sensitivity to the conclusion of things was one of many key ingredients in the Rebbe's Positivity Bias. This expressed itself in numerous ways throughout the Rebbe's life and teachings. One way in particular was the Rebbe's preference for ending things—whether books, conversations, or *farbrengens*—on a positive and uplifting note. There are dozens of reported stories that attest to this particular practice of the Rebbe; here are but a few.

In 1973, R. Leibel Schapiro, along with a team of colleagues, had just finished the final edits on a Haggadah which contained the Rebbe's commentary and insights. They sent a finished copy to the Rebbe for approval. The Rebbe wrote back to them and requested that they alter one small detail in the book—it did not end on a positive note. Indeed, the final words were in a footnote dealing with the mitzvah of circumcision: "...due to the pain of the child." The Rebbe asked the editors to rearrange the text so that the book would conclude on an explicitly positive note.

The editors immediately wrote back that they would make the appropriate edits for the next printing, but it was too late to change anything for the many books already printed. The Rebbe replied that they should buy rubber stamps, have them engraved with the words *l'shanah habaah biYerushalayim*—next year in Jerusalem—and stamp each book by hand.[374]

We see in this story the Rebbe's profound awareness of the impact of endings, as well as his commitment to doing anything in his power to ensure that every ending was portrayed in a positive light.

In a related incident, a visitor to the Rebbe's library, home to hundreds of thousands of Jewish books, came upon a book that documented the sad and final chapter of Jewish history in Warsaw, Poland. To his amazement, after leafing through this rather obscure book, he noticed a few handwritten words on the book's final page detailing the devastating end of that segment of Polish Jewry. The words read, "*Umesaymim betov.*" "We conclude with good." The handwriting was the Rebbe's. Again, we see the Rebbe's consistent expression of this general principle of framing all endings in the positive, down to the smallest detail.[375]

It is also worth noting that the Rebbe's sensitivity to positive endings was not only limited to books—it extended to other forms of media as well. When Joseph (Joe) Cayre and his brothers started their company, GoodTimes Home Video, and began producing children's movies, Joe went to confer with the Rebbe about his new venture.

The Rebbe said to him: "A lot of children's movies are violent—especially at the end—and they scare the children. Why don't you make yours with a happy ending?"[376] Mr. Cayre took the Rebbe's advice and implemented it to great effect, positively influencing a generation of children who grew up on his company's movies!

Significantly, the Rebbe's practice of ending on a positive note expressed itself in interpersonal exchanges as well. When R. Chaim Citron was in high school, he and his parents had some disagreements as to his future direction. At a certain point when their conversation had stalled, they agreed it would be beneficial to ask the Rebbe for his input.

During a moment of charged silence that followed a lengthy and emotional discussion, the Rebbe turned to Chaim's mother and said, "I want you to smile." His request was so unexpected and disarming that she couldn't help but do just that. Seeing her smiling from ear-to-ear, the Rebbe said, "Now that you're smiling, you can go. I want people to be happy when they leave here."[377]

This story says so many things, but in the context of our discussion, it is worth noting the Rebbe's conscious decision to cap an almost certainly difficult conversation with kindness. We can learn from this that no matter how wide the gap between perspectives, it is always worth maintaining a sense of shared connection and goodwill for the benefit of all involved.

Another example is recorded in a series of letters between the Rebbe and bestselling author Herman Wouk, who was an Orthodox Jew. The exchange was initiated when Mr. Wouk wrote to the Rebbe requesting his opinion on a particular communal education project. The Rebbe,[378] for various reasons, critically rebuffed it. But that is not where the Rebbe's letter ended. Directly following his critique of Mr. Wouk's proposal, the Rebbe proceeded to express his heartfelt appreciation of Mr. Wouk's efforts in support of Jewish education, referring to him as "not merely a 'supporter' but as a real partner." The Rebbe continued that this was "consistent with your participation in the work of Lubavitch in other parts of the U.S.A. and in the Holy Land, as well as other places—always readily responding to a call, whenever the opportunity presented itself."

Again, we see the Rebbe balancing a firm and unflinching stance on important and potentially contentious issues with an unwavering commitment to concluding every interpersonal exchange on a positive note. This story powerfully demonstrates the Rebbe's ability to stand up for his principles without losing his respect for and connection to each individual.

Truly, the Rebbe did everything possible to make sure that everyone walked away from an encounter with him—whether it was in person or in writing—on better terms than they were before they met.

As a final example of this expression of the Rebbe's Positivity Bias, it is touching to remember how the Rebbe would so often conclude *farbrengens*—when the Rebbe would gather with his Chasidim for a night of spirited teaching and prayerful song. Following hours of intense learning and reflection, as the *farbrengen* was coming to a close and the Rebbe was preparing to take his leave, he would frequently encourage the Chasidim to close the night by singing a joyous song whose lyrics, taken from Isaiah,[379] are a perfect reflection of the theme of this chapter: *You shall go out with joy, and go forth in peace*. This song would accompany the Rebbe as he left the building and would continue to echo in the hearts of the Chasidim as they went home to their families and individual lives. In some small way, this song continues to echo for those who are open to hear it, reminding us all to end every experience and interaction on a positive note!

CHAPTER 29

Where is our World Heading?

THE REBBE ONCE SAID to a Gerer Chasid named Rabbi Neiman, "The world says that I am crazy about Moshiach—and they are absolutely right!"[380]

Indeed, if there is one thing that the Rebbe and Chabad in general are known for, it is their fervent belief in the imminent arrival of Moshiach. This teleological driving force was at the root of everything the Rebbe said and did. But what does this actually mean, and what does it have to do with the Rebbe's Positivity Bias?

Without getting too deep into the finer points of Jewish philosophy and prophecy, Moshiach is the main developing character, both perpetually absent and potentially present at all times, throughout our story of Creation and Redemption. His inevitable arrival will signal the ultimate redemption and goal of history, when the world will be made right and truth will be as clear as day for all to see.

The Rebbe's belief in *Moshiach* as the culmination of the Divine/human drama gave him and all those he inspired more than a hope, but rather a vivid faith in the ultimately positive outcome to all of the world's bitter exiles and alienations.

A foundational aspect of this is that we all have our work cut out for us in order for it to occur; we are charged with spiritually preparing ourselves and the world for redemption. From this perspective, history has been a millenia-long crash-course on bringing Moshiach into our midst from out of the hovering realms of pure poetic potential.

It is this very combination of belief in G-d's ultimate goodness and in our own personal power to positively impact the world that forms the basis of the Rebbe's Positivity Bias.

The Rebbe believed that we are living in Messianic times. From when he was a small child, the Rebbe dreamed of that imminent great day, and despite the immensely challenging times he lived through, he never stopped nursing that dream. In a letter[381] addressed to Yitzchak Ben-Zvi, the second president of Israel, the Rebbe wrote:

> From the time when I was a child attending cheder, and even earlier than that, there began to take form in my mind a vision of the future redemption—the redemption of Israel from its last exile, redemption such as would explain the suffering, the decrees, and the massacres of exile....

In many ways, this dream is what made the Rebbe unique among other towering Jewish figures of our time. Most leaders see their life and impact in terms of their specific generation, but the Rebbe viewed his role through the wider lens of history in its entirety. He saw his generation as a whole, while at the same time also as a small but critical part of a much larger super-structure and meta-process.

Therefore, wherever you look in the Rebbe's teachings, there it is: the dream of Moshiach. Sometimes implicit, but more often explicit, in almost every one of his talks and letters, the Rebbe reveals the aspiration that is closest to his heart: A burning desire to see our imperfect world enter into an era of peace and wholeness, devoid of war and suffering, replete with revealed goodness and the pursuit of G-dly knowledge.

Indeed, the Rebbe most clearly articulated the contours of this dream on the very night he assumed the mantle of Chabad-Lubavitch leadership, 10 Shevat, 5711 (1951), in his discourse entitled *Bati L'gani.*

In this, his first public teaching as Rebbe, he cites centuries of Midrashic history, revealing this world's ultimate importance to G-d as His "garden" and most-desired "abode," as well as its simultaneous spiritual vacancy—"the *Shechinah* (the Divine Presence) is in exile"[382]—waiting to be welcomed back home. And this is where we come in. As G-d's entrusted "gardeners," it is our job to maintain and cultivate the world for G-d's eternal residence.

In the words of the Rebbe on the very night he assumed that name, after thousands of years of baby steps and quantum leaps, going all the way back to Adam and Eve in the

Garden of Eden, "it is up to us to complete the job and usher in the final redemption."

There it is: The Rebbe's world-redeeming dream. Nothing less than bringing humanity across the finish line of history and ushering in the Messianic era.

But how?

Not to Change Reality, but to Open Our Eyes

One of the axiomatic teachings regarding Moshiach that the Rebbe would often share is that Moshiach will not come to change reality; rather, he will expose reality for what it truly is.

In support of this idea, he would often say that the Hebrew word for exile has the same letters as the Hebrew word for redemption except for the addition of the letter *alef*. The addition of the *alef* shows that the redemption will not negate the work we did during the exile; rather, it will include and elevate the exile itself by revealing the *alef* of the *Alufo shel olam*—the Master of the world—within the exile. In other words, the way G-d is in control and runs the world even during exile.

It also shows how the redemption will only be accomplished through our service of G-d during exile—just as the word for redemption is made up of the letters of the word for exile with the addition of the *alef*—similar to the concept of descent for the purpose of ascent, as mentioned earlier.

In this seemingly simple word-play, the Rebbe is pointing out a powerful paradigm shift in our understanding of Moshiach.

Moshiach does not mean the articulation of a totally different word or world. The letters or infrastructure of our lives and the universe will fundamentally stay the same, except that the *alef* will be revealed, quietly smiling at us out of the tumult of our experiences, revealing the garden of oneness within.[383]

Signs of the Times

The Rebbe was once asked: If you could choose any era in history in which to live, which would it be?

"This one," he answered immediately.[384]

Throughout his myriad spiritual teachings, his inspiring personal interactions, and his bold public outreach projects, the Rebbe spiritually developed and actively expressed the idea that we are "the last generation of exile and the first of Redemtion."[385]

We are thus living on the transitional cusp of an unfathomable evolution of consciousness—a spiritual revolution. This is both an unbelievable privilege and an awesome responsibility, as our individual and collective lives are literally and metaphorically laying the final stones for the bridge between exile and redemption.

Based on this eschatological understanding of where we are in the process of history, the Rebbe saw the signs of Moshiach's imminent arrival everywhere—from world events to social trends, and advances in technology and medicine. From his inaugural address, and on thousands of occassions thereafter, the Rebbe declared it his mission to empower others to see the world through a similar lens, to understand and appreciate the nature of the miraculous and meaningful times we are living through, to get a glimpse of the hidden *alef* within the world and events swirling around us.

Traditionally, the vast multitude of Biblical prophecies relating to the redemption have been viewed through a supernatural lens, and were thus considered as being irreconcilably removed from our daily reality and experience. They were understood as miraculous "aberrations," and therefore as clear signs of Divine intervention.

Today, however, according to the Rebbe, many of the prophesied "miracles" pertaining to the Messianic era have begun to come into existence at varying degrees of actualization. As such, the fulfillment of the words of the prophets no longer requires a wild imagination or blind leap of faith to behold. According to the Rebbe, it is more a matter of "opening our eyes" to see beneath the surface of "natural" events and advances, in order to recognize the Hand of the Creator at work in history.

For instance:

The Rebbe saw in the rise of feminism the beginning stages of Jeremiah's prophecy: *For the L-rd has created something new on the earth, a woman shall rise above a man.*[386]

In many countries and cultures the world over there has continued to be a general shift in the direction of including and advancing women's voices, issues, and rights. Today, women are increasingly gaining political power and make up more than a fifth of members of national parliaments, and counting.[387]

Similarly, as we have explored, the Rebbe saw in the

emergent counterculture of the 1960s, many examples of prophesied socio-generational shifts and conflicts that would occur leading up to the arrival of Moshiach; for example, the words of Isaiah that *the youth will be insolent and rebellious towards their elders.*[388]

Rather than interpreting those words apocalyptically, the Rebbe chose to focus on the potential positive outcomes of such radical expressions of youth, and thereby sought to validate them and strengthen their good points.

The Rebbe, along with various other Chasidic leaders, including his father-in-law, the Previous Rebbe, felt what they considered to be the beginnings of the "birth pangs"[389] of Moshiach in the various cataclysmic events of the 20th century, particularly World War II.

In related fashion, the Rebbe saw[390] the Six-Day War, and the corresponding mass spiritual awakening and immigration of impassioned Jews moving to Israel, as a symbolic nod to Isaiah's prophecy that *It will come to pass on that day that the great shofar will sound....*[391] The prophecy goes on to describe the in-gathering of Jews "lost" and "dispersed" in exile, as they return to Jerusalem in the final redemption.

With the appearance of various communication technologies over the course of the 20th century—from the phone to radio to television to the beginnings of the internet—the Rebbe saw the potential, not for more discord and confusion, but for more communication and connection. Additionally, with the introduction of the World Wide Web, by making all information accessible to the furthest reaches of the globe, the groundwork has been laid for the *world to be filled with the word of G-d,*[392] literally!

This redemptive view of the world is the ultimate expression of the Rebbe's Positivity Bias. Wars, revolutions, uprisings, rapid shifts in consciousness—as unsettling as these things may be to our lives in the moment and to the established order of the day—are ultimately leading us towards a more perfect union, a higher system of truth and harmony. This was the unyielding faith of the Rebbe.

The Time is now! The world is ready for more light! Are we?

Can we keep our composure and direction amid what appears to be the madness of a new world being born? Can we hold on to the promise of goodness and G-dliness revealed? Can we see through the brokenness and not lose hope? This takes work and faith. The work of developing and maintaining a positive outlook to keep moving toward the light. We need faith that the sparks really are there, waiting to be acknowledged and uplifted.

Indeed, despite what the pessimists will have us believe, we are actually living in unprecedented good times. Rather than regressing, which is what it often feels like, our world is progressing, and at breakneck speed. But it often takes the cultivation of a positive and expansive outlook to see the resplendent forest through the smoldering trees.

In January 2018, *Time Magazine* welcomed Bill Gates as its first guest editor in its 94-year history. Gates designed the edition around a mindset that he had endorsed for years: optimism. He then invited the world's greatest minds and experts on world progress to share their findings. In an interview he gave explaining why he decided to edit an issue of *Time*, he explained:[393]

"Reading the news today doesn't exactly leave you feeling

optimistic. But many of the awful events we read about have happened in the context of a bigger, positive trend. On the whole, the world is getting much better."

This is not some naively optimistic view; it's backed by data.

According to Swedish economic historian named Johan Norberg, who wrote an important book on the topic called "*Progress*":

"If someone had told you in 1990 that over the next 25 years world hunger would decline by 40%, child mortality would halve, and extreme poverty would fall by three quarters, you'd have told them they were a naive fool.

"But the fools were right. This is truly what has happened."[394]

And not just that:

For most of human history worldwide, life expectancy was around thirty years. Today, in most developed parts of the world, it is over eighty. By 2030, it will reach over ninety years in certain parts of the world.

In the 1990s there were more than 60,000 nuclear arms around the world, but by 2018, that number had fallen to approximately 10,000 nuclear arms.[395]

Two hundred years ago, 90% of the world lived in extreme poverty; today that number is 10%.

Indeed, according to the prominent Israeli public intellectual Yuval Harari, more people die today from eating too much than from eating too little.

Through too many medical advances to count, today the "lame are dancing" with the aid of prosthetics, the "blind can see," as 80% of visual impairment has already been cured,[396] and through stem cell research scientists are well on their way to curing deafness,[397] bringing to life the Messianic prophecies of Isaiah:[398] *Then will the eyes of the blind be opened and the ears of the deaf unstopped. Then will the lame leap like a deer....*

As pointed out by the Rebbe in one of his talks,[399] even the UN, despite its many intrigues and imperfections, channeled this Messianic energy of the time when it decided to prominently display the prophetic words of Isaiah:[400] *And then they will beat their swords into ploughshares, and nations will learn war no more* in the entrance hall, expressing an intention to work towards the redemptive cause of lasting international peace.

The list goes on. And each new "miracle" reveals the fulfillment on some level of yet another prophetic vision related to the dawning of the Messianic age of Redemption according to our prophets of old.

Gates concludes his interview: "This issue of *Time* [is] a crash course in why and how the world is improving. I hope you'll be inspired to make it even better."

Passing the Baton

On a cold Tuesday night in February, 1992, just two years before passing away at the age of 92, the Rebbe could be seen standing at the front of Chabad Headquarters at 770 Eastern Parkway for hours and hours on end. Personally greeting the thousands who had lined up, the Rebbe handed each person a freshly printed copy of what would be the very last discourse he edited and distributed before his passing.

Opening with the verse (Exodus 27:20) *Ve'atah*

Tetzaveh—And you will connect/command—this discourse has come to be considered the Rebbe's last ethical will and testament.

Along with his first public discourse, *Bati L'gani,* it provides a kind of bookend to the more than forty years of his transformational teachings.

In it, among many other things, the Rebbe acknowledges[401] and articulates certain unique historical and spiritual aspects of Jewish experience in the current day and age. The Rebbe cited the well-known rabbinic metaphor comparing the Jew to an olive, because his inner oil and light are only revealed when he is crushed. The Rebbe then states that historically speaking, the Jewish People were most "productive" and pious when they were "crushed" through harsh decrees, oppressions, and massacres.

These externally-imposed conditions activated a super-rational dimension of the soul, which allowed our ancestors to stubbornly and miraculously hold fast to their Jewish traditions and faith in the face of death, disgrace, and ostracization.

But we are all familiar with the saying, "It is easier to fight for one's principles than to live up to them." According to the Rebbe, this is precisely the existential situation in which contemporary Jews find themselves. For now, with the disappearance of the vast majority of daily, systematic threats to the Jewish ways of life, the modern Jew is faced with an even bigger challenge: To find the inspiration within to be willing to live as a Jew, and not just to be willing to die as one.

Additionally, following the European Enlightenment, the general societal trend in the Western World has been a decrease in organized expressions of religiosity and a corresponding increased slide towards secular humanism. While outwardly this may appear to many as a sign of spiritual degeneration, the Rebbe recognized it for the opportunity that it was. For this is but another way in which the Jew of today is free of many of the external pressures to engage and express his commitment to Jewish faith and identity that prevailed in the past. The modern Jew, according to the Rebbe, is increasingly left to his or her own devices to connect with their Jewish community, heritage, and tradition.

The Rebbe saw Jewish history through the lens of a human life. Like a baby, whose first steps and development require constant hands-on attention and reassuring affection, the Jewish People in their national infancy during Biblical times required overt miracles and revealed G-dliness to help them learn to walk out of Egypt. This spiritual caretaking continued as Israel grew up through Divine revelations, and under the wing of priests and prophets, judges and kings. But as time passed, the Jewish People continued to mature spiritually, and along with this maturation the revealed presence and providence of G-d diminished correspondingly. This journey has created the conditions for us to grow into our own faith and develop a connection with G-d and a spiritual worldview that comes from within, without external pressure or even revelation. This has given us the exceptional opportunity to manifest the ultimate, deepest, and highest level of faith.

"For so long as a Jew's compliance with the Will of G-d is externally motivated—however commendable such motivation is in itself—it is not yet quite complete," said the Rebbe in 1991.

Indeed, it is clear from many public talks and pronouncements during this period, that the Rebbe was very consciously preparing his followers and future admirers for his departure. Through it all, one radical message consistently rings loud and clear: We all must become self-starters. We cannot rely on "help" from without, not even through faith-awakening hardship, let alone external positive support, constant guidance, and new teachings. We must find that eternal light within our own souls and ignite it, not once, but over and over again, through good deeds, the cultivation of a positive and providential perspective, and passionate expressions of holiness and faith.

"What else can I do so that all Jewish People should agitate, truthfully cry out, and effectively bring Moshiach in actuality.... We are still in exile.... and more importantly, in an internal exile with regards to serving G-d," cried out the Rebbe in the spring of 1991. "The only thing I can do is give it over to you: Do all you can... to actually bring our righteous Moshiach, immediately and directly.... I have done my part, from now on you must do all that you can."[402]

In the winter of 1992, around the same time as the publication of *V'atah Tetzaveh,* Gabriel Erem, the CEO and publisher of *Lifestyles Magazine,* approached the Rebbe as he distributed dollars. "On the occasion of your 90th birthday," Erem told the Rebbe, "we are publishing a special issue... What is your message to the world?"

"Ninety," the Rebbe replied, "is the value of the Hebrew letter *tzaddik*. The meaning of the word '*tzaddik*,' is 'a truly righteous person,' [the highest spiritual attribution]. And that is a direct indication that it is in the power of every Jew to become a real *tzaddik*, a righteous person, and indeed they should do so for many years, 'until 120' (for the rest of their life)."[403]

This message, the Rebbe added, applies equally to non-Jews as well.

Traditionally, the word *tzaddik* has been applied exclusively to saintly leaders of exceptional spiritual stature, but in this instance, and increasingly towards the end of his life, the Rebbe applied it to everyone.

It is no longer enough for an elite caste of holy leaders to tend to G-d's garden. We must, each and every one of us, accept G-d's invitation to play our role in the final phase of the meta-historical drama of world redemption.

This democratization of Divine responsibility is precisely the paradigmatic shift the Rebbe sought to inspire and strengthen within each individual, the Jewish People, and humanity as a whole.

From the redemptive dream of a precocious child to a daring vision of cosmic renewal, the stories and teachings explored throughout the course of this book all in some sense culminate in the Rebbe's clarion call to action:

Our generation is uniquely positioned to calibrate the conditions for monumental shift. The future is up to each one of us. Become the *tzaddik* you already are. The world is G-d's garden; we are each its humble gardeners. Care for it and beautify it in the way that only you can.

We are no longer waiting for Moshiach, Moshiach is waiting for us!

A new day is approaching; let's awaken the dawn.

CHAPTER 30

Positivity Works – Suggestions for Practical Action

PART I: THE THEORY

THE REBBE ONCE ENCOURAGED a man seeking guidance to use his unique talents to the fullest. At a subsequent meeting, the Rebbe said, "I hope you are fulfilling what we discussed. Don't turn me into a sinner!"

Taken aback, the man asked, "How could I possibly do that?"

The Rebbe replied, "Our Sages teach that 'whoever engages in excessive talk brings on sin.' If our previous conversation led to no practical outcome, it was merely 'excessive talk.'"[404]

The Rebbe's every word and teaching was designed to inspire and elicit practical and positive change in the lives of the people with whom he interacted. He saw no need for empty pontification; therefore, he relentlessly pushed all those with whom he was in contact to see Torah as a guide for life—a G-d-given instruction manual that teaches us how to sanctify every aspect of our lives through concrete actions.

"The Torah is the blueprint of Creation,"[405] the Rebbe would often say. If one would look into the Torah's illuminating passages, they would be sure to find life's passageways illuminated before them.

But for the Torah to have such benefit, we need to see it as such. Imagine reading a computer manual as poetry or studying it solely for arcane grammatical principles! Accordingly, the Rebbe was fond of reminding people that the word *Torah* is etymologically related to the word *hora'ah*, instruction. Similarly, a *moreh*, also from the same root, is not just a teacher, but a guide who shows people the way to live their lives in accordance with Jewish teaching.

In this respect, the Rebbe would highlight the difference between Torah and secular wisdom by pointing out that secular knowledge is judged and valued on its intellectual merits alone, not on its practical applicability. Therefore, in the secular world, the merit of philosophers and scholars is not related to or measured by their personal behavior. How they live is deemed irrelevant to their intellectual discoveries and contributions.

On a number of occasions,[406] the Rebbe told a related story about Aristotle, whom he would stress was admired greatly by Maimonides as a wise man. Aristotle was once confronted by his students in the midst of engaging in immoral behavior. When asked how he—the author of *Ethics*—could stoop so low, he responded: "At this moment, I am not Aristotle the teacher, but Aristotle the person," implying that he was not to be judged by his inability to live up to his own philosophical ideas and ideals.

From this perspective, the veracity of a person's knowledge or even ethical philosophy need not be linked to their behavior. Therefore, their intellectual contributions are valued independent of their behavioral integrity, or lack thereof.

Contrast that approach with *Pirkei Avot*, the Ethics of Our Fathers, where each and every teaching is connected to a specific author to make the point that we must look not only at the message itself, but also to the messenger, in order to validate its credibility. This means that if a Jewish teacher does not live up to or by his teachings, they are essentially invalidated. As the Talmud teaches:[407] "One who says 'I have only Torah' (meaning learning without practice), lacks even Torah"; revealing that the ultimate purpose of Jewish learning is practical action.

This idea was fundamental to the Rebbe's theology and overall worldview.

A Practical Guide to Life

A scholar once came to see the Rebbe to ask a question that was bothering him. His exploration of Jewish texts had brought him to study Maimonides, the great Jewish teacher and philosopher of the Middle Ages. Maimonides authored several monumental works, including *Mishneh Torah,* a comprehensive compendium of practical Jewish Law, and *Moreh Nevuchim—A Guide for the Perplexed*—which is a work of philosophy.

The man observed, "Each of these works reflects a very different, and sometimes contradictory, face of this legendary Jewish teacher! But which of his works represents the real Maimonides?"

The Rebbe responded: "The true Maimonides is seen in his work on Jewish law. It is a practical work with clear instructions for life."

With a hint of a smile, the Rebbe advised: "Better to study the *Mishneh Torah* and learn how to live as a Jew than to memorize *A Guide for the Perplexed* and know the answer to questions you didn't even have."[408]

Indeed, this idea was so important to him that, as the following story conveys, he saw it as an essential feature in religious and spiritual leadership, and criticized its absence as a fundamental shortcoming in other approaches to leadership.

I Think, Therefore I'm Not

A writer researching a book about great Jewish scholars and leaders mentioned a well-known and important modern figure during a conversation with the Rebbe.

"He was a wonderful man," the Rebbe commented, before his voice trailed off.

"What is it?" the writer prodded.

"Well," answered the Rebbe, "if there were one critique I would offer, it would be that his writings lack *tachlis*—a bottom line or focused points of action. His followers are left unsure of how to act upon the knowledge and inspiration he imparted."[409]

When a great speaker finishes speaking, his audience

erupts in applause and goes home. When a great leader finishes speaking, his audience jumps up and exclaims, "Let's march!"

Organize or Mobilize

The following is an excerpt from an interview with Ariel Sharon, the former prime minister of Israel:

"The Rebbe was perhaps the greatest believer I've ever met in the G-d-given strength of the Jewish People. He most definitely believed in the strength of the Jewish Nation, and he felt that Jews don't believe enough in their own strength.

"The Rebbe once said to me, 'The Jewish People must be mobilized.' When I concurred that they must be organized, he corrected me, meanwhile demonstrating his exceptional wisdom and wit: 'Not organized,' he said, 'mobilized.'

"What does it mean to organize the Jewish People? A few Jewish leaders get together for dinner, and the next day the newspapers report that they came to the conclusion that they must get together for another dinner....

"When it comes to the Jewish People, a different approach must be taken. The Jewish people must be directed and instructed—they must be shown what needs to be done. It's not about organizing the Jewish People, it's about mobilizing them."

Further on, their conversation turned toward Jewish education and identity. Here, too, the Rebbe stressed the importance of actual experience over abstract identification. In the words of Sharon: "Although I am not a religious Jew, I am a Jew, and for me, to be a Jew is the most important thing. I worry about the future of the Jewish People, and I believe that Jewish education is very, very important.... Whenever I had an opportunity, I would speak to university students. I would say to them, 'The Jewish People are a nation. Judaism is not only a religion—it is a combination of religion and nationalism. Take pride that you are part of the greatest nation in the world.'

When I shared this with the Rebbe, he asked me, "But what did you tell them to *do*?"

"To identify as Jews," I replied.

The Rebbe said, "For a young person who grew up in a traditional Jewish household, perhaps identifying as a Jew will hold him for one generation, but this alone will not guarantee the future of the Jewish People. Identification must be coupled with action—with practical observance of the commandments."

The Rebbe went on to explain that everything in Judaism is connected with action; settling the Land of Israel is an action, keeping Shabbat is an action...

"One can always add," the Rebbe continued. "No one is perfect. I, too, am not complete in the *mitzvot*. The fact that I do not live in the Land of Israel makes me incomplete."[410]

So many people stop their Jewish journey before it has even begun, because they are afraid that there's no point if they don't fulfill every commandment. This all-or-nothing approach robbed so many people of their own Jewish experience. It also deprived the world of their good deeds. In the Rebbe's eyes, it was not about doing everything, but about doing something. Each act has unlimited potential to bring light into our lives and into the world.

This focus on the practical expressed itself in many areas. Below are but a few stories that further highlight this point.

We Were Created to Act

A group of Chabad *shluchim* from across Canada arranged to meet with Canadian Prime Minister Brian Mulroney.

They purchased a beautiful silver Kiddush cup to present to the prime minister as a gift. They planned on explaining to the prime minister that every human being, especially a government leader, has the ability to figuratively "make Kiddush"—to sanctify his or her surroundings. The gift of a Kiddush cup would symbolically remind the prime minister of this noble thought and intention.

The day before the meeting, R. Zalman Aaron Grossbaum, a senior *shliach* in Canada, wrote to the Rebbe telling him of their planned appointment with the prime minister and the gift they had prepared.

The Rebbe's response proved enlightening.

"Of what practical use is a Kiddush cup to the prime minister? [As he was not obligated by Jewish Law to recite the Kiddush.] I would suggest, instead, that you present him with an English prayer book, as it includes prayers such as *Modeh Ani*—a prayer recited each morning thanking G-d for giving us life—which are relevant and meaningful to all humans, Jews and non-Jews alike."[411]

Don't Forget to Include the Instructions

During the 1960s, a newly-appointed campus rabbi placed an

advertisement in the university paper promoting his activities and offerings for the upcoming festival of Pesach. The clever ad played on contemporary themes that would resonate with Jewish students, calling on them to "Take up arms for the cause of liberty, like your radical ancestors in Egypt!"

Proud of the contemporary aesthetic and current terminology, the rabbi sent a copy of the ad to the Rebbe, expecting to be congratulated.

The Rebbe sent back the following message: "In future advertisements for Jewish festivals, remember to mention the relevant *mitzvot* that must be fulfilled."[412]

Take-Away

A seasoned rabbi and motivational speaker once shared his self-doubts with the Rebbe. "Rebbe," he said, "I am considered a gifted public speaker, and I must have given thousands of talks, yet I wonder: how many of my talks actually hit home? I don't see practical changes in the lives of my listeners."

The Rebbe responded: "Our Sages teach, 'Words that come from the heart enter the heart.' If you speak sincerely and with passion, you can be assured that your words will enter people's hearts, whether you see it or not.

"If, however, you want to be able to *observe* the actual change you inspire in your audiences," the Rebbe continued, "I suggest that you not speak in abstract terms. Teach your audiences a practical Jewish tradition, and leave them with an action point, even if it's only one thing, and even if it seems minimal. This is how you inspire change."[413]

One would be hard pressed to find a talk of the Rebbe

that did not contain or conclude with a call to practical action. In this way, the Rebbe transformed every one of his teachings, no matter how esoteric, abstract, or impractical it may have seemed, into a direct marching order.

PART II: TEN STEP PROGRAM FOR DESIGNING A LIFE OF POSITIVITY

THE REBBE WOULD OFTEN cite a teaching of the Mishnah[414]—"*hamaaseh hu ha'ikar,*" which means that the essential thing is the deed, not abstract study. Otherwise, teachings and words, no matter how beautiful, wise, or aesthetic, are *devarim beteilim* "empty expressions" and their power to move and inspire actions was wasted.

To that end, we will now highlight ten practical steps that will empower you to design a life of positivity. While there are countless other powerful instructions throughout the recorded encounters with the Rebbe, we have designed a program of ten essential directives to help you reframe your perspective in order to see yourself and the world in a more positive way. In Part III of this chapter, "A User's Guide to Practical Action," we conclude this work with a beginning for you: A program of specific written exercises to help you establish and maintain your own personal "Positivity Bias" in every aspect of your life.

You may want to keep a journal to record your progress

and share it with others. When you make a decisive shift in your life, it becomes easier for others to do so as well. Imagine creating a wave of positivity in the world!

It all starts with you.

I. Choose Your News

One of our main interfaces with the world is the news. We understand both current and historical events through the narrow prism and the naturally biased narrative of the news we watch, the websites we visit, and the books and papers we read. These usually present the most urgent, sensational, tragic, and fear-inducing viewpoints. We are fed only the things that draw attention, and they shape our view of life.

It is thus in the nature of news media to be disproportionately filled with disturbing and depressing stories. But that is not the whole picture of life—even though readers may think it is.

In an encounter with *New York Times* correspondent Ari Goldman, the Rebbe urged him to remember to "report good news."[415] This humble but pointed request influenced Goldman to report more regularly about things that were going right, not just those that were going wrong.

The Rebbe's advice to an influential journalist can be expanded to consumers of media as well. Meaning that as consumers, we need to be conscientious about our media diet. When we recognize how deeply our moods and mindsets are affected, and how influential such information is upon our psyche, we become aware of how important it is to consciously curate our data intake and nurture a healthy, balanced, and positive worldview.

Don't just passively read the bad news that is broadcast everywhere; rather, actively look for the good news that is quietly happening all around you!

2. Delete Cynicism

We live in a world that is more cynical than ever. Satire, sarcasm, and scorn have replaced compassion and civility in national discourse and have become the chosen tone of communication among many news outlets. Public scandals are used to teach and reinforce the general mistrust of leaders of any kind. Cynics and skeptics are seen as sophisticated, witty, and enlightened. People of faith and open-minded idealism, on the other hand, are viewed as naive, child-like, and uncritical.

The problem with cynicism is that it shrinks and darkens our belief in the power and potential for positive change within ourselves, in others, and in the world around us, further perpetuating a vicious cycle of distrust and despair.

In private encounters and public addresses,[416] the Rebbe emphasized that only through countering default cynicism and actively embracing educated optimism can we see the true import of our lives and move toward reaching our highest potential.

3. Share Good News

The Rebbe once followed up with an individual who had previously asked for a blessing for someone undergoing a difficult challenge. "How is he doing?" the Rebbe asked. "Thank G-d, everything worked out in the end," the man answered. "Why is it," said the Rebbe, "that people freely share their bad news, but fail to follow up when there is good news?"[417]

After a day of working or running errands, we often readily share the negative things that happened. If we have ten interactions with people and nine are positive and one is negative, we usually dwell on the negative one and feel a need to talk about it. This is only natural; we're holding onto it because it still needs resolution.

In fact, a number of scientific studies have suggested that negativity and complaints are powerful attention magnets and create a "negativity bias." Therefore, it requires an equally powerful intentionality and consciousness to become free of its gravitational field and create a "positivity bias" within our inner universes.

One practical way to make the shift toward positivity is to proactively change our default responses to questions about our day or life. Instead of immediately offering the most negative experience or challenge we are currently dealing with, try to mention something positive—at least as a starting point. This is not to say that we should ignore the negativity or challenges in our lives; we can always come back to them. The point is to begin by mentioning a highlight of our day or something exciting we are working on.

Prioritize sharing positive reports about your experiences.

Another deceptively simple way to positively influence the course and cadence of our conversations is to make a point of greeting others warmly, with a smile, and with a positive demeanor. By turning up the joy and warmth levels in our greetings and interactions, we elicit the same in others, thus generating an undercurrent of goodwill and positive energy that can elevate each encounter.

In a related anecdote: When media outlets began asking for a photograph of the Rebbe for publishing purposes, he requested that a photograph with a smile be selected.[418] Additionally, when a celebrated Chasidic artist was painting a portrait of him, the Rebbe asked that his serious expression in the painting be changed to a smile if this would not be too expensive.[419]

Not only does consciously crafting a positive demeanor impact our own joy and positivity levels, but as a side effect, our company will be more enjoyable and desirable to others due to the magnetic power of positivity.

4. Drop Negative Self-Talk

A man visiting the Rebbe bemoaned his spiritual state. "Rebbe, something must be wrong with me! I have spent a lot of time in the company of saintly individuals, but their example doesn't seem to affect me. I must be insensitive to spirituality!" The Rebbe interjected, "Just as it is forbidden to speak disparagingly about someone else—even if speaking the absolute truth—it is also forbidden to speak negatively about oneself!"[420]

It is important to free ourselves from limiting and self-deprecating words and thoughts. These create and reinforce negative beliefs about our capabilities and only serve to hold us back. Some seem to think that self-judgment is positively motivational. But as Chasidic thought teaches, emotions are like children. Just as a healthy parent would not insult their child, so too, we shouldn't insult our inner selves. Whatever you wouldn't say to someone else in decent company, don't say to yourself.

When negative self-talk is habitual, changing it requires proactive effort. By becoming aware of the pattern and identifying our triggers, automatic reactions, and words of self-denigration, we can begin to eradicate them from our mental vocabulary. The secret to this process is expressed in the following anecdote:

A woman who once complained to the Rebbe that she regularly experienced unwanted thoughts received this directive: "The mind cannot think two different thoughts at the same time. The next time you want to get rid of a thought, don't try to fight it; simply replace it with a different one."[421]

Through this process of becoming aware of and actively replacing our negative self-talk with kind words of affirmation, our inner narrative and resultant self-image will gradually be transformed into one that is confident and empowered.

5. Praise Effusively, Not Economically

A *shliach* who was stationed in a particularly challenging location once came to see the Rebbe. The Rebbe gently asked, "How is your relationship with your wife?" He then asked the *shliach* to write down the dynamics of his marriage. The *shliach* freely elaborated on his wife's many virtues, and ended with the words, "Perhaps I should not have been so profuse in describing my wife's qualities."

The Rebbe examined the page, crossed out the word "not," and underlined the word "should," leaving the sentence to read: "I **should** have been so profuse in describing my wife's qualities."[422]

Create a habit of regularly offering others generous words of praise and compliment. It may not seem obvious, but every human being, no matter how accomplished or altruistic, feels uplifted when acknowledged and affirmed.

Also, avoid qualifying your compliments—they need not be earned, deserved, or reciprocated. Be full-hearted, not begrudging, and do not take others for granted.

Some people fear that freely giving compliments will place them at a disadvantage in a relationship. The truth is, however, that kindness begets kindness and generosity of spirit is contagious.

6. Focus on the Present

Following the terrifying Crown Heights Riots in 1991, a community leader suggested arranging tours of Crown Heights to show that the area was back to normal. The Rebbe advised: "In principle, it's a good idea, but it [might highlight] that there was something negative here in the past.... Emphasize the positive [in the present], not mentioning that it was once otherwise."[423]

The Rebbe was saying that the community or certain locations on the tour shouldn't be defined negatively by what happened in the past, such as: "Here is where a terrible event in the riots occurred, and as you can see now things are fine again." The Rebbe wanted to allow visitors to see and experience the community's joy, sincerity, and togetherness in the present, untainted by the negative context of a previous tragedy.

In a related encounter, the Rebbe told a man who had been incarcerated, "Focus on the benefits of being free rather than dwelling on memories of your prison time. This may be difficult at first, but you can do it."[424]

Sometimes we view our current life circumstances through the lens of previous negative experiences. Comparing good with bad colors the good. When we carry anger, fear, or sadness from the past into the present, it makes room for its continued influence.

One area in our lives where this issue is particularly pertinent is in our personal relationships, especially with our loved ones, with whom we can fall into the trap of holding onto previous mistakes and disappointments.

We often engage with them as if the past is present, and we view them through the prism of our judgments. The images that we have created of them do not reflect reality. Visualize how different our relationships would be if we released our grip on past hurts and saw people with new eyes.

G-d creates the world and our lives every day—and moment—anew. Let us emulate our Creator and live our lives in kind, approaching each day and every encounter afresh.

7. Surround Yourself with Good People

Mr. Freddy Hager, a businessman from London, visited the

Rebbe in search of guidance and blessing. During a private audience, the Rebbe advised:[425] "Make it a point to meet upbeat, positive people.... Look for and interact with people of good will at work."

We are deeply affected by our environment and the people around us. Our Sages taught that a neighbor—a close stranger—can be more influential than even a friend or a loved one. Make it a point to find and associate with the positive people in your environment. Let go of socializing with individuals who are negative or cynical, or who make you feel inadequate, insecure, drain your energy, or bring out the worst in you. Even if an interaction with such a person seems enjoyable and exciting in the moment, sense how you feel afterward.

In the words of R. Yosei the Kohen,[426] the Talmudic sage who traveled the world searching for the best advice for a happy life: "A good neighbor [is paramount]!"

8. Do What You Love

A British school teacher visited the Rebbe for a private audience. He handed the Rebbe his note, outlining some of his innovations and accomplishments in the classroom over the previous year. After reading the note, the Rebbe looked up and responded gently: "While it is obvious from your report that you are devoted to your mission, I do not perceive that you find joy in your work."[427]

It's not enough to be good at what you do; the key to success is loving what you do. You can do something you don't enjoy for a few years, perhaps, but there will come a time when it starts to build resentment. We are programmed to pursue contentment; we are not meant to force ourselves to be productive.

This is reflected in another story. The Rebbe once asked a leading rabbi to continue at his community position in South Africa rather than moving to Israel. "But I do not want you to stay there because you 'received an order' from me. You should only do it *out of conviction and love*."[428]

Similarly, when a young couple decided that they were ready to serve as *shluchim*, they signed a letter of commitment. The Rebbe met with them and asked the wife, "Did you sign this letter happily or because you felt compelled?" Only when she confirmed that she was willing and glad to selflessly serve any Jewish community did the Rebbe give the couple his blessing and approval.

In all of these stories, the Rebbe consistently expresses the liberating truth that we only reach the ultimate joy and fulfillment in life when our passion and profession intersect, and where our source and sense of purpose, productivity, pleasure, and profit converge and coalesce.

If you do what you love, you will love what you do.

9. Lose Yourself

A person once wrote a letter to the Rebbe while in a state of despondency: "I wake up each day sad and apprehensive. I can't concentrate. I find it hard to pray. I keep the commandments, but I find no spiritual satisfaction. I go to synagogue, but I feel alone. I begin to wonder what life is about. I would like the Rebbe's help." The Rebbe replied without writing a single word. He merely circled the first word of every sentence and sent the letter back. The person understood and entered a path of spiritual recovery. The circled word at the beginning of every sentence was "I."[429]

Over-focusing on ourselves is the root cause of suffering and negativity. Stop thinking about yourself so much. Your ego can never be a source of happiness. Instead of seeing yourself through your own eyes, start seeing yourself through the eyes of G-d, Who chose to be in a relationship with your soul. Real joy comes from stepping out of yourself and into the Infinite.

A student once asked the Rebbe, "How can one be joyful all the time, as taught in Chasidic philosophy?" The Rebbe replied, "Reflect upon the fact that you are a finite creature whom the Creator has given the privilege to be bound with the Infinite through the *mitzvot*. If you keep in mind that your soul is a part of G-d, how can you not be constantly joyful?" From then on, whenever the Rebbe would see him at a Chasidic gathering, he would ask with a twinkle in his eye, "So, how is the joy going?"[430]

Only when we shift our focus from our personal productivity and achievements to our unconditional bond with G-d do we have a framework for consistent joy. Ego-driven achievements are dependent on external expectations and circumstances. G-d's unconditional love for us is not dependent on anything. A soul-based life is rooted in the bliss of "being" rather than the anxiety of "becoming."

10. Become Other-Centered

The Rebbe once inquired about a woman's father who was unwell and in the hospital. In response to the daughter's report, the Rebbe said: "When he sets out to teach others and raise their spirits, this will automatically have a positive effect on him."[431]

A central teaching of the Rebbe is to replace our constant thoughts about our own wellbeing with thoughts about the wellbeing of others. Through this practice, we can craft an other-centered life regardless of our circumstances. Actively attuning ourselves to the lives and struggles of others will help us take notice of—and reach out to—those in need.

This shift can also involve major life decisions. A young man consulted the Rebbe on choosing a career path. "If making money is not the main priority for you, I would encourage you to go into education," the Rebbe replied.[432] As a teacher, he would have the opportunity to produce and nurture emotionally healthy children and set them on course for a successful life.

The beauty of this story is that the Rebbe did not tell the man to choose one way or another. He merely pointed out that if becoming wealthy was not his priority, he would be free to choose a career overtly guided by a deeper calling. This would allow him to earn a living while bringing life to others.

In a related story, a newly engaged couple wrote to the Rebbe asking that they be blessed with warmth and positivity in their home. "See to it that others have warmth and positivity," urged the Rebbe, "and as a result, your lives will be warm and positive, as well."[433]

Helping others is the *most effective form of "self-help."*

PART III:
A USER'S GUIDE TO PRACTICAL ACTION

AS CHASIDUT TEACHES, THE goal of the Torah is to be manifest on the level of action, particularly in the performance of the spiritual practices called *mitzvot*. Therefore, it is never enough to allow its teachings, no matter how inspiring or wise they are, to remain in the realm of thought alone. Truth seeks expression in the world and in our lives. This last chapter concludes with an effort to help the reader put the transformative principles contained within this book into practice. For it is only through such practice and experience that we are able to personalize, internalize, and actualize these teachings, empowering us to create a positivity bias of our own.

With this in mind, I have selected nine practices that can be helpful toward this redemptive end. You may find these practices easier to implement with the aid of a mentor or friend with whom you can share your commitment and experiences.

1. Create a Daily Gratitude List

Set aside a few minutes each day, after reciting the morning blessings[434] and before reciting the Shema prayer when retiring at night,[435] to write down a minimum of five things that you currently have in your life that you are grateful for. Think about each for a moment, relish it. Now say "Thank You" to G-d for each one of these blessings. The next time you feel yourself starting to become preoccupied with anxieties, stop for a moment and recall some of these fundamental blessings. For further insight, see Chapter 2: Dwell on the Positive.

2. Identify and Reframe Your Negative Language

Commit yourself for one day to be aware of your language. Record any negative speech or even any negative phrasing that you use, and review the list at the end of the day. Do you notice any patterns or repeated phrases of negative speech?

Select a particular person, subject, or saying from this list that you often use or speak about in negative terms. How might you rephrase or reframe your language in this case to reflect a more positive outlook? Now commit yourself to implementing that verbal shift in a positive direction. For further insight, see Chapter 10: Positive Language.

3. Identify the People You Resent and Reframe Your View of Them

Think of a particular person of whom you have a negative opinion. Write down the most recent incident that gave rise to your negative interpretations of their actions or motives. Now, think about the same situation from the other person's point of view. What might they be dealing with or trying to balance in their handling of the situation? What commitments might complicate their involvement or intentions in the situation? What interests or goals of theirs might be threatened or compromised by you directly or by this situation in general? Is it possible that there is a major problem in their lives—even a tragedy—that you know nothing about? On a separate sheet of paper, write down all of these counter-points or contextualizing factors to balance out your prior judgments. Read both pages and breathe in compassion and patience, while exhaling judgment and arrogance. For further insight, see Chapter 6: Seek Merit, Not Mistakes.

4. List the Positive Qualities of Three People in Your Life

Think about three people in your life: a) Someone you are close with, b) someone you work with, and c) someone you find challenging but must interact with. Write down three positive things for each person: a) A compliment, b) some sort of empowerment, and c) something unique about them that you appreciate. Try to remember these positive aspects of each person and look for an opportunity to verbally express them to them. This is, of course, a good general practice to adopt for anyone you come in contact with—constantly strive to say something positive or empowering in every interaction. For further insight, see Chapter 9: Lashon Tov.

5. Record a Setback and See How It Was a Springboard

Think of a setback you have experienced in your life that was especially challenging and difficult. Try to locate the positive outcomes of that setback and write them down. What did you learn? What were you forced to overcome? In what areas did you grow? How are you a better, stronger, more conscious or caring person because of that experience? Then, insert the answers into this formula (tweaking as necessary for your personal purposes):

"Before I...(insert setback or challenge here), I...(insert old paradigm here—thought/felt/acted/etc.). Now I...(insert new paradigm here—know/feel/do/etc.)."

After the writing exercise, read the list aloud to yourself. Keep it and return to it—or add to it—as needed. For further insight, see Chapter 20: Setback or Springboard?

6. Make a List of Your Five Highest Values

Think about and write down five of your highest Jewish values. What morals, ideals, commitments, or allegiances do you hold most dear? Now choose your three most core principles from this list. Which of these values are non-negotiable or most worth living for? Write out these three pillars of your conscience on a separate paper, so you can return to and contemplate these sacred commitments regularly and impress them deep into your soul. For further insight, see Chapter 23: A Rebbe Revealed.

7. Redeem Unresolved Issues from Your Past

Call to mind a past experience that was challenging or painful at the time and still feels unresolved; something that has impacted the way you view and define yourself and the world. It could be a blown opportunity, a broken trust, an injustice, or a seemingly random "act of G-d" or catastrophe. Through the lens of redemptive reframing, imagine having a conversation with your past self, the "you" who lived through that experience. What would you say to that person to bring a sense of healing and understanding to their soul? Either write these consoling words down or speak them out loud in a form of personal prayer. For further insight, see Chapter 25: Reframing and Redeeming the Past.

8. Identify the Silver Linings You've Experienced

Think about an experience from your more distant past that you felt you could not possibly survive or recover from. Now take a moment to recognize that here you are, and you have indeed survived. Now, if possible, think back on the situation and write down for yourself: What were the specific events, people, practices, or experiences that helped you get through that challenging time? Did you recognize them in the moment for the redemptive role they were playing? Write a letter to a person, teacher, book, teaching, practice, event, or anything else that helped you survive and grow from that place of fear, pain, or brokenness. You can choose to send the letter or keep it as your own reminder of the hidden redeemers in your life. For further insight, see Chapter 26: Silver Linings.

9. Commit to Good Deeds as a Positive Approach to Loss

Who is someone you were close with or means a lot to you who has passed on? What is the anniversary of their passing? What is a good deed or mitzvah you could do in their name and honor that would bring their soul *nachas,* deep pleasure? A few examples from Jewish tradition are wrapping *tefillin* (for men), lighting Shabbat candles (for women), giving *tzedakah* (charitable gifts) or studying Torah in their honor. Commit yourself to this holy deed on their *yahrtzeit*. For further insight, see Chapter 27.

L'CHAIM!

ONE BITTERLY COLD NIGHT, R. Shmuel Munkes embarked on a journey to his Rebbe, R. Schneur Zalman of Liadi. The wind pierced his bones, and he was relieved to see a wagon passing by. The wagon stopped, and the driver happily offered R. Shmuel a ride. The driver was a liquor merchant, and R. Shmuel made himself comfortable among the many bottles of liquor that filled the wagon. Still chilled to the core, R. Shmuel realized that drinking some of the vodka would warm him. The driver agreed, and after drinking the vodka, R. Shmuel felt warm through and through.

When R. Shmuel entered the room of R. Schneur Zalman for a private audience, he said, "The Rebbe has taught his Chasidim that they must take lessons from every life experience," and went on to recount the events of his journey. "The air had chilled me to the bone. I sat among the bottles of liquor for quite a while, and although liquor has the power to warm a person, I still remained ice-cold. Only when I actually drank the vodka did I become warm."

R. Shmuel said that this taught him an important lesson about Divine service. A person might dwell in an environment of Torah, surrounded by inspiration, yet it can only have a great effect on him and warm his soul once it is internalized.[436]

Books, like bottles, are exceptional vessels. But every book needs a reader to open it in order for its light to enter into the world. Similarly, words and ideas also contain great power to motivate and transform people—but only if they are taken seriously enough to be acted upon. If a word remains inert on a page or trapped inside our heads, it is as good as fine wine in a corked bottle. Its true flavor and potential is only fulfilled when it is taken deeply into the core of the person's very being. For this to occur, we must "taste and see that G-d is good."[437]

It is our sincere prayer that each of you, in your own way, imbibe these teachings, bringing them into your lives and relationships through continued reflection, passionate conversation, and practical action. May we all merit to see the Infinite light and Divine goodness shining out from within ourselves, within each other, and within the world, always and forever! This is the essence of the Rebbe's Positivity Bias.

ENDNOTES

INTRODUCTION

1 *My Encounter* interview (JEM) with Mr. Charles Roth, March 2, 2010.

2 *Igrot Kodesh*, vol. 20, p. 41.

3 As told by his son, R. Menachem Junik.

CHAPTER 1

4 Ch. 5, v. 1.

5 This is the work of transforming reality into that which it already is by shifting our dualistic perspective to see the unity of G-d, revealing the inherent goodness beneath the surface of all phenomena. This is what is meant by the Kabbalistic concept of accessing the "fruit that is beneath the peel." Our physical eyes see only the shell of reality. The eyes of spirit perceive the sweet and nourishing fruit within. Acknowledging this truth and living from that place is what enables us to fulfill our purpose to tend G-d's garden.

6 *Sichot Kodesh 5732*, vol. 1, p. 362; *Living Torah* (JEM) program 19, accessible at www.chabad.org/253998.

CHAPTER 2

7 See above, Introduction, footnote 3.

8 The Rebbe's letter can be seen at www.chabad.org/1910419.

9 See *Igrot Kodesh*, vol. 4, p. 261.

10 *Igrot Kodesh*, vol. 12, pp. 270-271. This letter can also be seen at www.chabad.org/72907.

11 *Dawidowicz-Kulski Wedding Memento*, 11 Elul 5778, p. 8. The full text of the Rebbe's note can be seen at: www.teshura.com/teshurapdf/Dawid-owicz%20-Kulski%20-%2011%20Elul%205778.pdf —translation provided by *A Chassidisher Derher*.

12 See *Menachot* 43b.

13 As told by R. Dovid Schochet, One by One (JEM) p. 74, accessible at www.chabad.org/4445923.

14 As told by R. Nochum Stilerman, Here's My Story (JEM) No. 234, accessible at www.chabad.org/3728424.

15 Of interest is that the Rebbe chose the *Modeh Ani* to explain the unique contribution of Chasidism in interpreting the Torah beyond the four traditional levels of *peshat, remez, drush,* and *sod* (the plain, the allusive, the homiletic, and esoteric meanings). See *On the Essence of Chasidut* (Kehot, 2003).

16 Additionally, the *Modeh Ani* prayer thanks G-d for another day before it has begun. This is a truly beautiful expression of Judaism's positivity bias! By consciously connecting to such inherent goodness at the outset, we are that much more likely to activate or appreciate it throughout the day.

17 *Igrot Kodesh,* vol. 12, pp. 270-271. The Rebbe's letter can be seen at www.chabad.org/72907.

18 As told by R. Chaim Jacobs, *Here's My Story* (JEM) No. 119, accessible at www.chabad.org/2948324.

CHAPTER 3

19 As told by R. Jacob Biderman, *Living Torah* (JEM) program 459, accessible at www.chabad.org/2243631.

20 *Man's Search for Meaning,* p. 66.

21 See *Igrot Kodesh,* vol. 22, p. 227.

22 The Rebbe's relationship with Frankl is evident also from the following episode. In the early 1970s (around 1973-74), an individual studying psychology at the University of Leeds visited the Rebbe. He had begun exploring the teachings of Judaism at the Rabbinical College of America in Morriston, NJ, and asked the Rebbe how to deal with the numerous conflicts between the contemporary study of psychology and the paradigms of Judaism. The Rebbe suggested that he correspond with Victor Frankl on the matter. "If you wish," the Rebbe added, "you can use my name as a reference." (www.theyeshiva.net/896)

23 For example, a religious Jewish psychiatrist, Jacob Greenwald, related that he was once invited by the Rebbe for a visit. The Rebbe wanted to know if he was familiar with the writings of Victor Frankl and if they could be integrated into a Torah perspective of therapy. For more on this, see essay by R. Yosef Yitzchak Jacobson, at: www.theyeshiva.net/896.

CHAPTER 4

24 As told by R. Baruch Oberlander, Chabad *shliach* to Hungary.

25 *The Letter and the Spirit*, vol. 1, pp. 52–53.

26 What is unique about this letter is that it was written a week after the Rebbe suffered a massive heart-attack on the holiday of Shemini Atzeret 5738 (1977).

For weeks following the heart attack, the Rebbe remained confined in his office-turned-hospital-room. It is amazing to note that at this difficult time, the Rebbe took the time to address a small detail that the child wrote in his letter.

27 Written in 1975.

28 From a letter dated 21 Sivan, 5725 (June 21, 1965), which can be seen at www.chabad.org/1899570.

29 *Hilchot Geirushin* 2:20.

30 *Chagigah* 27a, *Berachot* 57a, et al.

31 As told by R. Alter Bukiet, *shliach* to Lexington, Massachusetts, who heard the story from the man with whom it happened.

32 *Sanhedrin* 44a.

33 See *Tanya*, ch. 24.

34 *Sotah* 3a. The basis for this Talmudic exegesis is the biblical verse (Numbers 5:12) describing the *sotah*, a woman suspected of adultery: *Any man, if his wife will go astray* (*tisteh* in Hebrew). Instead of using the more linguistically correct word *titeh*, the Torah uses *tisteh* (from the root word *shtut*, folly), to teach that people sin only because of a spirit of folly.

35 Genesis 1:27.

36 Deuteronomy 32:26.

37 *Torat Menachem—Hitvaaduyot 5742*, vol. 1, pp. 109-110.

38 See *Likkutei Sichot*, vol. 2, p. 409.

39 *Niddah* 30b.

40 As told by R. Tzvi Hersh Weinreb, *One by One* (JEM), p. 26. Video accessible at www.chabad.org/2618592.

41 Accessible at www.chabad.org/66878. As stated there, this is clearly a paraphrase of the conversation based on Mr. Shamir's recollections.

42 In a similar vein, the Rebbe once shared: "The term "returning to the source" [used to describe people who embrace the path of the Torah] is inappropriate. The word "source" implies a faraway entity, one that one must travel great distances to reach. The reality, however, is that because (as stated in the beginning of the *Tanya*) we all have a divine soul, we do not need to traverse great distances to arrive at our source. It is there already in our hearts and minds; we need only to remove the cover that conceals it." See *Torat Menachem—Hitvaaduyot 5723*, vol. 2. pp. 224-225.

43 Deuteronomy 33:4.

CHAPTER 5

44 Accessible at www.chabad.org/66877

45 As told by Mr. Len Weksler, *One by One* (JEM), p. 260. Video accessible at www.chabad.org/1339436.

46 The full conversation is accessible at: www.chabad.org/392177.

47 Cited in J. Immanuel Schochet, *Chassidic Dimesions*, p. 210 (Kehot, 1990). See also Adin Steinzaltz, *My Rebbe*, p. 3.

48 *Igrot Kodesh*, vol. 22, pp. 129-130; translation of the latter can be seen at www.chabad.org/64036.

49 *Shabbat* 97a.

50 As told by Mr. George Rohr at a convention for the Rebbe's emissaries in 1996. A video of the exchange is accessible at www.chabad.org/4429924.

51 *Likkutei Sichot*, vol. 2, p. 499.

52 *Sefer Hasichot 5705*, p. 41.

53 Accessible at www.chabad.org/1200.

54 *Seeds of Wisdom*, vol. 2 (JEM), p. 52. Accessible at www.chabad.org/395794.

55 *Living Torah* (JEM) program 59, accessible at www.chabad.org/319001.

56 Isaiah 8.

CHAPTER 6

57 As told by R. Yehudah Leib Dubov, citing R. Eliyahu Simpson, secretary of R. Yosef Yitzchak who was present at the time.

58 *Avot* 1:6.

59 *To Know and to Care* (SIE), vol. 1, p. 75, accessible at www.chabad.org/78663.

60 In a letter dated 16 Tammuz 5720 (July 11, 1960), can be seen at www.chabad.org/2187478.

61 *Kfar Chabad Magazine*, Issue 1737, p. 54.

62 *Sichot Kodesh 5741*, vol. 1, p. 345.

63 Highlights of the interview are accessible at www.chabad.org/61921.

64 For more on the Rebbe's vehement opposition to justifying tragedy—and the Holocaust in particular—on religious grounds, see *A Time To Heal: The Rebbe's Response to Loss & Tragedy* (Ezra Press, 2015), ch. 26.

65 I heard the following story from my father-in law, R. Yosef Katzman, who heard it directly from the manager of the original organization with whom it happened.

66 *Sanhedrin* 18b.

CHAPTER 7

67 *Chagigah* 15a.

68 *Torat Menachem—Hitvaaduyot 5742*, vol. 3, p. 1456 ff.

69 *Avot* 4:20.

70 Ibid.

71 See *Likkutei Sichot*, vol. 3, pp. 747-750.

72 Ibid.

73 *Sanhedrin* 38b.

74 Genesis 25:28.

75 *Torat Menachem—Sefer Hamaamarim 5724*, p. 54.

76 See *Likkutei Sichot*, vol. 4, pp. 1041-1047.

77 *Shabbat Parashat Shelach*, 5740 (1980).

78 *Torat Kohanim*, beginning of *Acharei*. See also *Vayikra Rabbah* 20:8, *Bamidbar Rabbah* 3:23, *Tanchuma, Acharei* 6.

79 *Vayikra Rabbah* 20:9.

80 Ibid.

81 Ibid.

82 Leviticus 10:1.

83 See Nachmanides and *Rabbeinu Bechaya* ad loc.; *Raavad* to *Sifra*; *Ritva* to *Yoma* 53a.

84 R. Eliezer in *Torat Kohanim* 10:1.

85 Bar Kapara in *Vayikra Rabbah*.

86 R. Yishmael in *Vayikra Rabbah* 12:1.

87 See Exodus 30:21. This the opinion of R. Mani of She'ab, R. Yehoshua of Siknin, and R. Yochanan in the name of R. Levi in *Vayikra Rabbah*, ibid.

88 Exodus 24:9-11. This opinion is recorded in the Midrash, ibid.

89 *Likkutei Sichot*, vol. 3, p. 987. See also vol. 7, p. 125.

90 Leviticus 16:1.

91 See *Likkutei Sichot*, vol. 18, pp. 187–195.

92 Isaiah 11:1-9.

93 Numbers 16:3.

94 The basis of this idea can be found in *Likkutei Torah, Korach* 54b. See also *Or Hatorah, Korach,* p. 686; *Likkutei Sichot,* vol. 18, pp. 187–195.

95 *Megillah* 11a.

96 *Shemot Rabbah* 1:30.

97 *Yalkut Shimoni,* Exodus 167.

98 *Shemot Rabbah* 1:29.

99 *Midrash Tehilim* 106:5.

100 *Shemot Rabbah* 1:30.

101 See *Likkutei Sichot,* vol. 31, p. 6.

102 *Nachalat Yaakov,* quoted in *Siftei Chachamim,* Exodus 5:15.

103 Exodus 5:15.

104 Ibid. 5:14.

105 Ibid. 5:21.

106 End of *Sukkah.*

107 6 Tishrei 5735 (1974). To view a video of this talk, see *Living Torah* (JEM) program 225, accessible at www.chabad.org/942194.

108 An audio recording of the talk is accessible at www.chabad.org/551950.

109 See *Hayom Yom,* 21 Sivan and 25 Tammuz.

110 See *Likkutei Sichot,* vol. 11, p. 144; vol. 24, p. 5 ff.

111 Exodus 32:1.

112 Deuteronomy 34:10-12.

113 Exodus 32:32.

114 *Shabbat* 87a.

115 See *Hayom Yom,* 28 Nissan. See also, *Igrot Kodesh* by R. Yosef Yitzchak Schneersohn, vol. 3, p. 425.

CHAPTER 8

116 *Avot* 2:9.

117 R. Avraham Yaakov of Sadigura (1928-2013), on 14 Tevet, 5744 (1983). Transcript published in *Torat Menachem—Hitvaaduyot 5744,* vol. 2, p. 750 ff. For a recording of the conversation, see *Living Torah* (JEM) program 619, accessible at www.chabad.org/3377076.

118 From time to time, the Rebbe would send emissaries to the former Soviet Union. Posing as a tourist, an emissary would have clandestine meetings with members of the Lubavitch underground who lived in constant fear of detection and could only dream of leaving Russia and living in a place where they could practice Judaism openly. Once, when an emissary came, all the students of the underground *yeshivah* wrote "prayer request" notes to the Rebbe, asking that he pray that they be able to leave Russia. The emissary could not carry the notes out as they were, because his luggage might be searched and the notes confiscated. So the students baked a cake and put the notes into the batter. The emissary packed the cake carefully, deciding that if he were questioned by the authorities, he would tell them that a relative had baked it for his father. The emissary was not questioned, and he was able to bring the cake to the Rebbe, who, upon reading the notes, commented that this was the sweetest cake he had ever received. See *To Know and to Care,* vol. 2, p. 19 (SIE, 1996).

119 *Tanya,* ch. 12.

120 As told by R. Moshe Feller, *Living Torah* (JEM) program 238, accessible at www.chabad.org/858590.

121 *To Know and to Care* (SIE), accessible at www.chabad.org/62097.

122 *To Know and To Care* (SIE), vol. 2, p. 141, accessible at www.chabad.org/79689.

CHAPTER 9

123 See *Shulchan Aruch Harav, Orach Chaim* 156:10.

124 *Rambam, Hilchot Dei'ot* 7:3.

125 *Hayom Yom,* 29 Tishrei.

126 *Likkutei Sichot,* vol. 27, pp. 158-166.

127 Accessible at www.chabad.org/694406.

128 *One by One* (JEM), p. 232, as told by Mr. Jack Hardoff. A video is accessible at www.chabad.org/724794.

129 *Here's My Story* (JEM) No. 241, as told by Mr. Raphael Nouril, accessible at www.chabad.org/3771100.

130 This letter can be seen at www.chabad.org/1105275.

131 For a video of this exchange, see *Living Torah* (JEM) program 241, accessible at www.chabad.org/878368.

132 *Here's My Story* (JEM), as told by Mrs. Susan Shuster, accessible at www.chabad.org/4445922.

133 *To Know and to Care* (SIE), vol. 2, p. 237, accessible at www.chabad.org/222947.

134 For a video of this exchange, see *Living Torah* (JEM) program 416, accessible at www.chabad.org/1923555.

135 *Shirat Yisrael,* p. 156, where the author, R. Moshe Ibn Ezra, quotes it as a previously known saying.

136 *One by One* (JEM), p. 198, as told by R. Gedalia Schreiber, accessible at www.chabad.org/4445925.

137 *Here's My Story* (JEM) No. 136, as told by Judge Jerome Hornblass, accessible at www.chabad.org/3044539.

138 *To Know and to Care* (SIE), accessible at www.chabad.org/79689.

139 For a video of this exchange, see *Living Torah* (JEM) program 318, accessible at www.chabad.org/1317511.

CHAPTER 10

140 *Pesachim* 3a.

141 A photo of this incident can be seen at www.chabad.org/1316518. For a video, see *Living Torah* (JEM) program 88, accessible at www.chabad.org/377132.

142 See www.psychologytoday.com/gb/blog/words-can-change-your-brain/201208/the-most-dangerous-word-in-the-world.

143 See www.psychologytoday.com/us/basics/teamwork.

144 See www.chabad.org/2993147.

145 As told by the Rebbe's personal secretary, R. Yehuda Krinsky.

146 Ch. 4.

147 As told by R. Zalman Gafni, who received this directive from the Rebbe during a private audience. Another source of this directive is Mrs. Sara Labkowski, who is head of a seminary for women who are exploring their Jewish heritage; *My Encounter* interview (JEM).

148 In a related story, while delivering a Chasidic discourse on Shabbat Shuvah, 5740 (1979), the Rebbe cited Isaiah 43:25, which reads in full, *It is I, I Who erase your transgressions for My own sake, and your sins I will not remember.* When the editors sent a copy to the Rebbe for reviewing for print, he crossed out the words "erase your transgressions" and presented the verse thus: *It is I, I etc. for My sake.* In a marginal comment, the Rebbe wrote, "During the address I *intentionally* did not quote these words." The Rebbe pointed out that this verse, which talks about repenting begins with the word I said twice. Even in the very first words of the Ten Commandments the word I is said only once, which teaches us that through repentance a person can reach a deeper level of G-dliness than even through the straightforward practice of Torah and *mitzvot*. This is very powerful, because the Rebbe was quoting a verse and not spelling out a point in the verse relevant to the point he was making, which is that this verse speaks about the erasing of transgressions. The Rebbe didn't include those words, because they recall the transgressions of the Jewish People that need to be erased, and he didn't even want to make reference to it if at all possible. Instead, he wrote, "etc." (As told by R. Chaim Shaul Brook).

149 As told by R. Moshe Kotlarsky.

150 As told by R. Yisroel Deren, who heard it from the couple with whom this exchange took place, *My Encounter* interview (JEM).

151 From a letter by the Rebbe dated 3 Adar, 5737 (February 21, 1977). *Igrot Kodesh*, vol. 32, p. 130.

152 As told by Dr. Mordechai Shani, *Here's My Story* (JEM) No. 192, accessible at www.chabad.org/4448813. A video is accessible at www.chabad.org/3323934.

153 This letter can be seen at www.chabad.org/1865694.

154 As told by R. Yosef Goldstein.

155 As told by Mrs. Chana Sharfstein, *Living Torah* (JEM) program 296, accessible at www.chabad.org/1180695.

156 *A Time to Heal* (Ezra Press), accessible at www.chabad.org/3244230.

157 As told by R. Yitzchak Meir Gurary, *Living Torah* (JEM) program 370, accessible at www.chabad.org/1638118.

158 See *Brachah V'hatzlachah*, vol. 3, p. 96.

159 As told by R. Chaim Ciment, *Living Torah* (JEM) program 339, accessible at www.chabad.org/1441945.

160 *A Chasidisher Derher*, Iyar 5778, p. 38.

161 See Chaim Dalfin, *Conversations with the Rebbe*, p. 124.

162 *Torat Menachem—Hitvaaduyot 5711*, vol. 1, p. 211. *Likkutei Sichot*, vol. 16, p. 291.

163 *Torat Menachem—Sefer Hamaamarim Cheshvan*, p. 340, fn. 11.

164 *Torat Menachem—Hitvaaduyot 5724*, vol. 1, p. 101.

165 *Torat Menachem—Hitvaaduyot 5712*, vol. 1, p. 188.

166 *Torat Menachem—Sefer Hamaamarim Adar*, p. 85.

167 *Likkutei Sichot*, vol. 1, p. 215.

168 *Torat Menachem—Sefer Hamaamarim Tishrei*, p. 67.

169 *Likkutei Sichot*, vol. 1, p. 279.

170 *Igrot Kodesh*, vol. 6, p. 19.

171 *Likkutei Sichot*, vol. 2, p. 610.

172 *Torat Menachem—Hitvaaduyot 5751*, vol. 2, p. 24.

173 14:15.

174 *Shemot Rabbah* ch. 3.

175 As told by R. Chaim Shaul Brook.

176 116:15.

177 *Torat Menachem—Sefer Hamaamarim Elul*, p. 227, fn. 36.

CHAPTER 11

178 See www.chabad.org/1007604.

179 The response was written on Saturday night, July 29, 1978. A transcript can be seen at www.col.org.il/show_news.rtx?artID=77904.

180 *Seeds of Wisdom*, vol. 1, p. 92.

181 Joseph Telushkin, *Rebbe*, p. 431.

182 As told by R. Chaim Jacobs, *shliach* of the Rebbe to Scotland, with whom this took place.

183 *Toward a Meaningful Life*, p. 28.

184 As told by Mrs. Sara Labkowski.

185 *Living Torah* (JEM) program 367, accessible at www.chabad.org/1600168.

186 See www.chabad.org/60696.

187 *Igrot Kodesh* by R. Yosef Yitzchak Schneersohn, vol. 2, p. 537; vol. 7. p. 197.

CHAPTER 12

188 See www.scientificamerican.com/article/the-power-of-negative-thinking.

189 See www.newsweek.com/2016/09/23/positive-thinking-myth-498447.html.

190 *Likkutei Sichot*, vol. 26, p. 95 ff.

191 As told by R. Avraham Rottenberg, *Living Torah* (JEM) program 588, accessible at www.chabad.org/3144781.

192 As told by R. Zalman Gurary, with whom this took place.

193 As told by R. Yehoshua B. Gordon, *Here's My Story* (JEM) No. 144, accessible at www.chabad.org/4448935. A video is accessible at www.chabad.org/3107162.

194 *Igrot Kodesh*, vol. 6, pp. 286-287.

195 Based on the principle that verbalizing negativity can bring about negativity, the Rebbe once explained the sequence of verses that describe Moses' second foray into public life: *He went out on the second day, and behold, two Hebrew men were quarreling, and he said to the wicked one, "Why are you going to strike your friend?" And he retorted [to Moses], "Who made you a man, a prince, and a judge over us? Do you plan to slay me as you have slain the Egyptian?" Moses became frightened and said, "Indeed, the matter has become known!" Pharaoh heard of this incident, and he sought to slay Moses, etc.* The Rebbe explained that the Torah records not just Moses' fear but also his verbalization of the fear (an irrelevant detail, it would seem). It was speaking aloud his fears that caused Pharaoh to hear of the incident and want to kill him.

196 *Meah Shearim* 28a-b. *Maamarei Admur Hazaken Haketzarim*, p. 446.

197 This statement recalls a well-known line attributed to David Ben-Gurion, who said, referring to Jewish history as a whole: "A Jew who doesn't believe in miracles is not a realist." (*Note by the editor.*)

198 This letter can be seen at www.chabad.org/3006265.

CHAPTER 13

199 *Against Silence,* vol. 3, p. 63. Cf. *Memoirs* (Wiesel), p. 402 ff.

200 Ibid.

201 An account of that visit is accessible at www.chabad.org/260048.

202 Accessible at www.chabad.org/61921.

203 Accessible at www.chabad.org/143508.

204 See the *Algemeiner Journal,* Issue 196.

205 *Sichot Kodesh 5736,* vol. 1, p. 632 ff.

206 II Samuel 6:16.

207 *Hilchot Lulav* 8:14-15.

208 *Chullin* 63a.

209 Zechariah 10:8.

210 Isaiah 7: 18. See also ibid. 5:26.

211 Ibid. 27:12.

212 An article on the history of Chasidic joy is accessible at www.chabad.org/1211258.

213 *Igrot Kodesh by R. Schneur Zalman,* ed. 2012, pp. 270-271.

214 Deuteronomy 28:47–48.

215 Psalms 100:2.

216 See the introduction to *Chareidim, Tna'ei Hamitzvot, Tnai* 4.

217 See *Tzava'at Harivash* §110.

218 *Avot* 2:12.

219 R. Yehudah Chitrik, *Reshimot Devarim,* p. 112 (ed. 2009).

220 See *Zohar* II, 184b.

221 As told by R. Zalman Gurary.

222 See *Sefer Hamaamarim 5657,* p. 223 ff., at length.

223 See R. Shlomo Yosef Zevin, *Sippurei Chasidim, Moadim.*

224 R. Moshe Leib of Sassov, *Likkutei Ramal, Parashat Vayeitzei.*

225 *Sefer Hasichot 5748,* vol. 2, p. 628 ff.

226 In the *kol koreis* (announcements) published in *Hakriah V'hakedushah* (Sivan-Tammuz, 5701 [1941]; Elul, 5702 [1942]).

CHAPTER 14

227 See *Tanya*, chs. 1-2.

228 *Tosfot Chaim* by R. Chaim Yosef Brukstein of Postin (1775-1865), who records having heard these arguments firsthand. Cited in *Heichal Habesht*, Issue 21, p. 52 ff. See further there.

229 Psalms 37:27.

230 Interestingly, the Mussar movement, which arose among Orthodox Lithuanian Jews in the 1800s, held the same view—that Jews must examine their individual shortcomings and negative inclinations closely, in deep thought, in order to correct them.

231 *Tanya*, ch. 28.

232 *Igrot Kodesh*, vol. 4, p. 404.

233 *Tanya*, ch. 12.

234 As told by the individual with whom this took place.

235 As told by R. Shlomo Zarchi.

236 *Here's My Story* (JEM), accessible at www.chabad.org/4449205.

237 See, for example, *Full Devotion* (Kehot, 2010), p. 63 ff.

238 *Berachot* 28b.

CHAPTER 15

239 As told by Mr. Charles Samuel Ramat, *Here's My Story* (JEM) No. 206, accessible at www.chabad.org/4449206. A video is accessible at www.chabad.org/3840613.

240 Accessible at www.chabad.org/393257.

241 Accessible at stories770.blogspot.co.uk/2013/04/hisorerus-tshuva.html.

242 As told by Mr. Louis Gavin, *Here's My Story* (JEM) No. 239, accessible at www.chabad.org/3758240.

243 As told by Professor Alan Dershowitz, *Here's My Story* (JEM) No. 101, accessible at www.chabad.org/2799672. See also www.chabad.org/525279.

244 As told by Mrs. Ruth Benjamin, *My Encounter* interview (JEM).

245 A transcript and video of Prime Minister Netanyahu's address at the UN are accessible at www.chabad.org/1394394.

246 See *Torat Menachem—Hitvaaduyot, 5742*, vol. 4, p. 2171.

247 *Berachot* 10a.

248 Psalms 104:35.

249 *Torat Menachem—Hitvaaduyot, 5742*, vol. 4, p. 2171.

250 *Tanya*, ch. 12.

CHAPTER 16

251 *Igrot Kodesh*, vol. 22, p. 472.

252 *My Story* (JEM), pp. 47-48. A video is accessible at www.chabad.org/462845.

253 *Sotah* 49b. See also *Sanhedrin* 97a.

254 *Sichot Kodesh 5730*, vol. 1, pp. 610–611.

255 Accessible at www.chabad.org/66878.

256 *Likkutei Sichot*, vol. 9, pp. 451-452.

257 *Torat Menachem—Hitvaaduyot 5728*, vol. 3, p. 131.

CHAPTER 17

258 See www.chabad.org/60700.

259 Proverbs 31:30.

260 For a video of this exchange, see *Living Torah* (JEM) program 353, accessible at www.chabad.org/1547903. For a similar exchange, see *Living Torah* (JEM) program 424, accessible at www.chabad.org/1974202.

261 *Living Torah* (JEM) program 510, accessible at www.chabad.org/2615418.

262 As told by Dr. Yaakov Hanoka, *One by One* (JEM), p. 245. A video is accessible at www.chabad.org/675644.

263 As told by Dr. Naftali Loewenthal, *One by One* (JEM), p. 162, accessible at www.chabad.org/3834796.

264 *Hilchot Matnot Aniyim* 10:8.

265 See *Likkutei Sichot*, vol. 16, p. 341.

266 See Peter Kalms, *Guidance from the Rebbe*, p. 83.

267 As told by R. Simon Jacobson, *My Encounter* (JEM) interview.

268 *Torat Menachem—Hitvaaduyot 5715*, vol. 1, p. 58.

269 As told by R. Chaim Nisenbaum, *Living Torah* (JEM) program 597, accessible at www.chabad.org/3226539.

270 *Reb Mendel*, p. 220.

271 *Torat Menachem—Hitvaaduyot 5750*, vol. 2, p. 139.

272 *Sanhedrin* 4:5.

273 As told to me by R. Levi Avtzon, who heard it from the individual with whom this took place, and who is now a renowned Talmudic scholar.

274 *Avot* 4:1.

275 As told by Ambassador Yehudah Avner, *Seeds of Wisdom* (JEM), vol. 1, p. 13.

276 As told by R. Yitzchak Maier Gurary, *Seeds of Wisdom* (JEM), vol. 1, p. 21.

277 Exodus 20:17.

278 *Bava Batra* 22a.

279 Dated 24 Nissan 5727 (May 4, 1967).

280 Exodus 32:9.

281 As told by Adinah Singer, *My Encounter* (JEM) interview.

282 Accessible at www.chabad.org/66878.

283 *Avot* 1:14.

284 As told to me by R. Naftali Loewenthal.

285 *Igrot Kodesh*, vol. 3, p. 370.

286 *Living Torah* (JEM) program 519, accessible at www.chabad.org/2660937.

287 *Avot* 6:11.

288 See, for example, *Likkutei Sichot*, vol. 20, p. 260.

289 See *One Hour. Forty Years* (Merkos L'Inyonei Chinuch and American Friends of Lubavitch, 1990).

290 See www.meaningfullife.com/vices-and-virtues-of-technology.

291 As told by R. Moshe Feller, *My Encounter* (JEM) interview.

292 An example can perhaps be seen in the following story, where Mr. Michel Schwartz was told by the Rebbe that his art should have the look of the Dick Tracy series. See www.chabad.org/1624160.

CHAPTER 18

293 For the correspondence between Dr. Wilkes and the Rebbe see *Inclusion and the Power of the Individual* (Ezra Press, 2019).

294 Currently, there is much discussion regarding the appropriate language to refer to or address people with disabilities. The use of the term special itself has indeed become a flashpoint for debate, with some people with disabilities claiming that it feels condescending and unnecessarily othering. However, it is important to note that the term was not meant in the way it is most commonly used (i.e., to refer to someone's special needs); rather, it was intended as an altogether more empathic acknowledgement of each individual's special gifts and unique potential.

295 Accessible at www.chabad.org/1202.

296 For a video of the Rebbe's remarks, see *Living Torah* (JEM) program 278, accessible at www.chabad.org/1076652.

CHAPTER 19

297 As told by R. Shabtai Slavaticki.

298 *Avodah Zarah* 3a. See also *Pitchei Shaarei Haavodah,* ch. 1.

299 Jerusalem Talmud, *Orlah* 1:3. *Likkutei Torah, Tzav* 7d.

300 *Kiddushin* 31a, *Tosfot.*

301 *Sukkah* 52a.

302 See www.portraitofaleader.blogspot.com/2010_08_15_archive.html.

303 This letter can be seen at www.chabad.org/821811.

304 *Torat Menachem—Hitvaaduyot 5745,* vol. 4, p. 2274.

305 *Sichot Kodesh 5736,* vol. 1, p. 670 ff.

306 Proverbs 3:12.

CHAPTER 20

307 This letter can be seen at www.chabad.org/821812.

308 See *Torah Or, Bereishit* 30a.

309 As told by Mr. Mendel Greenbaum, *Living Torah* (JEM) program 468, accessible at www.chabad.org/2289730.

310 This letter can be seen at www.chabad.org/4380025.

311 *Avot* 4:2.

312 From a letter to F. A. Van der Kemp (Feb. 16, 1809), Pennsylvania Historical Society.

313 From a letter to F. A. Van der Kemp (Dec. 31, 1808), Pennsylvania Historical Society.

314 Indeed, Jewish law expressly states that one cannot gain forgiveness if he sins with the intention of repenting thereafter.

315 See *Maamar Bati L'gani 5731*(*Torat Menachem—Sefer Hamaamarim Bati L'gani,* vol. 1, p. 20 ff.). See also *Tanchuma, Vayeishev,* 4.

316 For more on this, see *Likkutei Sichot,* vol. 3, p. 66-67.

317 At the conclusion of Chanukah, 5735 (1974). An audio recording of this talk, is accessible at www.chabad.org/551973. See also *Sefer Hamaamarim 5735,* p. 290.

318 See www.chabad.org/67623.

319 See www.ou.org/jewish_action/06/2014/unparalleled-leader.

CHAPTER 21

320 As told by Mr. Benzion Rader, *One by One* (JEM), p. 262. A video is accessible at www.chabad.org/1248289.

321 This letter can be seen at www.chabad.org/1899566.

322 As told by Dr. David Luchins, *Living Torah* (JEM) program 153, accessible at www.chabad.org/548435.

CHAPTER 22

323 As told by Mrs. Miryam Swerdlov, *Here's My Story* (JEM) No. 121, accessible at www.chabad.org/2949985. A video is accessible at www.chabad.org/4098684.

324 R. Yosef Yitzchak Schneersohn, sixth Lubavitcher Rebbe (1880-1950).

325 R. Yisrael Baal Shem Tov (1698–1760), founder of Chasidism, taught that "everything that occurs, and every detail thereof, is by Divine Providence. If a leaf is turned over by a breeze, it is only because this has been specifically ordained by G-d to serve a specific function within the purpose of creation." Thus, "every single thing that a person sees or hears is an instruction to him in his conduct in the service of G-d."

326 Accessible at www.chabad.org/2855443.

327 *Likkutei Sichot*, vol. 23, pp. 227-8.

328 As told by R. Simon Jacobson, who is the son referred to in this story.

329 As told by R. Yisroel Deren, *My Encounter* (JEM) interview.

330 As told by R. Avraham Glick, *Here's My Story* (JEM) No. 238, accessible at www.chabad.org/3752414. A video is accessible at www.chabad.org/4210605.

331 See https://www.chabad.org/parshah/article_cdo/aid/2511133/jewish/Worth-The-While.htm.

CHAPTER 23

332 *Igrot Kodesh*, vol. 2, p. 14.

333 *To Know and to Care* (SIE), accessible at www.chabad.org/78663.

334 As told by Mrs. Faygie Levy, *My Encounter* (JEM) interview. See also www.chabad.org/4449208.

335 As told by R. Dovid Aaron Neuman, *Here's My Story* (JEM) No. 99, accessible at www.chabad.org/2787070.

336 As told by R. Menachem Teichtel, *Living Torah* (JEM) program 421, accessible at www.chabad.org/1974187.

337 To read more about the *Reshimot*, see www.chabad.org/1210901.

338 Proverbs 3:18.

CHAPTER 24

339 As told by R. Mendel Lipskar, *Here's My Story* (JEM) No. 161, accessible at www.chabad.org/4449210.

340 As told by Mrs. Sheindel Teichtel, *My Encounter* (JEM) interview.

341 Accessible at www.chabad.org/1395114.

342 *Kiddushin* 82a.

343 As told by R. Yoel Kahan.

344 Proverbs 3:6.

345 As told by R. Avraham Glick, *Here's My Story* (JEM) No. 238, accessible at chabad.org/3752414.

346 Furthermore, the thirty-nine categories of work forbidden on Shabbat are based on the thirty-nine types of work employed to construct the *Mishkan*, the Tabernacle in the desert. The Rebbe was comparing the facilitating of child education to the building of the Tabernacle, the highest honor.

CHAPTER 25

347 As told by R. Bentzion Wiener, *Here's My Story* (JEM) No. 182, accessible at www.chabad.org/4449211.

348 *Sichot Kodesh 5733*, vol. 2, pp. 30-33.

CHAPTER 26

349 See www.chabad.org/2619820.

350 The complete letter is published in *To the Sons and Daughters of Our People Israel, Everywhere...*, vol. 1, (Elul-Adar), pp. 82-83, Kehot, 2019.

351 Deuteronomy 6:4. These words embody the heart of the Jew's faith, and are the words he endeavors to recite in his final moments of physical life. Perhaps the Rebbe's intention here is that if the stricken young woman was not in a state that allowed her to do so, the fact that she was in a home with a *mezuzah* on its door compensated for this.

352 The Holy of Holies was the innermost chamber of the Holy Temple, and the most sacred place on earth. Only the High Priest entered there, and only for a few minutes on Yom Kippur, the holiest day of the year. Nevertheless, the law is that is that the High Priest is obligated to leave the Holy of Holies to attend to a body that has no one to take care of it.

353 *Likkutei Sichot*, vol. 35, p. 345.

354 *Likkutei Sichot*, vol. 19, p. 511.

CHAPTER 27

355 For more on this, see *A Time To Heal: The Rebbe's Response to Loss & Tragedy* (Ezra Press, 2015).

356 Accessible at www.chabad.org/392177. See also *Torat Menachem—Hitvaaduyot 5720*, vol. 1, p. 396.

357 From a letter of the Rebbe dated 25 Elul, 5738 (September 27, 1978). The letter can be seen at www.chabad.org/941840.

358 Ibid. In other words, the departure of the soul from the body is a great advantage and ascent for the soul, and the loss is only for the bereaved, and to that extent it is also painful for the soul, of course.

359 From a letter of the Rebbe dated 5 Tammuz, 5743 (June 16, 1983). The letter can be seen at www.chabad.org/1852670.

360 *Torat Menachem—Menachem Tzion*, vol. 2, p. 558.

361 *To Know and to Care* (SIE), vol. 2, p. 237, accessible at www.chabad.org/79697.

362 *Igrot Kodesh*, vol. 26, p. 271. *Torat Menachem—Menachem Tzion*, vol. 2, p. 543. For the full text of the letter, see *A Time To Heal: The Rebbe's Response to Loss & Tragedy* (Ezra Press, 2015), p. 199.

363 From a letter by the Rebbe dated 25 Elul, 5738 [September 27, 1978]. For the full text of the letter, see *A Time To Heal: The Rebbe's Response to Loss & Tragedy* (Ezra Press, 2015), p. 193.

364 *Igrot Kodesh*, vol. 6, pp. 175-176.

365 *Igrot Kodesh* vol. 13, p. 30.

366 See *Sefer Hasichot 5748*, vol. 1, p. 332.

367 Isaiah 26:19.

368 *Igrot Kodesh*, vol. 25, pp. 3-5. *Torat Menachem—Menachem Tzion*, vol. 2, pp. 536-537.

CHAPTER 28

369 See www.psychologytoday.com/blog/fulfillment-any-age/201209/happiness-it-s-all-about-the-ending.

370 *Berachot* 55b.

371 *Berachot* 31a.

372 Lamentations 5:22.

373 Ibid. 5:21.

374 As told by R. Leibel Schapiro, *My Encounter* (JEM) interview.

375 *Heichal Menachem*, vol. 1, p. 249. A fascimile of similar handwriting is printed in *Tzaddik L'Melech*, Issue 5, p. 149. A detailed overview of related incidents is accessible at www.chabad.org.il/Magazines/Article.

asp?ArticleID=2966&CategoryID=845 www.chabad.org.il/Magazines/Article.asp?ArticleID=2935&CategoryID=841 forum.otzar.org/forums/viewtopic.php?t=4224.

376 A told by Mr. Josef Cayre, *Here's My Story* (JEM) No. 130, accessible at www.chabad.org/3000764. A video is accessible at www.chabad.org/640812.

377 Dated 4 Iyar 5745, the letter can be seen at https://crownheights.info/letter-and-spirit/435012/letter-and-spirit-no-compromise-in-education/ Mr. Wouk's response can be seen at http://crownheights.info/letter-and-spirit/435653/letter-and-spirit-an-exchange-with-herman-wouk.

378 *Living Torah* (JEM) program 528, accessible at www.chabad.org/2725134.

379 55:12.

CHAPTER 29

380 *Sippurim Meichadar HaRabbi*, p. 76.

381 Dated 11 Nissan 5716, the Rebbe's 54th birthday. *Igrot Kodesh*, vol. 12, p. 414.

382 *Mechilta of R. Yishmael, Bo* 14.

383 See *Sefer Hasichot 5751*, vol. 2, p. 520 ff.

384 As told by R. Tzvi Telsner.

385 *Sefer Hasichot 5751*, vol. 2, p. 595.

386 Jeremiah 31:22.

387 See www.time.com/magazine/us/5087338/january-15th-2018-vol-191-no-1-u-s/.

388 3:5.

389 Isaiah 27:16.

390 *See Torat Menachem—Sefer Hamaamarim 5728*, p. 10.

391 Isaiah 27:13.

392 Habakkuk 2:14.

393 See www.time.com/magazine/us/5087338/january-15th-2018-vol-191-no-1-u-s.

394 See www.theguardian.com/global-development-professionals-network/2017/feb/14/despite-many-obstacles-the-world-is-getting-better.

395 See ourworldindata.org/nuclear-weapons.

396 See www.medicalnewstoday.com/articles/291090.php.

397 See www.sciencedaily.com/releases/2010/05/100513123720.htm.

398 35:5-6.

399 A free translation of this talk was published in *Sichos in English*, vol. 51 (SIE), accessible at www.chabad.org/2465331.

400 2:4.

401 For an English translation of the discourse see *Nurturing Faith* (Kehot, 2005).

402 A free translation of this talk was published in *Sichos in English*, vol. 48 (SIE), accessible at www.chabad.org/2487406.

403. See www.chabad.org/2619824. A video is accessible at www.chabad.org/372587.

CHAPTER 30

404 *Living Torah* (JEM) program 574-575, accessible at www.chabad.org/3046548 and www.chabad.org/3046553.

405 See *Yalkut Shimoni, Mishlei* 942.

406 See talks by the Rebbe dated 12 Tammuz, 5726; *Shabbat Parashat Mikeitz* 5732; second day of Shavuot, 5734.

407 *Yevamot* 109b.

408 A told by R. Marvin Tokayer, *Living Torah* (JEM) program 349, accessible at www.chabad.org/1515869.

409 As told by Herbert Weiner, *My Encounter* (JEM) interview.

410 As told by Prime Minister Ariel Sharon, *One by One* (JEM) p. 219, accessible at www.chabad.org/2562002.

411 As told by R. Zalman Aaron Grossbaum, *Living Torah* (JEM) program 455, accessible at www.chabad.org/2222319.

412 As told by R. Laibl Wolf, *Here's My Story* (JEM) No. 198, accessible at www.chabad.org/4449212. A video is accessible at www.chabad.org/3637140.

413 As told by R. Mordechai Gutnick, *Here's My Story* (JEM) No. 294, accessible at www.chabad.org/4121657. A video is accessible at www.chabad.org/2725135.

414 *Avot* 1:17.

415 See *Rebbe*, p. 174.

416 See talks by the Rebbe dated 10 Shevat, 5732; 8 Shevat, 5747. See also *Living Torah* (JEM) program 434, accessible at www.chabad.org/2081434.

417 *Seeds of Wisdom* (JEM), vol. 2, p. 118.

418 As told by the Rebbe's personal secretary, R. Yehuda Krinsky, *My Encounter* (JEM) interview.

419 See www.chabad.org/3929896.

420 As told by R. Yosef Goldstein, *Seeds of Wisdom* (JEM), vol. 1, p. 11.

421 As told by Mrs. Ruth Benjamin, *Seeds of Wisdom* (JEM), vol. 2, p. 20.

422 As told by Rebbetzin Bassie Garelik, *Here's My Story* (JEM) No. 31, accessible at www.chabad.org/2308655.

423 For a video of this exchange, see *Living Torah* (JEM) program 157, accessible at www.chabad.org/548455.

424 For a video of this exchange, see *Living Torah* (JEM) program 503, accessible at www.chabad.org/2552703.

425 As told by Mr. Freddy Hager, *Living Torah* (JEM) program 31, accessible at www.chabad.org/675634.

426 *Avot* 2:9.

427 As told by Mr. Naftali Deutsch, *Seeds of Wisdom* (JEM), vol. 1, p. 25. A video is accessible at www.chabad.org/2316181.

428 Recounted by his son, R. Michoel Katz, *Here's My Story* (JEM) No. 277, accessible at www.chabad.org/4454479. A video is accessible at www.chabad.org/3296364.

429 Jonathan Sacks, *Celebrating Life*, p. 47-48.

430 As told by Mr. Bentzion Bernstein, *Here's My Story* (JEM) No. 205, accessible at www.chabad.org/4449216. A video is accessible at www.chabad.org/1600159.

431 *To Know and to Care* (SIE), accessible at www.chabad.org/79693.

432 As told by Mr. Meir Bastomski, *Living Torah* (JEM) program 697, accessible at www.chabad.org/3908664.

433 As told by Mrs. Masha Lipskar, *Here's My Story* (JEM) No. 105, accessible at www.chabad.org/2842569.

434 *Siddur Tehillat Hashem* (Kehot), p.5.

435 Ibid. p. 141.

L'CHAIM

436 A related idea can be found in *The Divine Commandments*, by Nissan Mindel (Kehot, 2010), p. 55, citing *Sefer Hasichot 5680*, p. 5.

437 Psalms 34:9.

ACKNOWLEDGEMENTS

A work of this kind, drawing as it does from hundreds of the Rebbe's talks, letters, and private audiences, requires considerable research and support. I would like to acknowledge the following people and institutions:

Rabbi Zalman Shmotkin, the executive director and driving force behind the legendary Jewish website, Chabad.org, for his enthusiasm and support for this book.

Rabbis Yehuda Krinsky, Simon Jacobson, Yossi Jacobson, Dovid Olidort, Shlomo Zarchi, Chaim Shaul Brook, Shmuel Lew, Naftali Loewenthal, Michoel Seligson, Yosef Katzman, Levi Garelik, and Tzvi Telsner, for agreeing to be interviewed and for their valuable input.

My gifted editor, R. Eden Pearlstein, a man of many talents, whose unique blend of philosophy, psychology, and poetry is deeply imprinted on this book, and Elke Reva Sudin, for facilitating our fateful and fruitful collaboration.

Rabbi Mattisyahu Brown, whose purity, precision, and expert editing has greatly enhanced this book.

Yaakov Ort, whose incisive clarity and insight have helped refine this manuscript substantially. Professor Susan Handelman, for her valuable feedback and guidance.

Mendel Katzman, for his insightful review of the manuscript.

Rabbi Meir Simcha Kogan, director of Chabad.org, for his constant wisdom and patience.

Rabbi Motti Seligson, who has been a constant source of support for this project.

The editorial team at Kehot Publication Society, for their rigor and professionalism. In particular, Rabbis Dovid Olidort, Mendel Laine, and Avraham D. Vaisfiche.

Chanie Kaminker of Hannabi Creative, for the creative cover design. This is our third book together, and I look forward to future collaborations.

Rabbi Elkanah Shmotkin, the executive director of Jewish Educational Media, and the My Encounter Project team, who do a masterful job at preserving the Rebbe's legacy through the hundreds of first-hand interviews they have taped documenting the Rebbe's life. This book has been greatly enriched by these valuable interviews, and for that I am grateful.

My dear and esteemed friend, Alec Sellem, for co-sponsoring this book in honor of his dear wife, Sonia, and their beautiful children. I am profoundly grateful for their friendship.

My dear brother, Yekusiel, for co-sponsoring this book. His constant support and friendship are truly one of life's greatest gifts, for which I am profoundly grateful.

My dear and esteemed friend, Sacha Gaydamak and his beautiful family, for their role in facilitating the creation of this book. I am profoundly grateful for their friendship.

My wife and life partner, Chana, whose unwavering support and dedication helped facilitate this book. Her clear thinking and discerning comments have enhanced this book immeasurably. I would also like to express our gratitude to G-d for our beautiful children, Geula, Dov, Esther, and Zelig, who bring unlimited joy to our lives.

My dear parents, Rabbi Yosef Yitzchak and Hindy Kalmenson, my beloved grandparents, Rabbi Sholom Ber and Sara Shanowitz, and my dear father- and mother-in-law, Rabbi Yosef and Tamara Katzman, for their constant counsel, love, and support. My life and that of my family is greatly enriched by their living example of Jewish and Chasidic values.

My dear brothers and sisters, Chanie, Nechama Dina, Menucha, Yekusiel, and Moishy. I feel so blessed to have you in my life.

Lastly, I would like to express a profound sense of gratitude to the Rebbe, of righteous memory, whose living and loving wisdom I have tried to communicate in this book. His example and teachings continue to inspire and guide me daily.

Mendel Kalmenson

ABOUT THE AUTHOR

Rabbi Mendel Kalmenson is the rabbi of Beit Baruch and executive director of Chabad of Belgravia, London, where he lives with his wife, Chana, and their children. He is also the author of the popular books *Seeds of Wisdom* and *A Time to Heal*.

A woman of valor who can find!
Her worth is beyond that of pearls.
Proverbs 31:10

This book is dedicated
to my dear wife

Sonia

and to the wisdom and care
she surrounds me with.

Alec Sellem

Dedicated to
our dear Rebbe

whose endless positivity
and boundless optimism
has inspired and changed
the lives of so many.

Lovingly sponsored by

Yekusiel Kalmenson
and family